JOURNALISM Made Simple

The Made Simple series
has been created
primarily for self-education
but can equally well
be used as
an aid to group study.
However complex the subject,
the reader is taken
step by step,
clearly and methodically,
through the course. Each volume
has been prepared by experts,
using throughout the
Made Simple technique of teaching.
Consequently the gaining
of knowledge now becomes
an experience to be enjoyed.

Accounting
Acting and Stagecraft
Additional Mathematics
Advertising
Anthropology
Applied Economics
Applied Mathematics
Applied Mechanics
Art Appreciation
Art of Speaking
Art of Writing
Biology
Book-keeping
British Constitution
Business and Administrative
    Organisation
Calculus
Chemistry
Childcare
Commerce
Company Administration
Company Law
Computer Programming
Cookery
Cost and Management
    Accounting
Data Processing
Dressmaking
Economic History
Economic and Social
    Geography
Economics
Electricity
Electronic Computers
Electronics
English
English Literature

Export
Financial Management
French
Geology
German
Human Anatomy
Italian
Journalism
Latin
Law
Management
Marketing
Mathematics
Modern Electronics
Modern European History
New Mathematics
Office Practice
Organic Chemistry
Philosophy
Photography
Physical Geography
Physics
Pottery
Psychology
Rapid Reading
Retailing
Russian
Salesmanship
Secretarial Practice
Social Services
Soft Furnishing
Spanish
Statistics
Transport and
    Distribution
Typing
Woodwork

JOURNALISM Made Simple

David Wainwright

Made Simple Books
W. H. ALLEN   London
A Howard & Wyndham Company

© W. H. Allen & Co. Ltd, 1972

Made and printed in Great Britain by
Butler & Tanner Ltd, Frome and London,
for the publishers, W. H. Allen & Company Ltd,
44 Hill Street, London W1X 8LB

First Edition, January 1972
Second Edition, August 1978

ISBN 0 491 00229 7 Paperbound

Foreword

There is one way to enjoy a career in journalism—journalism made simple. Start your own paper. Many men have done it. They discovered a small town, got together enough money to buy a printing press, and launched the *Hometown Chronicle*. Proprietor, editor, advertising and circulation manager (and often printer and sub-editor in one), they had a great life.

A few years later when radio started, the same sort of man started radio stations (particularly in North America). That was journalism made simple—though it meant hard work.

Today communications are in a process of transition. Journalism in newspapers, radio and television is being refashioned by a new technology, which in the few years since this book first appeared has advanced from a series of ingenious ideas to a practical reality in daily use round the world. This revised edition takes into account the fact that much 'information storage and retrieval' is now done by computer, and that the computer can effect all the processes between the creation of words and the reading of them, whether on paper or on the television screen or visual display unit (VDU). Satellites now beam facts around the world by the million in a few seconds, to produce a deafening cacophony of information.

This book tries to unravel the complication. It is designed to be useful to all students of communications who are interested in the impact of these new developments on the world, and the opportunities they offer for further change.

While the book is designed to be helpful as background reading for new entrants into journalism working for the Proficiency Certificate of the National Council for the Training of Journalists (and detailed reading lists are given to help such students), it will also give students of General Studies courses at 'O' and 'A' level GCE valuable insights into the way the press, radio and television journalists go about their work.

Journalism is the day-to-day operation of gathering and transmitting news. It affects everyone, and this book therefore should also interest those members of the public who are concerned about the standards, content and presentation of the media.

DAVID WAINWRIGHT

Acknowledgments

I am grateful to Arthur Davidson, MP, who read the section on newspaper law, to Barry Phelps who wrote the chapter on financial journalism, and to David Smith, newspaper printer, who saved me from a number of blunders in the section on printing as (over the years) he and his colleagues have helped me as a journalist 'on the stone'. Many other friends and colleagues have helped me in the preparation of this book and while it would have been a less informative work without their assistance, I must make clear that any mistakes are mine and not theirs.

For permission to quote, I thank the following: Terry Coleman and the *Guardian* for his interview with Lord George-Brown; Harold Evans for an article in the *Listener*; the Executors of Lord Francis-Williams for *Dangerous Estate: an Anatomy of Newspapers* (Longmans); Fred W. Friendly for *Due to Circumstances Beyond Our Control* (Random House); Victor Gollancz Ltd for *In My Way* by Lord George-Brown; J. D. Halloran for *Demonstrations and Communications: A Case Study* (Penguin Books) and *The Effects of Mass Communications* (Leicester University Press); Louis Heren and *The Times* for an article in that paper; International Publishing Corporation for *Cassandra at His Finest and Funniest* (Daily Mirror); Tony Lane for *Strike At Pilkingtons* (Penguin Books); Penguin Books Ltd for *I, Claud* by Claud Cockburn; Leslie Sellers for *A Simple Sub's Book* (Pergamon Press); and Nicholas Tomalin for an article in the *Sunday Times Magazine*.

For permission to reproduce cartoons I thank Associated Newspapers Group Ltd for those by Cookson and Trog; Express Newspapers Ltd for Giles, Jak, Sir David Low and Vicky; International Publishing Corporation for Will Dyson and Philip Zec; John Murray Ltd for the Osbert Lancaster cartoon from his book *Graffiti*; Punch for that by Sir Bernard Partridge; and Mrs Jocelyn Starling for the pocket cartoon by Timothy Birdsall.

I apologise for any omissions.

D. W.

Barbican, London, Easter 1978

Table of Contents

'Congress shall make no law respecting an establishment of religion, or prohibiting the free exercise thereof; or abridging the freedom of speech or of the press; or the right of the people peaceably to assemble, and to petition the Government for a redress of grievances.'—First Amendment to the Constitution of the United States, 1791.

'The first duty of the press is to obtain the earliest and most correct intelligence of the events of the time, and instantly, by disclosing them, to make them the common property of the nation.' —*The Times* (John Delane), 1852.

'It is a newspaper's duty to print the news and raise hell.'— *Chicago Times*, 1861.

'Freedom of the press is perhaps the freedom that has suffered the most from the gradual degradation of the ideal of liberty. . . . A free press can of course be good or bad, but, most certainly, without freedom it will never be anything but bad. . . . Freedom is nothing else but a chance to be better, whereas enslavement is a certainty of the worse.'—Albert Camus, *Resistance, Rebellion and Death*, 1960.

'As the free press develops, the paramount point is whether the journalist, like the scientist or scholar, puts truth in the first place or in the second.'—Walter Lippmann.

CHAPTER ONE

INTRODUCTION

(1) What is Journalism?

What is journalism? Journalism is information. It is communication. It is the events of the day distilled into a few words, sounds or pictures, processed by the mechanics of communication to satisfy the human curiosity of a world that is always eager to know what's new.

Journalism is basically news. The word derives from 'journal'; its best contents are 'du jour', of the day itself. But journalism may also be entertainment and reassurance, to satisfy the human frailty of a world that is always eager to be comforted with the knowledge that out there are millions of human beings just like us.

Journalism is *The Times* and the *Guardian*, the *Daily Mirror* and the *Sun*. It is the *Huddersfield Daily Examiner* and the *Kidderminster Shuttle*. It is the 'Today' programme and 'World at One' and 'P.M.' on BBC radio. It is 'Newsroom', 'Panorama', 'Twenty-Four Hours' and BBC television news: it is Independent Television News.

Journalism is *Private Eye* and the *International Times* and *Oz* and *Rolling Stone*, and every 'underground' news sheet. It is the disc-jockey on Radio One chattering about the latest group to emerge in the pop-rock culture.

Journalism is the television picture beamed by satellite direct from some war zone, showing men dying in agony and accurate colour. It is the television picture of a man stepping on to the surface of the moon, seen in millions of homes as it happens.

Journalism can communicate with as few people as can a classroom news-sheet or a parish magazine, or with as many people as there are in the world.

The cave-man drawing a buffalo on the wall of his home did so to give other hunters the news that buffalo were nearby. The town-crier reciting the news in the market-place provided a convenient way in which a number of people could simultaneously learn facts affecting all their lives.

Even now in Britain when a new king or queen comes to the throne the first act of the new reign, by the Accession Council, is the ordering of the proclamation of the new Sovereign. This is a historic curiosity, since of course this method of informing the people has long been superseded by the press, radio and television. Yet even today a herald, Garter King of Arms, stands on the balcony of St James's Palace and reads the proclamation. The same reading is repeated three times in London, at Charing Cross, Temple Bar, and on the steps of the Royal Exchange.

The proclamation is said to date back to the Witan, the Anglo-Saxon parliament that elected the King. In those days it was necessary to let people know as quickly as possible to whom they owed loyalty. Otherwise rival tribes might attack and find the district in disarray, not knowing which chief was now the rightful leader whom they must follow.

The death of a leader, the accession of a new leader—these are straightforward facts. The proclamation is the announcement of a provable truth.

(2) The Time Change

Not all journalism is so simple. Today the news media are swamped by the very availability of news. There is simply more of it than ever before—unmanageably more, available to many more people. This is a transformation that has been achieved in little over 100 years.

When Admiral Lord Nelson died aboard the *Victory* after the Battle of Trafalgar in 1805, it took two weeks for the news to reach the Admiralty in London (a young lieutenant of the Royal Navy brought the despatches personally, sailing in the sloop *Pickle* to Plymouth and then riding to London). It was some hours before important people in London heard the news, some days before it reached the other cities of Britain. There must have been outlying hamlets that the news took even longer to reach; and on some isolated farms the labourers no doubt heard of it from the broadsheet peddlers travelling from inn to inn.

When President John Kennedy was assassinated in Dallas, Texas, in November 1963, the news of his death was known around the whole world in a matter of seconds. The political leaders of Russia and China, the financial manipulators of Geneva, the obscure tribesmen of Borneo all heard the news simultaneously.

This is a profound change in the pattern of human communication. It has taken place in hardly more than one man's lifetime.

Even forty years ago, most people in the developed world obtained their news from the newspapers. The newspapers had changed little from the days of Caxton. The process of printing had hardly changed at all, and the only modernisation had been in machinery to produce and distribute a greater number of copies of each issue. Then radio arrived.

At first, newspapers regarded it as a passing technical fad. One director of the Press Association returned from America in 1923 and said that 'broadcasting is on the wane. . . . People are getting so tired of it that it reminds one of the almost-forgotten skating-rink craze.' He was, of course, profoundly wrong. In America, the effects of radio were more rapid in appearing, due to the springing up of hundreds of small-town radio stations. In Britain, radio was put under the control of a non-profit-making body financed by government-collected licence fees and charged with the duty of providing a nationwide broadcasting service.

The war reports of BBC radio from 1939 to 1945 should have warned newspapers that radio could rival them in the presentation of news. But it was not until two-channel television was introduced in Britain in 1956 (with the commercially backed Independent Television Authority rivalling the BBC's television service) that the television set entered 80 per cent of British homes and the way in which most people learnt their news changed radically.

(3) The Customers Change

Journalism is about people. It is produced for people. So how has the ordinary man's receptivity to journalism changed in twenty years?

Even twenty years ago, a family might listen to a news bulletin on the living-room radio over breakfast. Father would read his morning paper over breakfast or on the bus or train going to work. After work, he would buy an evening paper and read it on the way home, handing it over to his wife who would read it when she had washed up after the evening meal. Then they might listen to the BBC nine o'clock radio news.

What happens now? The bedside transistor radio switches itself on with the alarm. Mother has her transistor on in the kitchen as she cooks breakfast. The kids have their transistors switched to Radio One with its mixture of pop and news flashes. Father glances at the morning paper over breakfast, then gets into the car and turns on 'Today' as he drives to work. Mother carries the transistor around the house as she dusts and makes the beds to the voice of Jimmy Young. Father buys an evening paper as he leaves work, glances at the headlines, then turns on the six o'clock radio news as he drives home. After eating, they turn on the telly and sit down to an evening's viewing. Mother may read the evening paper if there is a sports programme which she finds boring. They watch the BBC's television nine o'clock news or ITN's 'News at Ten'.

It is an immense change. These are people for whom journalists are working. They have to take account of these social changes, which can be equated in most countries of the world.

The newspaperman has to be aware of the changes in the lives of his readers. It is not enough for him to print the 'hard news' of the evening before (most national newspapers start printing their major editions around 10 pm, with further editions for the city in which they are produced coming out until 4 am), since his readers who look at the paper over breakfast will have heard most of that and seen many of the public figures and significant events on television the night before. Or they will hear on the early morning radio news items that are three hours later than the latest possible edition of the morning paper.

The press has been slow to catch on to this change, and to revise its methods of operation so that the newspaper still has a function. That it has a function, there can be no doubt: for the television or radio news bulletin is tightly encapsulated, containing only a few of the main facts in a highly abbreviated form.

Newspapers are archives, objects of record. They can be referred to, checked back on, in a way that the television or radio news cannot. They can describe events at greater length, add more relevant detail, give authoritative comment from people in a position to detect trends and the likely lines in which a news story will develop.

But the old concept of a newspaper 'scoop', the presentation of a startling hard news story a day before its rivals, is virtually dead—killed by radio and television.

(4) What is Newsworthy?

During the day, newsworthy events will happen that are quite unpredicted. A passenger plane may crash, a bank raid take place, a fim star arrives at Heathrow without her husband and announces she is getting a divorce.

'Newsworthy?' But are these things newsworthy? Who says they are newsworthy? Different countries have different customs. In Russia, for example, the newspapers would not cover or report the bank raid, because Russian newspapers (for reasons we shall discuss later) do not report crime.

So who says these things are newsworthy? Who chooses to report a bank raid rather than the one hundredth birthday of Mrs Jemima Snooks, who has had a telegram from the Queen?

Let us look at the finished product and work back from there. Every newspaper, every radio and television news bulletin has a 'lead' story—the first story, given greatest prominence on the front page or put first in the bulletin. The editor—or more usually the chief sub-editor, since the editor is usually too busy to be concerned with the minute-by-minute running of the organisation—chooses which story he thinks will be most important to the readers, listeners or viewers.

If there is an earthquake in Peru with an estimated 2,000 dead, the quality papers in Britain would probably put that prominently on their front pages. The popular papers would try to discover whether any Britons were working in the area, and if they found that an English girl was there—and particularly if the picture department could produce a photograph of her—that might rate the front page. Otherwise, if the death toll were entirely local, the popular press would probably place the disaster on an inside foreign page.

If a house fell down in Liverpool trapping a family, the *Liverpool Echo* would put that prominently on the front page. The national papers might put it briefly lower down their front pages, and the popular tabloids would probably put the story inside the paper.

Each newspaper, each news bulletin is thus a product manufactured from what is available. No newspaper ever comes out with blank columns and the comment that there is 'no news today', except in those countries where governments impose press censorship.

The quality papers, sometimes called the 'papers of record', do however print stories that they feel should be recorded, even if they are dull and unlikely to appeal to many readers. Claud Cockburn maintains that there used to be a competition on the foreign desk of *The Times* to write the dullest headline, which he once won with the headline: 'Small Earthquake In Chile: Not Many Dead'.

(5) Sex, Money and Crime

But how do the executives measure what is important and what is interesting to their readers? In part, they go by their own intuitive rule-of-thumb judgement. They are ordinary men, they travel to work by train, they belong to suburban golf clubs and they drink in various pubs: they talk to people and hear people talking, and they form their judgement of what is interesting from these influences. The popular papers may assume that sex, money and crime interest many readers.

Every journalist is sooner or later buttonholed by the critic who asks 'Why do you always print the seamy side of life? Why are you always writing about crime, and violence, and abortion and racial conflict?' The critic will go on to say that he doesn't live like that, he doesn't want to read about that sort of thing, and he doesn't know why papers are allowed to print such stuff and television news allowed to show such violence.

'Human kind cannot bear very much reality' as T. S. Eliot wrote. There was a theory—put forward, among others, by Clive Irving— that the 'quality' papers would increase in circulation as the spread of education led to a better-educated population who would demand a more serious press. Though the circulations for the 'quality' papers have indeed increased, they have not yet reached the point where they begin to rival the circulations of the popular tabloid press.

However, it has to be said that the spectrum of interest of the tabloids has widened. The *Daily Mirror*, with its 'Mirrorscope' feature, takes a serious and intelligent look at the major events of the day: and under Rupert Murdoch's control the *Sun*, edited by Larry Lamb, has not only made a custom of publishing scantily clad girls on page three, but has also published socially useful and well-researched features on breast cancer and on the social impact of industrial redundancy.

(6) The Circulation Race

'This is a democracy,' say the critics. 'We should be given what we want—and we do not want sex, crime and violence.' The newspaper executives listen—and look at the circulation figures. For the communications media are businesses. They are subject to commercial pressures. A newspaper's circulation—the number of copies it sells—is what governs the rates it can charge for advertisements. British newspapers depend heavily on advertising revenue to be viable: the popular press gains 40 per cent of its revenue from advertisements, the quality press an astonishing 70 per cent.

If people do not want the fare newspapers are providing for them, they show little reluctance to buy it. Newspapers, to survive, must deliver a product that the potential readers want to buy. (This is as true of the 'underground press' with its derision of the news values of Fleet Street, as of the national newspapers.) The television news-rooms are under similar pressures, though somewhat differently expressed. Independent Television News, for instance, depends for its revenue on contributions from the commercial television companies. If they are not profitable, then ITN would be at risk. This does not affect the editorial judgement of ITN, which has managed to be both popular (with high positions regularly in the 'ratings', the television viewing figures on which advertising still relies) and to maintain the highest standards of news reporting.

With the creation of ITN, a rival has been presented to the BBC's news services. Many feel the latter have been strikingly improved by this challenge.

The fact that the British press—and indeed the world's press, with some exceptions—depends so significantly on advertising is considered by some to be a threat to journalistic independence, since the advertiser may pay for space and try to influence editorial decisions. Few journalists are, in fact, ever told that they must suppress a story, or write it differently, because of the susceptibilities of the advertisers (though it has happened).

But what is the alternative? In communist countries, the press is a branch of the Government. The press publishes—with rare and brave exceptions, for short periods—what the Government tells it to publish. If you believe that governments are always right, and that the rights of the individual should be subordinate always to those of the State, expressed through the local Commissar on the directive of the Party Praesidium, then you are fully entitled to that belief. Russian journalists work under those inhibitions.

(7) Truth and Familiarity

There are those in the West—including Presidents, Vice-Presidents, and politicians of both left and right—who feel that the freedom of the press has gone altogether too far and needs to be restrained. The world is in a ferment, and the journalist has one of the most difficult tasks—to report what is happening, as honestly and as frankly as he can, so that his readers may be as fully informed as he can make them.

News may be uncomfortable and unpopular. Television pictures of warfare in Vietnam, beamed coast-to-coast across America, divided that country and ended in American withdrawal from the Asian front. News media have to do this, and be unpopular for doing it.

Some newspapers have an honourable record in this respect. When the British Government sent troops into Suez in October 1956, the *Manchester Guardian* (under its new editor, Alastair Hetherington) took an editorial stand against that operation. The newspaper lost circulation in the short term, but in the past few years has more than picked up. No one could doubt the honesty of that decision, or in the short term, its perilous consequences. The *Guardian* was prepared to take the risk.

But it is true that in general people do not like to be distressed or disturbed, and the news of the day is often distressing or disturbing. Therefore, one element of the popular press might be called the 'familiarity factor'—the leaven of nonsense, of pulp entertainment, of simple reassurance that the world is still turning, that the popular press feels it must include in its pages.

The 'familiarity factor' is important. It must not be despised. For to get through to his readers, his listeners or his viewers, the journalist must lay down some guidelines to lead the public from what is familiar to what seems strange, dangerous and frightening. The journalist is an agent of change in a society. He must seek it and not stay too comfortably in the familiar present. For society changes, media or no media: and the press that does not change wakes up to find that its readers have left it behind.

(8) The Social Effects of Communications

The young man who enters journalism expecting to be sent to foreign parts reporting revolutions, or to be exchanging clues with

Chief Inspectors of Police over some murder victim, the while shouting into a telephone 'Hold the front page!' is doomed to disappointment. Most journalists lead a life of pedestrian domesticity and sobriety.

But what qualifications do you need to succeed, to break through to the top in newspapers or television? The late Nicholas Tomalin wrote in the *Sunday Times*:

> The only qualities essential for real success in journalism are ratlike cunning, a plausible manner, and a little literary ability.
>
> The ratlike cunning is needed to ferret out and publish things that people don't want to be known (which is—and always will be —the best definition of News).
>
> The plausible manner is useful for surviving while this is going on, helpful with the entertaining presentation of it, and even more useful in later life when the successful journalist may have to become a successful executive on his newspaper. The literary ability is of obvious use.
>
> Other qualities are helpful, but not diagnostic. These include a knack with telephones, trains and petty officials; a good digestion and a steady head; total recall; enough idealism to inspire indignant prose (but not enough to inhibit detached professionalism); a paranoid temperament; an ability to believe passionately in second-rate objects; well-placed relatives; good luck; the willingness to betray, if not friends, acquaintances.
>
> A reluctance to understand too much too well (because *tout comprendre c'est tout pardonner*, and *tout pardonner* makes dull copy); an implacable hatred of spokesmen, administrators, lawyers, public relations men, politicians and all those who would rather pervert words than policies; and the strength to lead a disrupted personal life without going absolutely haywire.
>
> The capacity to steal other people's ideas and phrases—that one about ratlike cunning was invented by my colleague Murray Sayle—is also invaluable (*Sunday Times Magazine*, 26 October 1969).

Other qualifications of a more boring nature are listed in chapter eight ('Training for Journalism'). The 'little literary ability' is more important than Tomalin allows—since the first qualification of a journalist is to be readable. The second qualification is a healthy scepticism about what you are told, and not only by spokesmen, administrators and the rest.

The Blind Eyewitness

A reporter arriving at the scene of an incident—whether an accident, bank raid or whatever—must get his information from eye-witnesses. Some (such as the police) are trained observers. Most are not. The journalist learns—if not from his own experience, then by listening to witnesses in magistrates' courts—that the general public are not often observant, and have a remarkable capacity for remembering in detail things that they could not possibly have seen as they swear they did. Patently honest witnesses in court frequently tell substantially different stories about the same event; it is not surprising that newspapers get so much wrong.

For it has to be admitted that newspapers do get things wrong. Arthur Christiansen, the great editor of the *Daily Express*, wrote a memorandum to his staff in which he pointed out to them that whenever they saw anything in the paper concerning their own street, or some matter about which they had personal knowledge, the odds were that there would be some material fact wrong. The public can never understand why this should be, when so many supposedly competent journalists are earning comparatively large salaries for reporting events accurately: but Christiansen's point is valid.

Perhaps the public would appreciate the difficulties better if it was appreciated how many times, inside a newspaper office, some member of the public telephones to ask for details of some book or show or sports fixture. 'I read it in your paper last Thursday,' he says: and inevitably on looking through the files you discover it in the opposition paper, last Tuesday fortnight ago. People are cavalier with facts, let alone opinions.

News as Incident

Those who work in the field of news recognise that their treatment is episodic. This is because each day's paper, each day's news bulletin on the radio or television is a thing complete in itself. The pressures of working in communications tend to be such that journalists wake each new morning with a clean slate, proceed to spend the day scribbling on it, and then wipe off the recollection at the end of the day.

Life, of course, is not like that. Life is a continuing development with a 'before' and an 'after'. The media catch aspects of life in midair and fix them as rigidly as a posed smile in a photograph. The very mechanics of the process make for distortion.

This is one reason why the press has a reputation for superficiality. Few newspapers have so many reporters on the staff that they can afford to keep them studying a situation if they are not going to produce copy for the paper. The result is that the news editors tend to look for situations of crisis and drama that are going to produce instant copy. This is bound to seem unfair, perhaps deliberately unfair, to people who are caught up in a 'running story' that does not get continuous coverage.

What It's All About

Industrial disputes are frequently like this. Two sociologists, Tony Lane and Kenneth Roberts, recently studied a long and unofficial strike at the Pilkington glass works at St Helens, Lancashire. In their report (*Strike at Pilkingtons*, Collins/Fontana) appears this comment:

> The Rank-and-File Strike Committee was no more flattering about the press, though the 'heavies' like *The Times*, the *Guardian*, the *Financial Times*, the *Daily Telegraph* and the 'posh' Sundays were almost universally exempt from criticism:
> 'The *Sun*, the *Daily Mirror* and *Daily Express* are not worth the paper they are written on. They are papers I used to buy, but I don't any more. Papers I've never bought in my life are the *Financial Times* and the *Observer*—now I do because their people really did try to find out what it was all about.'
> As one of the militants put it:
> 'The *Guardian* and the *Financial Times*, papers the workers don't read, were much better than the others. The popular press doesn't want to educate the workers because the less they know, the safer they are. The *Financial Times* and papers like that don't constitute a danger because they are not read by shop-floor workers so they can print exactly what is going on.'

It is a fair criticism of the press that the populars gave episodic treatment to an event that was only episodic when there were confrontations at factory gates, and failed to get to grips with the fluid and continuing nature of the situation. But it is manifest nonsense to say, as this militant does, that the *Financial Times* only prints 'exactly what is going on' because it is not read on the shop floor. It is as available to the workers on the shop floor as any other newspaper, and its proprietors, editor and journalists would no doubt be delighted if more shop-floor workers took it.

Similarly it is nonsense to say that the popular press 'doesn't want to educate the workers': the *Daily Mirror*, for one, has made determined efforts (through 'Mirrorscope') to do so.

But the comment does reflect the unsatisfactory nature of much industrial reporting, where the reporter has to try to assimilate a vast mass of conflicting fact, much of it highly technical and detailed. Such analyses are much less readable than stories about instant conflict. In this, the press is probably suffering from the impact of instant conflict on the television screen, a phenomenon we shall deal with later.

The Treatment

The ways in which the media work have not yet been studied in great detail, particularly since satellite communications introduced immediate awareness of world events and destroyed the old time-lag between an event happening, and the need for reactions to it (by politicians, world leaders, or individuals).

But the way in which the media prepare to deal with one event, and then cover that event, has been studied by James D. Halloran, Philip Elliott and Graham Murdoch of the Centre for Mass Communication Research at Leicester University (*Demonstrations and Communications; a Case Study*, Penguin, 1970).

On 27 October 1968, there was a march through London to the American Embassy in Grosvenor Square. Before that date, the media carried reports of militant groups who were threatening violence. A large police contingent was drafted into London in the anticipation of violence. Then, on the day itself, the march took place. There was an occasional scuffle, but none of the serious violence that had been predicted.

The researchers were concerned to establish how far the anticipation of the event influenced press and television coverage, what preparations were made by the media to cover the event, and finally how they did in the end report it. Incidentally they dealt with such factors as what the marchers expected, what groups were controlling the march, and whether they had been influenced by the advance publicity that had been given by the media.

Two newspapers, the *Daily Mirror* and the *Guardian*, co-operated with the researchers, as did the BBC newsroom and the ITN. The report is interesting, even though it states concepts that are obvious to anyone with a basic knowledge of journalism. By implication, however, it throws light on the troubled area in which the communicators are now challenged: the area in which, in Marshall McLuhan's phrase, 'the medium is the message'.

The researchers summarise the pattern of communications thus:

PRE-EVENT COVERAGE defines the nature of the EVENT-AS-NEWS. OCTOBER 27TH COVERAGE works within this definition. The general framework of the event-as-news is elaborated in the direction of the three main NEWS ANGLES:
NEGATIVE ASPECTS: the violent behaviour of the demonstrators; squabbles among the marchers;
PERSONALITY ASPECTS: PC Rogers; Tariq Ali;
POSITIVE ASPECTS: behaviour of the police; predominantly peaceful nature of the march.

The Media as Message

The study demonstrates the selectivity that journalists must apply when faced with a large and diffuse news event. Those who are planning coverage must make certain assumptions about the value, in news terms, of certain aspects of the event. These assumptions are derived from what the researchers call the 'event-as-news'. This limitation is best symbolised by the predicament of the television executives as they try to decide at what points along the route they will site their limited numbers of cameras. The problem then arises— it will be referred to later—of the impact of the presence of television cameras in an explosive situation: whether, that is, the television cameras will not by their presence spark off the violence they are placed to capture.

Some of the conclusions that the researchers came to included these:

> Events were not so much deliberately distorted or otherwise falsified by presentation, as selected and interpreted for their relevance to the basic and pre-determined news issue. The single negative image built up for the demonstration story was the only image made widely available to the public by press and television news. . . .
>
> The concentration on events itself makes some aspects of a story more likely to emerge as newsworthy than others. The issue of violence, for example, is directly related to the visible form of events on the streets. In contrast, the preoccupation with events and incidents tends to exclude consideration of background development and of the issues involved. . . .
>
> In one sense television appears to be dependent on the press, as well as in competition with it. The morning newspapers are an important source of information about the likely stories of the day, and are used at the morning planning conferences of both television organisations. . . .

The media, say the researchers, tend to create stereotypes— 'goodies and baddies'.

> It is not enough to state, as many do, that there is no freer, fairer, more accurate system in the whole world—although it is probably true. It is not even enough to recognise shortcomings in the present system and to accept the need for increased vigilance, accuracy and fairness in news-reporting. The area of discourse needs to be widened to include an examination of what is a much more complex system of news selection and presentation than one would gather from the current debate. . . .

This research demonstrates how the great change in communications produced by television has reflected back on the press, and on the profession of journalism. 'Ratlike cunning, a plausible manner and a little literary ability' are perhaps still the qualities required of the lone operator, the individualistic reporter for newspapers or television.

But there is a deep questioning going on concerning the effect of the media on society: journalists cannot ignore it. Indeed, those entering the profession, while studying the existing framework, must also study the assumptions that created that framework, and see how and when these should be changed in the light of the latest technological and social change.

(9) The Exercise of Power

'Power without responsibility—the prerogative of the harlot throughout the ages.' Prime Minister Stanley Baldwin (using words provided for him, it is supposed, by his cousin, Rudyard Kipling) summed up the way the newspaper proprietors intervened in a parliamentary election. By exercising their legitimate function of revealing something that someone doesn't want known, the press and television lay themselves open to this criticism.

In Britain the laws of libel firmly restrict the press media. In the United States journalists are much more free to publish allegations about criminal acts, without—as in Britain—the criminals being able to shelter under the protection of lengthy legal proceedings.

What power does the press in fact have, and how is it exercised? Harold Evans, editor of the *Sunday Times*, has urged the need for a code of conduct in reporting racial matters. Since the conflict of race is perhaps the most critical in the world today, this small example illustrates a *possible* (though not proved) connection between a reported fact and its consequences. But here again, it is for the reader to decide whether Mr Evans is linking cause and effect artificially. The following quotation can be read on two levels: first, as a study by an experienced national newspaper editor of the responsibility of the press in one field, and secondly as a piece of writing which raises additional questions in the professional journalist's mind.

It is my basic submission that newspapers have effects at two reciprocal levels on ethnic tension. By the information they select and display and the opinions they present, they have effects at ground level on the creation of stereotypes and the stimulation to behaviour. Because of the volatility of the subject, they also have swift effect at government level on the creation of policy. The press must first recognise that what it prints or broadcasts about ethnic groups can directly affect ethnic tension.

Any organisation not in league with the devil, which makes this first positive recognition, must then recognise the commitment which follows. It must have a positive policy to avoid unnecessary damage. These are responsibilities which many in the press refuse to acknowledge. They do so basically—since they none of them professes to like the devil—by insisting that they are mere mirrors and that news is neutral.

A small but typical example was provided by the *Middlesex County Times*. A study of several London weekly newspapers by the National Committee for Commonwealth Immigrants, published in 1967, showed that this paper published a high proportion of ethnic stories, ran a considerable number of unfavourable stories related to housing, and had a strongly anti-immigrant column written by 'Looker-On'. Looker-On gave particular attention to the news of a West Indian family moving into a council house. The week it happened, the front page of the paper headlined the story 'Council Home for Immigrant', and the story began: 'A Trinidad man, his wife and two children have moved into a council house on the Lady Margaret Road, Southall.' Looker-On's column the same day made a great deal of the secrecy with which the political decision had been made.

Three days after this, vandals attacked the new home of the immigrant family. They broke the windows. They harassed and abused the family. What did Looker-On think about this? 'The fact that it took place at this particular house so recently occupied by this family could be a coincidence—I hope it is, but on the surface there is every indication of race hatred. This kind of action disgusts every responsible thinking person.' That is typical of the schizophrenia of race reporting.

The *Middlesex County Times* columnist sought to escape responsibility by calling on coincidence. But the inflammatory stuff apart, the simple news story itself shows how shallow is the defence of the newspapers which say they must simply reflect the neutral facts. Hundreds of people in Middlesex move into council homes every week. They are not news. But this move was made news by the *Middlesex County Times*, made news by the identification of the new council house tenant as a Trinidadian. He had met all the council's qualifications. He had met the qualification of five years' residence. He was no different from other tenants except in this one respect. The man's ethnic group was irrelevant. It would have been relevant only if he had been given a house or refused a house *because of this ethnic group*.

A more damaging irrelevance is the selective identification of ethnic groups in court and crime reports. The survey of the London weekly press showed that ethnic identification was reserved almost exclusively for those stories which conveyed an unfavourable image, most of them about crime. People in court and crime stories were not identified ethnically as English, Welsh or Scots; but they were identified ethnically if they were Indian or West Indian.

The impression left on the reader over a period of time is that crime is concentrated among immigrants. Selective perception is encouraged. Stereotypes are formed. Yet the truth in Britain happens to be that immigrants are at least no more prone to crime than the rest of us. The statement of ethnic origin therefore conveys a factual accuracy—but a real untruth. This is a fundamental distinction for evolving proper guide-lines for ethnic reporting (*The Listener*, 16 July 1970).

This commentary by a highly responsible journalist implies a great deal more about a journalist's responsibility to search out the facts and give a full and fair picture than it does even about the particular subject that concerns Mr Evans. It shows also the depth of research that may be necessary before such an article can legitimately be written.

Mr Evans has studied a report by the National Council for Commonwealth Immigrants. He briefly summarises its conclusions about one newspaper. He then takes a single, particular example. In dealing with a diffuse general subject, it is always good to particularise: in this case, because the reader can identify with one family, which has much more impact than if the article continued to report solely in general terms.

Then the incident itself. The vandals struck 'three days later'. Does the *Middlesex County Times* circulate in or near the housing estate mentioned? Do the police know from which street the vandals came? Is there any direct causal connection between the vandals and the comment by Looker-On? These are questions a journalist would ask. No doubt Mr Evans asked them and was satisfied with the answers.

But Mr Evans has gone further. He has asked himself whether there was some reason other than race why 'vandals' should have resented this West Indian family moving into a council house. Had they 'jumped the queue' of the council's housing waiting list? Had they been given some preferential treatment? Mr Evans has discovered that the family was fully entitled to the house, having lived in the area for the appropriate time, and thus having the necessary residential qualification. This narrows down the reason for violence.

You may, of course, believe that racial purity is a good and desirable thing. You may believe that people with black skins are inferior to people with white skins, or that people with white skins are inferior to people with black skins. But the comment by Looker-On about 'race hatred' suggests that he does not think that race hatred is a good thing. So Mr Evans is right in referring to the 'schizophrenia' of race reporting. If either of Looker-On's quoted comments is valid, the other is inconsistent.

So journalists do have power, and must always remember the fact. Public reaction is not necessarily expressed in letters to the paper (writing letters to newspapers is something of a trade among some people, and there is no evidence that they represent a reasonable cross-section of public opinion).

If newspapers have this power, how much more does television have? Some commentators argue that television has now taken over from Parliament as the forum for the discussion of vital national issues, and television interviewers have much more power in the eyes of the public than do Members of Parliament. This is where the conflict between politicians and the media, now almost paranoid on both sides worldwide, begins.

Pictures of Violence

The job of the journalist in television is that of the analyst and the commentator. Though there has not been enough research to be certain of this, it seems likely that the effect of repeated pictures of war and violence on the television screen in the living-room is a brutalising effect. Such pictures increase callousness.

> Broadcast journalism needs more, not less analysis [writes Fred Friendly, for so many years assistant at CBS of America to the great Ed Murrow]. To take only one example: Vietnam today is not only the first war that television has been able to cover fully; it is also the news analyst's greatest challenge.
>
> No conflict in modern history has been obscured by so many subtleties and implications; in South-East Asia, black-and-white words like 'victory', 'defeat', 'majority', 'democracy', and 'appeasement' have relatively little meaning, and the complexities and nuances of the situation demand interpretation. As James Reston has said, 'today's reporter is forced to become an educator more concerned with explaining news than with being first on the scene' (Fred W. Friendly: *Due to Circumstances Beyond Our Control*, Random House).

The need for the reporter-as-expositor is all the greater because the mechanics of television mean that (particularly in news bulletins) the picture of any event is necessarily distorted by compression. Viewers see a two-minute clip of a woman searching among the ruins of her house, wrecked in an earthquake. It may be a vivid image, but the picture cannot say that the earthquake devastated a square mile, that a thousand people were killed and that thousands more are homeless. These facts, perhaps more important, can only be put across in words, and are almost impossible to express in pictures.

The firecracker effect of the television picture may distort in another way. The late Richard Crossman, former Labour cabinet minister and journalist, pointed out:

> Scarcely a Sunday passes without an evening bulletin, three or four minutes of which are devoted to covering a political meeting. What the viewer sees is an extract lasting 30 or 40 seconds from a main speech. It may well have been a 50-minute treatment of a serious issue, but all the viewer gets is a couple of sentences before the camera turns to a heckler, and the rest of the item shows the procession with banners which takes place after the meeting closes. I know I shall be told that heckling is news. But one ought to be clear what kind of impression this news selection makes on the viewer. In the first place it strengthens his suspicion that politicians never in their speeches treat issues seriously on their merits. In the second place it strengthens the natural feeling of many of the young people that the most exciting kind of protest to stage is violence, particularly when it gets you on to the television screens (R. H. S. Crossman: Granada Lecture, 1968).

What Crossman is saying here, in effect, is an extension of the criticism previously recorded of the press—that it treats events as episodic, even when they are part of a slowly evolving process. In addition the television treatment is a still tighter constriction of the time-scale. While the newspaper takes the single day as the boundary, television narrows the boundary down to one or two minutes.

So how does the journalist cope with this? The ultimate presentation, of course, is the business of the editor or the television news producer, or those whom they authorise to select and filter the news.

The Context of Facts

But the journalist has a duty too. It is the duty to exercise his power with restraint and responsibility. It is the duty to check his facts, and to assess in as much depth as he can, the context in which those facts exist.

Can journalism change a great deal? There are 'campaigning' newspapers which have uncovered abuses. There are 'campaigning' journalists—many of them on local newspapers—who have exposed malpractices and made their towns altogether more healthy places. They achieve success not, usually, by some sudden blaze of discovery, but by the slow piecing together of relevant information until the whole picture emerges, like a photograph coming into view in a developing-tank. In this, the investigative journalist is like a detective. Police work is seldom romantic: often the results are achieved by slow, solid digging over a long period. The same is true of newspapers.

But (despite the ambitions of leaderwriters and television commentators) people seldom change their deeply held opinions, but approve what they see on television when it goes along with those opinions, and disapprove of it when it challenges them.

Such evidence as is available suggests that the influence is likely to be at its maximum when we are not aware of being 'got at' and when the context is one of which we generally approve. Generally, however, reinforcement is more likely to occur than change, and this is largely due to the part played in the communication process by the various mediating factors. These mediating factors include (*a*) the individual's predispositions and the derived processes of selective exposure, perception and retention; (*b*) group membership and group norms; (*c*) inter-personal dissemination of the communication content; and (*d*) opinion leadership (J. D. Halloran: *The Effects of Mass Communication*—Television Research Committee working paper no. 1, Leicester University Press, 1968).

As I understand it, this means that our opinions are influenced by (*a*) our background and experience, (*b*) the neighbours and what they think, (*c*) the people we discuss TV programmes with in the train and the office or factory, and (*d*) the opinions of people we trust and admire.

Some journalists would deny that it is their purpose to form opinions or change society, but 'simply to give the facts'. But as we have seen, the relevant facts are not identified as easily as all that; and whether we like it or not, journalism in the press or on radio or television is a contributory factor—mingled with other factors—in the transformation of society.

But there *are* facts that are right or wrong. There are areas of reporting where the journalist can get his facts right or wrong, and report them accurately or inaccurately.

It is in those areas that most working journalists operate. But even here, the effects can be dramatic, as Hugh Cudlipp of the *Daily Mirror* demonstrates:

Herewith two intelligence tests for would-be executive newspapermen. Time to answer: 15 seconds.

1. You arrive at the office at nine o'clock one morning to find the Dog Expert, pale and distraught, awaiting you on the doorstep. In his right hand he is waving a copy of the current issue.

'My God!' he exclaims. 'In my column today I give a prescription for puppies with a cold in the nose. It included a poison which is perfectly safe when mixed with water, and I mean lots of water. Some idiot has deleted my reference to the water. This means that hundreds of our readers' pets are being bumped off at this very moment.'

The question is: what does one do?

2. The telephone rings at eleven o'clock one morning, and you answer it. The voice on the phone says:

'I am Professor A. M. Low. I have just been reading some advice given by one of your readers this morning in the column called Women's Parliament. She describes a method of saving fuel. Her idea is that you wrap a wet newspaper around a few handfuls of powdered coal, then wrap another wet newspaper around that, placing the result on the fire. I thought you might like to know that any reader who follows her advice is likely to blow up her husband's house. Good morning.'

The question is: what does one do? (Hugh Cudlipp: *Publish and be Damned*, Andrew Dakers).

Unfortunately, there are no satisfactory answers—except to get the thing right in the first place.

(10) The Freedom of the Press

Two consequences have sprung from the speed and efficiency of modern communications. One is that the right of the press to have access to all available information is being seriously challenged, by governments and the general public. The second is that as communications become so universal and dominant, organisations (governments, local authorities, industrial companies and societies of all kinds) are developing ways of protecting themselves against the release of information that is adverse to them, or that they think is adverse.

The first consequence is demonstrated by the growing number of attacks on the communications media by politicians and public figures, and by the arrival of pressure groups in favour of censorship and against what they regard as undue permissiveness. The second consequence is demonstrated by the expansion of the public relations industry, whose function it is to disseminate information favourable to its clients, and shield its clients from the publication of information detrimental to their interests.

There *is* a running conflict between politicians and the media. But the problem is accentuated today because the politicians need the media so desperately. It is now a serious quality in a public figure that he should 'come across' well on television. Unfortunately it is not true, as some commentators once believed, that television reveals the phoney. It may do. It may not. Edward R. Murrow, one of the greatest of the radio and television journalists, who exploded the Senator Joe McCarthy communist witch-hunting in the United

States, wrote this warning as early as 1949: 'Is it not possible that an infectious smile, eyes that seem remarkable for the depth of their sincerity, a cultivated air of authority, may attract a huge television audience regardless of the violence that may be done to truth or objectivity?'

Ed Murrow, from inside the world of communications, was voicing a fear that has lately been voiced by many public figures, who are beginning to question the motives of the communicators. Often the politicians' intentions are of the highest probity. Consider Lord George-Brown's comment:

> Every Foreign Secretary comes up against the BBC's refusal even to listen to, let alone take guidance on some matter that is causing concern. This is because of the BBC's insistence that it must be free from any suggestion of the taint of government control. That is a fine conception, but there are occasions when the Foreign Office, or some other Ministry, may in fact know more about a subject than BBC's own reporters or commentators. If what the BBC broadcasts is known to be wrong, or is known to be doing actual harm to British interests in some other country, should there not be some method of inducing the BBC to accept guidance? (Lord George-Brown: *In My Way*, Gollancz, 1971).

The answer, simply, is no—however one interprets that curious word 'inducing'. A free press (and I include in that an unfettered radio and television service) is essential to a free society, and a perpetual source of irritation and annoyance to the politicians of free societies. The alternative, after all, is a press regulated by governments, as in communist and totalitarian states. It is significant that the BBC has been criticised for its reporters' motives and views both under Labour and Conservative administrations.

The Resentment of Politicians

The same conflict is seen in an even more bitter battle in the United States, where the press has traditionally preserved its right to print the fullest account of what it thought should be printed irrespective of what the politicians considered the national interest, even during wars. President Roosevelt is said to have presented one American reporter at the White House with a German Iron Cross as a rebuke for printing a story that the President felt was damaging to the American war effort.

There are occasions when American newspapers have held back— and later were sorry. A notable example was the Bay of Pigs fiasco, early in the Presidency of John F. Kennedy, when the CIA supported an 'invasion' of Cuba by Cuban exiles based in Miami. Shortly before the invasion was due to take place stories began to filter back to Washington—notably a report written by Karl Meyer for the *New Republic*, and another by Tad Szulc for the *New York Times*. Both journals were persuaded by the White House not to publish these reports as this would endanger security. Afterwards it was felt that had the reports been published, they might have caused the cancellation of what proved to be a disastrous and ill-conceived venture: and its cancellation would certainly have been 'in the public interest' of the United States.*

The growing resentment of the politicians, and of some sections of the public, against those who work in the communications media has been voiced by the Vice-President of the United States. Power in television, according to Mr Spiro T. Agnew (and he later made the same criticism of the most distinguished American newspapers), is concentrated in the hands of . . .

> a tiny and closed fraternity of men, elected by no-one, and enjoying a monopoly sanctioned and licensed by Government. . . . Most Americans know little of these men other than that they reflect an urbane and assured presence and are seemingly well-informed on every important matter. . . . I am not asking for censorship; I am asking whether a form of censorship already exists, when the news received by 40 million Americans is determined by a handful of men responsible only to their employers and is filtered through a handful of commentators who admit to their own set of biases (Spiro T. Agnew, 13 November 1969).

The Suspicious Press

The best modern answer to such criticism has been given (after the then Labour Government had rejected his report on a matter concerning the press and national security) by Lord Radcliffe, the eminent British lawyer:

> Governments always tend to want not really a free press but a managed or well-conducted press. I do not blame them. It is part of their job. It is equally part of the job of the press to be wary about responding to these sometimes subtle, sometimes rather obvious inducements. Do not let us think of the Government as being powerless or ill-equipped in this issue. They have all the resources of modern public relations at their beck and call, they have all the subtle acts of pressure, the nods and the winks, the joggings of the elbow, the smile at what is called the responsible reporter, and the frown at the man who does not see quite clearly the Government's point of view. There is nothing evil about this, but it is one of the conflicts that goes on between the Government—

*The story is told by Arthur J. Schlesinger in *A Thousand Days*, André Deutsch, 1965.

B

whatever Government it is—and the press who are seeking to do their duty of telling the public the news.

I do not think that it is the duty of the press to have complete trust in what is advanced to them by the Government. I think they ought to be suspicious and they ought to be aware of a certain tension between the respective functions and duties of the two sides. I should be sorry to see a system under which complete trust is given (Lord Radcliffe, House of Lords, 6 July 1967).

Not only governments can become irritated by press 'intrusions' into privacy. Because of the increase in the number of cases involving 'bugging' devices—themselves a product of the new technology—the British Government in 1970 set up the Younger Committee on Privacy, 'to consider whether legislation is needed to give further protection to the individual citizen and to commercial and industrial interests against intrusion into privacy by private persons and organisations or by companies'.

Among the matters referred to this committee was 'the use by some newspapers and broadcasting authorities of certain recording devices'. Mr Jeremy Wallington, Executive Producer, Current Affairs, for Granada Television, was able in a subsequent article in *The Times* (31 January 1970) to cite four cases in which journalists had used 'bugging' devices or methods that would be regarded as breaches of the privacy of industrial or commercial companies in order to break stories.

The first was the Savundra affair, in which money paid in car insurance premiums was being diverted to a private company for the use of the directors. Journalists arranged for the files of the inner company to be extracted. In the second case, a journalist posed as a 'dim Australian' in order to send prohibited goods to Rhodesia, in breach of the sanction laws. In the third case, journalists posed as shipping dealers and secretly taped and filmed a meeting with a man supplying weapons to Biafra. In the fourth case, a firm of private detectives specialising in industrial espionage was tricked into 'bugging' a factory owned by a friend of one of the journalists. The exposure of all these matters, Mr Wallington (and many other people) believed, was in the public interest. Had the companies and individuals concerned been protected by a 'privacy' law, they might have continued their work unimpeded.

Lord Shawcross, himself a lawyer and chairman of the 1949 Royal Commission on the Press, has spoken strongly against any such privacy legislation designed to muzzle the press.

If enacted, [such legislation] would lead to restrictions on the press far outweighing any public disadvantage or alleged evils which the legislation is intended to cure.

In recent years some newspapers have engaged in deliberate probing, investigating or prying. Teams such as the Insight team of the *Sunday Times* have brought matters to light which it was clearly in the public interest to publish, but their efforts would have been defeated at the outset of the inquiry (Lord Shawcross speaking to the Commonwealth Press Union, 6 October 1970).

National Security

A rather finer line describes the responsibility of the press in the field referred to in the quotation above by Lord George-Brown: the field of national security. In Britain there have been repeated jousts between Government and press over this, leading ultimately to the '*Sunday Telegraph*' case when the editor of the *Sunday Telegraph*, Mr Brian Roberts, was acquitted of the charge of publishing an article (on an aspect of the Nigerian civil war) in contravention of national security. Earlier there had been the 'D-notice' affair (in Britain, matters which the Government feels are concerned with national security may be identified to the communications media by a Government-issued notice, a D-notice, which requests that such information should not be published).

At the time of the D-notice affair Lord Devlin, as Chairman of the Press Council, commented: 'There are too many people ready to prefer an official accusation to a newspaper denial.' Lord Devlin was touching on a matter which is of growing significance—the fact that there is an increasing body of public opinion that seriously believes, and vociferously states, that the press and television are only stirring things up, and that if only they would shut up and go away, half the trouble in the world could be safely ignored or forgotten.

No doubt this is a natural consequence of the ubiquitousness of news, and the fact that it tells us so many things that we got along fine without knowing, and do not wish to know. The feeling is understandable, particularly when it seems that every producer of television documentaries has suddenly latched on to the problem of abortion and the domestic screen is filled, night after night, with pictures of clinics, abortions, pregnant teenagers, and experts of every shade of opinion.

But there is a danger that—the media having cried 'Wolf!' so often and on so many subjects—when the wolf does really come down on the fold, the sheep turn blandly in disbelief. They turn on the journalists.

Louis Heren, then *The Times* correspondent in the United States, saw this happen after the Democratic Convention in Chicago, 1968:

Chicago was certainly not a novelty for reporters who had covered civil rights demonstrations in the south, but the American press is threatened by another despotism—not of governments, but of their readers. Many Americans, perhaps a majority, seem not to want to know what is going on in their country. They resent the press for telling them, and a common response is to blame reporters and not Mayor Daley's police or southern sheriffs for the national distemper.

There is little particularly new in this. It helps to explain the basic unpopularity of the press here and in Britain. American journalists have always claimed for themselves a higher status, professionally and in popular regard, than they have been prepared to yield to their British colleagues, but suspicion of their intentions has long been evident.

At the 1964 Republican National Convention in San Francisco, I can recall the wild applause when the former President, General Eisenhower, attacked the press. . . . They apparently believed that all would be well in the unreconstructed South if it were not for the press. . . . Press reports and national exposure on television were destroying their way of life.

Many at Chicago are well-educated, read newspapers regularly as well as watch television, but they are reluctant to believe what they read. Instead they blame the press for exaggeration or misrepresentation. They seem firmly to believe that the Chicago police were provoked and that television cameras attract trouble. All would have been well in Chicago, apparently, if the press had stayed away (Louis Heren: *The Times*, 10 September 1968).

'It takes two to speak the truth—one to speak, and another to hear,' wrote Thoreau.

There is the predicament of the journalist in the modern world. So much potential material that it is almost unmanageable, and the media are tempted towards superficiality. But superficiality in the press is nothing new. Thomas Jefferson, third President of the United States, remarked that 'the artillery of the press has been levelled against us, charged with whatsoever licentiousness could devise or dare'.

The journalist is today operating in a new world. It is the world of instant communication, worldwide (and indeed galaxy-wide). Ironically it is a world in which communication is so rich, so comprehensive, that many are turning away from its too strident voice.

Ed Murrow predicted a decade ago what would be the effects of satellite television.

A bus burning in Birmingham, Alabama, could be seen live throughout West Africa. A UN debate on the admission of communist China could be seen live throughout the Far East.

Fidel Castro may be seen as large as life from one end of Latin America to another. And all of South-East Asia can be drowned under a torrent of Instant Kruschev direct from Moscow.

Satellite TV will have no conscience, no principle, no morality. It will broadcast filth or inspiration with equal facility. It will speak the truth as loudly as the falsehood.

Murrow's prediction has already come true. The President of UPI, Roderick Beaton, foresaw in 1978 that news agencies worldwide might combine to use their own satellite, with the capacity to beam a newspaper full-page round the world in six minutes, or 'an entire news and stock service plus other special services, constantly and instantaneously updated, circulated continuously at 1,544,000 words per minute through a satellite channel'.

The problem will then be one of selection. That is the problem also facing the developing television information systems. In Britain these consist of Ceefax (BBC), Oracle (IBA) and Viewdata (Post Office). An adjustment to the domestic television receiver enables the viewer at any moment to call up, on his home screen, information deposited in a central computer and constantly updated. It may be the latest news, the stock exchange prices, the racing results. Viewdata was launched in 1978 with an 800,000-page storage.

This is the new world of communications, a world of computer-data-bases and information retrieval. Yet the function of the journalist does not change in spirit—to inform, to illuminate and to warn.

CHAPTER TWO

THE DEVELOPMENT OF COMMUNICATIONS

Printing was an ancient art long before it was used to reproduce lettering or books. The Japanese were engraving wood-blocks, inking them, and impressing them on paper in the eighth century A.D. A Chinese, Wang Chieh, printed a book in memory of his parents and dated it with the equivalent of 11 May 868. The Chinese are believed to have invented the first movable type, by using small blocks each carved independently with one character to make them interchangeable. Pi Sheng is said to have done this between 1041 and 1049. But the complex character of the Chinese alphabet, with its multiplicity of picture-symbols, made this a slow and tedious process.

It was not until the fourteenth century that moving type was introduced to Europe. Johann Gutenberg set up his press in Mainz, Germany, in 1454–5, and began to print Papal indulgences—the documents authorised by the Pope to grant forgiveness to sinners, for which there was an understandable demand. In 1456 Gutenberg and his assistants printed 300 copies of the Bible. It was in black Gothic lettering, and the initial letters were left blank and later ornamented to give the impression that the work had been hand-written by scribes (since Gutenberg did not want to give away the secrets of his achievement).

Unfortunately when the Bibles were sent to Paris to be sold, people noticed that each was absolutely identical with the next and supposed that Gutenberg had produced them by some evil magic. In 1457 Gutenberg produced a psalter. But the discovery of the technique of printing could not be long hidden. Within a few years the skill spread to Italy, and in particular to Venice. Printers began to devise new forms of lettering that were more appropriate to the physical requirements of print (the early printers either imitated handwriting, or copied the lettering on the classical monuments of ancient Rome). In Venice Nicolas Jenson added 'lower-case' (small letters, so called because they were usually kept in a case below the one in which capital letters were stored in the workshop) to the Roman capitals. A few years later Aldus Manutius Romanus (known as Aldus) added a sloping alphabet that came to be called Italic.

Before the end of the fifteenth century printing had started in France, and also in Switzerland where for a time the great scholar Erasmus was a press corrector. Then printing was brought to England by William Caxton. He had been born in Kent and apprenticed to a London mercer, but afterwards lived for thirty years in the Low Countries. He learnt printing in Cologne, and recognising the opportunities of this new technique began business on his own account in Bruges. Then in 1476 he returned to his native land and began printing in Westminster. He was an important innovator in another sense. Until Caxton, most books had been produced for religious purposes and in the language of the church—Latin. Caxton translated books into English and published them in his own tongue so that they could be read more widely. In fifteen years he produced about 100 books, and when he died in 1491 he left the business to his assistant Wynkyn de Worde.

Soon presses began to be set up all round the world. An Italian, Giovanni Paoli, began printing in Mexico City early in the sixteenth century; and with the opening up of the New World, printing went with the settlers. In 1638 the Rev. Jesse Glover set sail for America, taking a press with him. He died on the way, but the press was eventually set up at Cambridge Massachusetts, by Stephen Day and his eighteen-year-old son Matthew.

The press, then, was a means of increasing and deepening communications. As such, it was regarded as dangerous and subversive by many of those in authority. The history of the press has always been that of a battle for freedom against those who would stifle the open expression of opinion. Fortunately, there has never been a shortage of brave voices to shout against repression, whatever the personal consequences. In 1644 the British Parliament—in an effort to curb the proliferation of printing—imposed a licensing rule. It was against that system that John Milton published his *Areopagitica*, one of the noblest statements of the freedom of the press:

> Though all the winds of doctrine were let loose to play upon the earth, so Truth be in the field, we do injuriously by licensing and prohibiting to misdoubt her strength. Let her and Falsehood grapple; who ever knew Truth put to the worse, in a free and open encounter. . . . Give me the liberty to know, to utter and to argue freely, according to conscience, above all other liberties.

Despite Milton's efforts, it was another fifty years before the licensing of printing ended in Britain in 1695, and laid the ground for those fathers of journalism who are also respected as masters of literature: Defoe, Swift, Steele, Addison and Prior. In their writings they enriched the language—but their purpose was journalistic. As Defoe wrote: 'If any man was to ask me what I would suppose to be a perfect style of language, I would answer, that in which a man speaking to five hundred people of all common and various capacities, idiots or lunatics excepted, should be understood by them all.'

When in 1704 Defoe started his *Review* (at first a weekly, it was soon published three times a week) he became the chronicler of a changing Britain, and a journalist who introduced the country to itself. His main occupation was as a secret agent, first for a Tory politician, and then for a Whig. Some have called him a turncoat for this inconsistency. But he was a great reporter. As Francis Williams says of him:

> Each issue [of the *Review*] contained articles on political, commercial and social matters and there were from time to time a number of supplements. The whole of it Defoe wrote singlehanded and without outside help. To the task he brought an unexampled genius for plain writing and a superb never surpassed talent for the accumulation of significant detail. In so doing he not only established what journalism at this stage most needed—a tradition of responsible popular reporting—but also provided a pervasive antidote to the fierce partisanship that had earlier held almost undisputed dominance in the world of periodical journalism. He cultivated moderation. In matters of opinion his purpose was not to scarify but to persuade, a purpose so unusual as to seem almost eccentric. Like Swift he cast aside the pretentious journalism of the past and with it the dialogue form that had until then been almost the only mode for periodical writing.

Swift, in contrast, was a violent political pamphleteer, using brilliant language, and his works were not gentle breezes to civilise the climate of opinion but powerful blasts of diatribe. His pamphlet attacking the Duke of Marlborough and the Whig Government—the 'Conduct of the Allies in the Present War'—sold 10,000 copies in little more than two months in 1711–12. It is a vehement, inaccurate and exaggerated account, but probably helped to bring down that government. Such popular pamphleteering instilled terror into the politicians and led to the imposition of the Stamp Tax in 1712. This levied fourpence a copy on every newspaper and effectively restricted circulations.

Not that newspapers were at that time particularly militant. The first British daily newspaper was the *Daily Courant*, first published on 11 March 1702. This was a modest digest of extracts from European news sheets, often out of date, and provided no comment or opinion. Its editors wrote that they 'supposed other People to have Sense enough to make Reflections for themselves'.

A good deal more influence was held by the *Tatler*, when Sir Robert Steele started it in 1709 to circulate among the coffee-houses.

Two years later Steele combined with Joseph Addison to launch the *Spectator*, a daily journal that rapidly achieved the then remarkable circulation of 4,000 copies daily.

Addison and Steele devoted each issue to one essay, reflecting the thoughts and opinions of the time through the personalities of a group of representative 'clubmen'—Sir Roger de Coverley, the country gentleman; Sir Andrew Freeport, City merchant; Captain Sentry, a soldier; Will Honeycombe, 'man-about-town'; a lawyer and a clergyman. For nearly two years their experiences and opinions held London—for in those days road travel was slow and difficult (the mail coach only began in 1784) and publication was concentrated on the main centres of population. But Addison and Steele were deliberately non-political, reflecting society rather than the strongly doctrinaire opinions of the pamphleteers.

Parliament in the early eighteenth century kept its debates unreported. It was Edward Cave, founder and editor of the *Gentleman's Magazine* from 1731, who set out to break this embargo. He managed to bribe the doorkeepers of the Commons to allow one of his reporters, named Guthrie, to attend the debates. Guthrie had a remarkable memory. After each debate he would go back to his office and write down all he could remember of what was said, which was enough for Parliament to consider itself affronted. In 1738 the matter was raised before the Committee of Privileges and Edward Cave was threatened with terrible penalties if he continued to publish the reports.

But evidently the Commons had failed to identify Guthrie, for he continued to attend the debates. Cave published his reports— but instead of publishing them as the proceedings of the House of Commons, he called them the proceedings of 'the Senate' of the fictitious State of Lilliputa. The public were delighted. But if Guthrie had a good memory, he was not an attractive writer. So from 1740 to 1743 Cave employed a 'rewrite man' to improve the quality of the reports. The young man, newly arrived from Lichfield, was Samuel Johnson.

The reports of Parliament in that period in the *Gentleman's Magazine* have since been taken (by Cobbett, among others) as an accurate record. The MPs of the day were lucky to have the future great lexicographer to polish up their speeches.

The political newspapers had run into a sad decline. Bribery and corruption was general. An inquiry in 1742 discovered that as Prime Minister Sir Robert Walpole had paid out, over a period of ten years, about £50,000 to pamphleteers and the 'Treasury' newspapers—those that were putting out the Government's propaganda. Later, William Pitt is recorded as having paid £5,000 a year to the press. This made for complacent and weak newspapers, already hamstrung by the Stamp Tax. But late in the eighteenth century there began a groundswell of discontent with political management that led to articulate criticisms of Parliament. Eventually this produced a strong critic in the press.

In the columns of the *Weekly Advertiser*, published by Henry Sampson Woodfull, were published the 'Letters of Junius' which fiercely attacked Parliament. The attacks struck home to such an extent that there was a move to prosecute Woodfull for publishing them. In a London court the jury refused to convict him, despite a judge's direction to do so.

Junius wrote subsequently to the *Public Advertiser*:

Let it be impressed on your minds, let it be instilled into your children, that the liberty of the press is the palladium of all civil, political and religious rights of an Englishman, and that the right of juries to return a general verdict, in all cases whatsoever, is an essential part of our constitution, not to be controlled or limited by the judges, nor in any shape questionable by the legislature. The power of King, Lords and Commons is not an arbitrary power. They are the trustees not the owners of the Estate.

But it was the case of John Wilkes, MP for Aylesbury and proprietor of the *North Briton*, that broke open parliamentary reporting for all time. In the famous 'No. 45' of his journal, Wilkes attacked the King's Speech. George III was bitterly angry, and forty-eight people—printers, proof-readers and news-sellers, and including the proprietor Wilkes himself—were arrested for 'infamous and seditious libel'. Wilkes pleaded parliamentary privilege and to the general surprise the Lord Chief Justice upheld his plea and not only released the other prisoners but awarded them substantial damages for wrongful arrest. Wilkes fled to France, but five years later returned to stand and be elected as MP for Middlesex. Four times Parliament declared his election invalid. The City elected him an Alderman, and Wilkes began to report the proceedings of Parliament in the *Middlesex Journal*.

Other newspapers followed his lead, and soon three printers were before the courts. The printer of the *Middlesex Journal* found himself being tried by Alderman John Wilkes, who not unnaturally discharged him forthwith and committed to trial—for assault and wrongful arrest—those who had arrested him. Two other Aldermen MPs did the same for the printers of the *Gazetteer* and the *London Evening Post*. Outraged, Parliament committed them to the Tower. Disorder in the streets of London followed, until Parliament was obliged to give way. Thanks to Wilkes, parliamentary reporting continued, though formally remaining illegal until 1971.

But if this freedom had been won, the press was still severely restricted by law and custom. Until 1792, the judges decided libel cases, which did not go before a jury: and even after that, the Government could choose a 'special jury'. In the last thirty years of the eighteenth century there were seventy prosecutions of the press, with printers going to gaol and paying heavy fines.

Yet there were those arriving who looked forward to a free press, like Richard Brinsley Sheridan who in 1810 said to the Commons:

> Give me the liberty of the Press, and I will give the Minister a venal House of Peers, I will give him a corrupt and servile House of Commons, I will give him the full swing of the patronage of office, I will give him the whole host of ministerial influence, I will give him all the power that place can confer upon him to purchase submission and overawe resistance and yet, armed with the resistance of the Press, I will go forth to meet him undismayed.

Even if the eighteenth century was largely corrupt, it saw the foundation of several newspapers that survived for many years and provided the chronicles of the industrial revolution and the expansion of Victorian England. In 1772 John Bell started the *Morning Post* (his son later founded the *News of the World*), and made it a fashionable and well-laid-out newspaper. In 1790 James Perry took over the *Morning Chronicle* and gave it a great reputation for news coverage. In 1791 a young Irishman, W. S. Bourne, started the *Observer*. In 1795 James Stuart bought the *Morning Post* and turned it into a literate and literary paper, with Charles Lamb among the contributors, and a specialisation in fashion that attracted women readers.

On 1 January 1785 John Walter I launched a paper that he called the *Daily Universal Register*. Its purpose was largely to advertise an improved system of typography the rights in which John Walter had bought. The information it contained was mainly commercial, and the first proprietor had no concern with the freedom of the press such as agitated John Wilkes a few years earlier. John Walter accepted £300 a year from the Government for inserting useful paragraphs.

This did him little good, for two of the paragraphs were held to be criminal libels on the Prince of Wales and the Duke of York and John Walter was sentenced to two years in Newgate gaol, since he refused to reveal the source of his information. His paper also took money from individuals for agreeing not to mention them or their peccadilloes in the paper. By that time he had changed its title to *The Times*.

He learnt from the skill of his contemporaries. From John Bell's success he studied the improvement of his paper's layout and typography. From James Perry he copied the concept of detailed news coverage, particularly foreign news as up-to-date as could be got.

From James Stuart he deduced the importance of news about people, and particularly society people—the 'top people'. These were the editorial strengths that laid the foundation of one of the most potent influences on Victorian England. But it was in the constant modernisation of production methods that *The Times* was able to capitalise on the flair of its later editors.

From Caxton's day until the eighteenth century, more than 300 years, printing of all types was done on the wooden press hand-operated by screws—a cumbersome, often inaccurate and always time-consuming process. In the eighteenth century the most significant improvements were to type faces: William Caslon in 1720 cut a new version of Nicholas Jenson's Roman, and later in the century John Baskerville in Birmingham and Giambattista Bodoni in Parma cut alphabets that ever since have borne their names.

But as the art of printing spread, it was clear that the process must be speeded up. A Dutch printer, Willem Janszon Blaeu, improved the old wooden press at the beginning of the seventeenth century. But it was 1800, the dawn of the industrial revolution and of the age of the machine, when the Earl of Stanhope's iron press came into use. Presses were still flatbed. The metal impression had still to be inked separately and brought into contact with the sheet of paper, which itself was limited in size by the restrictions of papermaking.

Several men had the idea of using a cylinder to roll the impression on to paper. William Nicholson, in Britain, took out a patent for a cylinder press in 1790 but apparently never followed up the idea. At the same time, inventors were considering ways of introducing mechanical power to the press. In 1811 Frederick Koenig invented the first steam-driven press, in Saxony. Three years later a steam press was in use at *The Times*, quadrupling the output of the old hand press. The steam press could produce 1,100 papers each hour.

Soon it was adapted to print both sides of each sheet simultaneously, thus halving the printing time. And in 1827 Applegarth and Cowper of *The Times* made further modernisations that increased the speed to 4,000 impressions per hour. While *The Times* was thus creating the material context in which a mass circulation newspaper might be produced, the spread of the railways across England from the 1830s offered a speedy and efficient method of distribution. Meanwhile the climate of reform, culminating in the great Reform Bill of 1832, provided a middle class eager for information to armour them for that participation in public affairs that reform had granted them.

But below the middle classes were the vast numbers of workers recruited into the factories and workshops of industrial England, and fired by revolutions in Europe with the hope of social change at home. William Cobbett set himself up as their spokesman, and his *Political Register* became the notable and notorious voice of radicalism at the beginning of the nineteenth century. Cobbett, a farmer's son, had fought with the British Army in America and then, returning to Britain in 1800, set up his weekly first as a Tory periodical. But his own strong opinions moved steadily left and soon he was angering the authorities.

The Stamp Tax on newspapers meant that each copy of the *Political Register* cost 1s 1½d, an extraordinary sum. So Cobbett produced a 2d version containing only comment and no news, and therefore unstamped. He arranged for it to be distributed throughout the country and sold by small shopkeepers, and these marketing arrangements gave his 'Twopenny Trash', as he proudly called it, a staggering circulation for the times of between 40,000 and 50,000 copies a week. So powerful did Cobbett's *Political Register* and similar radical publications such as the *Black Dwarf* and the *Poor Man's Guardian* become that action was taken against them. The Habeas Corpus Act was repealed in 1817 (at which Cobbett fled to America for two years); and in 1819 the Six Acts were passed—they have been called the 'high water mark of legislation restricting the freedom of the press'.

Under a new editor, Thomas Barnes, *The Times* had ceased to be merely a commercial broadsheet and become a major political voice, and a loud and critical voice at that. The second proprietor, John Walter II, gave Barnes authority to turn the paper into an independent expression of popular opinion. This he did by publishing full and accurate accounts of the major events of the day at home and abroad, whether or not they were comfortable to the Government.

To those authorities who called such reportage 'dangerous radicalism' he replied: 'There is nothing which they so much dread as a free journal, unattached to any other cause than that of truth, and given to speak boldly of all parties.' By the Reform election of 1832 (when Cobbett was elected as MP for Oldham) *The Times* was the most influential daily newspaper in Britain.

Political reform led to the easing of repressions on newspapers. In 1836 the Stamp Tax was reduced to 1d. The main effect of this was the launching of several popular Sunday papers, particularly *Lloyds Weekly News*, the *News of the World* and *Reynold's News*. *Lloyds* reached a high circulation by using a new rotary printing press invented in America by Robert Hoe, the forerunner of the modern press—and by giving the widest coverage to the Jack the Ripper murders. The first issue of the *News of the World* had as its main headline—'Extraordinary Charge of Drugging and Violation', thus striking at the very beginning the note that carried it through 150 years of popular success. These Sunday papers were also the first to give detailed sports reports—for the Victorians were achieving leisure as one of the rewards of industrial progress.

As the railways were enabling newspapers to circulate across the country, the electric telegraph became the means whereby they could inform their readers of the latest news. In 1805 the news of Nelson's death took two weeks to reach London. In 1850 Paris, Brussels and Berlin were linked by the telegraph cable, and the first submarine cable was laid under the English Channel between Dover and Calais in 1851. In a few years this revolutionised foreign news coverage.

1851 was the year of the Great Exhibition in London. One visitor to it was a German, Paul Julius Reuter, owner of a pigeon post between Cologne and Brussels. He had watched the spread of the cable with apprehension since it was wrecking his business; so on the principle 'if you can't beat 'em, join 'em' he set up an international service of stock market prices using the electric telegraph.

Then he contracted with the leading newspapers to provide them with a foreign news service. For a time there was a fight with the telegraph companies which tried to impose a surcharge on press messages other than their own, sent via their cables. In New York, the newspapers appreciated what was going on and formed a co-operative, the Associated Press of New York, to collect and transmit foreign news. In Britain a similar system was set up by provincial newspapers, organised by John Edward Taylor, the proprietor of the *Manchester Guardian*, and the Press Association was founded to provide them with foreign news.

With the ending of the Stamp Tax in 1855 there was room for a cheap morning paper. This gap was filled on 29 June 1855 (the eve of the abolition of the tax) by the *Daily Telegraph and Courier*, which published four pages at 2*d* and soon reduced its price to 1*d*. This was not much welcomed by *The Times*, which until then had a near-monopoly of 'serious news'. Not that the *Daily Telegraph* was then 'serious' in its presentation. It adopted headlines that for the day were garish and bold, and some journalists sneered at its adoption of 'brash American techniques'. But they worked.

Under Barnes and his successor John Delane (who became editor in 1847 at the age of twenty-three) *The Times* was bitterly attacked by the politicians. Lord Derby said that if the press wanted the same influence as statesmen, the press must 'as a sacred duty, maintain that tone of moderation and respect, even in expressing frankly their opinions on foreign affairs, which would be required of every man who pretends to guide public opinion'.

John Delane was not having any of this, and on 6 and 7 February 1852 published a classic statement of press responsibility from which these are extracts:

The first duty of the press is to obtain the earliest and most correct intelligence of the events of the time, and instantly, by disclosing them, to make them the common property of the nation. The statesman collects his information secretly and by secret means, he keeps back even the current intelligence of the day with ludicrous precautions until diplomacy is beaten in the race with publicity.

The press lives by disclosure: whatever passes into its keeping becomes a part of the knowledge and history of our times; it is daily and for ever appealing to the enlightened force of public opinion—anticipating, if possible, the march of events—standing upon the breach between the present and the future, and extending its survey to the horizon of the world.

The responsibility [the journalist] really shares is more akin to that of the economist or the lawyer, whose province is not to frame a system of convenient application to the exigencies of the day, but to investigate truth and apply it on fixed principles to the affairs of the world. The duty of the journalist is the same as that of the historian—to seek out the truth, above all things, and to present to his readers not such things as statecraft would wish them to know but the truth as near as he can attain it.

Within a few years, upholding these principles, Delane and *The Times* were shocking public opinion in Britain by reporting the scandalous conditions under which British soldiers were living in the Crimea. Many were appalled by the 'irresponsibility' of *The Times*, among them Queen Victoria who felt that those responsible for such reporting should be excluded from 'higher society'.

The reputation of *The Times* had become worldwide. Welcoming a *Times* reporter on the eve of the American Civil War, Abraham Lincoln told him that 'the London *Times* is one of the greatest powers in the world—in fact I don't know anything which has more power, except perhaps the Mississippi'.

But the ending of the Stamp Tax and the founding of more cheap daily newspapers curbed this solitary eminence. Soon the *Daily Telegraph* had topped the circulation of *The Times*. The combination of large print-runs, advertising and rising costs meant that the old style of campaigning journalism was muted. It is significant that one of the most powerful press campaigns of the latter part of the nineteenth century was conducted not by a mass circulation daily but by W. T. Stead, editor of the small-circulation *Pall Mall Gazette*. Stead went to gaol for three months after his exposure of child prostitution (for having ostensibly 'procured' a child during his investigations).

Meanwhile other technical developments had paved the way for a new system of journalism. The fast rotary printing press invented in America by Robert Hoe was only practicable because the paper-making Fourdrinier brothers had in 1803 discovered how to manu-facture paper in long lengths that could be wound on to reels: until this invention, printing speeds were governed by the need to feed single sheets of paper into the press, by hand or by mechanical means. But it was 1865 before the American William Bullock perfected the system of linking paper reels to the press to offer near-continuous operation. This meant that newspapers could be produced fast and in a greater quantity.

From 1860 to the 1880s newspapers were started all round the world, many of which survive to this day. They joined—and chal-lenged—some which beginning in the eighteenth century learnt to keep up to date with modern techniques (for example, *Berlingske Tidende*, the Copenhagen paper, has published since 1749).

This selective list of some of the papers founded in those years gives an indication of the importance of the reel-fed rotary press:

1860   *Aftenposten* (Oslo, Norway)
1861   *L'Osservatore Romano* (Vatican)
1864   *Dagens Nyheter* (Stockholm, Sweden)
1867   *La Stampa* (Turin, Italy)
1874   *Manitoba Free Press* (Winnipeg, Canada)
1875   *O Estado de Sao Paolo* (Sao Paolo, Brazil)
1876   *Al Ahram* (Egypt)
1878   *The Hindu* (Madras, India)
1878   *St Louis Post-Despatch* (St Louis, USA)
1879   *Asahi Shimbun* (Osaka, Japan)
1881   *Los Angeles Times* (Los Angeles, USA)

The Elementary Education Act (the Forster Act) of 1870 is sometimes taken as a key reform in the history of journalism, since it led to the growth of a large literate reading public. Significantly, the profits went to those who provided what this new public wanted. In Manchester, Edward Hulton was notably successful with his halfpenny evening papers, mainly devoted to sport.

It was in Manchester, too, that George Newnes—then a salesman for a fancy goods firm—recognised the yearning of this new public for condensed information presented in a popular way. In 1881 he produced a sixteen-page magazine, costing one penny, with the title *Tit-Bits from All the Most Interesting Books, Periodicals and Newspapers of the World*. Within a short time *Tit-Bits* had achieved the startling circulation of 900,000 and Newnes had moved to London.

Newnes started a range of similar magazines based on the parti-cular interests of the time. There was among them a cycling magazine, published in Coventry. Newnes took on to the staff the young Alfred Harmsworth, son of a failed London barrister. Harmsworth made a success of cycling. Soon he came to London and started up his own magazine, *Answers*.

The first issue was published on 2 June 1888 (numbered 'No. 3', since Harmsworth realised that as the paper was to give 'Answers to Correspondents' (its full title), the first number must mysteriously have at least one predecessor—he published a limited number of fictional 'Nos. 1 and 2' later in the year for inclusion in bound volumes). He was married that spring, and he and his best man carried 'dummy' copies of *Answers* sticking ostentatiously out of their pockets at the wedding ceremony.

Such publicity methods paid off. But it was his famous competition offering a prize of 'one pound a week for life' that sent the circulation soaring. His brother Harold joined him as financial adviser, and the magazine empire was soon expanded to include *Comic Cuts*, *Home-Sweet-Home*, *Union Jack*, the *Sunday Companion* and other similar publications. By 1892 *Answers* had 'the world's largest circulation' of over a million: and Harmsworth was using the circulation figures to attract more advertising.

In 1894 he bought the London *Evening News*—a liberal paper founded in 1881 but by then suffering from the competition of the much livelier *Star*—for £25,000. By making the news reporting sharper and briefer, adding a strong sports page and powerful crime reporting, he made enough profit in the first year to cover the purchase price and turn the ailing paper towards its career as (for many years) the world's largest-selling evening paper. Two years later, in 1896, Harmsworth launched the *Daily Mail*. Lord Robert Cecil called it a 'newspaper for office boys written by office boys'. Harmsworth preferred to call it 'a penny paper selling for a halfpenny'.

Its foreign coverage was superlative, but Harmsworth kept to the theory he had learnt in magazines: 'There's no story that can't be told in 100 words.' Each day there was a 'daily magazine', a feature page of background information and matters of interest to women—the introduction of the feature page to newspapers. *The Times* had held an unchallengeable circulation for forty years early in the nineteenth century. From its foundation in 1865 the *Daily Telegraph* held sway for forty years. Now the *Daily Mail* took top circulation and held it for nearly the same period. As he had done with *Answers*, Harmsworth published certified circulation figures as a means of fixing high advertising rates.

Though he later for a time took over *The Times* and the *Observer* Lord Northcliffe (as he became, with his brother Harold becoming the first Lord Rothermere) always regarded the *Daily Mail* as his own creation and favourite paper. But even Northcliffe, the 'Napoleon

of the Press', could make mistakes. He was perhaps ahead of his
time when in 1903 he launched the *Daily Mirror*, 'written by gentlewomen for gentlewomen'. Because the women's features in the
Daily Mail had been such a triumphant success he had argued that a
newspaper devoted wholly to women's interests, and edited by women
would be bound to succeed.

It was a resounding failure, and after three months was renamed
the *Daily Illustrated Mirror*, a tabloid paper—appealing to both men
and women and making great use of the newly perfected half-tone
block for printing photographs. A near-disaster was turned into yet
another success.

Northcliffe's death in 1922 coincided with a major development in
communications that was to have an important effect on newspapers. He died just three months before (in November 1922) the
British Broadcasting Company began regular broadcasting from a
radio station, 2LO, on Savoy Hill, London. Despite press objections
to the broadcasting of news, the British Broadcasting Corporation
was set up—a state-financed institution not subject to commercial
pressures. John Reith (later Lord Reith) imposed upon it, as Director-
General, a philosophy of public service broadcasting based on his
own austere probity.

As newspapers became more competitive in Britain, there was a
feeling that as most of the proprietors were Conservative the political left—of growing importance—should have its own newspaper.
The *Daily Herald* was founded as a strike newspaper during a printing lock-out in 1911. By 1920 it was being financed by the Labour
Party and the Trades Union Congress (by means of a levy on the
unions) as a Labour paper. In 1929 a new company was formed, in
an alliance between the TUC and J. S. Elias, of Odhams Press, who
needed a morning paper to keep his presses occupied.

In 1930 the Communist Party founded the *Daily Worker*, 'the
only paper financed by its readers'. Distinguished by its high standard
of layout and design (by Allen Hutt) and by its racing service, the
Daily Worker changed its title in 1965 to become the *Morning
Star*.

The newspaper circulation war of the 1930s has been vividly
described by Francis Williams, himself a former editor of the *Daily
Herald*. The war was fought not by journalism but with free gifts—
books, clothing and insurance.

First the *Herald* passed the *News Chronicle*. Then the *Express*
passed the *Mail* ending its close on forty years' supremacy. Then
the *Herald* passed the *Mail* also and came up hard on the heels of
the *Express*. The two of them shot neck and neck down the straight
with the *Mail* and the *News Chronicle* racing for third place.

Between them the four were spending close on £60,000 a week, or at the rate of £3 millions a year, on clothing and equipping hundreds and thousands of people all over Britain. The *Herald* made a last sprint. It beat the *Express* by a cutlery set and became —although for a matter of days only—the first newspaper in the world to announce a circulation of 2 million copies a day.

This circulation war, ended by a truce shortly before the real war of 1939–45, was accompanied by a similar and parallel battle for control of provincial papers. It effectively divided the British press into two groups—the 'quality' papers (*The Times, Guardian* and *Daily Telegraph*) which drew most revenue from the distinction of their readers and therefore the expensive advertising they could attract; and the 'popular' papers (the *Daily Mirror* and *Daily Express*), a substantial part of whose revenue came from the sheer number of their readers, which in itself could attract lucrative advertising. From this point of view the newspapers whose appeal was between these poles began to feel the squeeze—and particularly the liberal *News Chronicle*, which combined a highly literate style of reportage and comment with a comparatively popular presentation.

Both the top-circulation British morning newspapers of the post-war period have been the creation of individuals of strong personality. The *Daily Express*, with its sister-papers the *Sunday Express* and the London *Evening Standard*, were built up by Max Aitken, Lord Beaverbrook. His combination of vigorous political (and partisan) comment, euphoric social reporting and vivid sub-editing and rewriting (inspired by the greatest of his editors, Arthur Christiansen) proved a money-spinner. It was beaten only by the *Daily Mirror* under Harry Guy Bartholomew, with Hugh Cudlipp as editor and William Connor ('Cassandra') as probably the greatest idiosyncratic columnist of the century.

Both papers had powerful effect, but at a tangent to the mainstream of British political change. Lord Beaverbrook told the Royal Commission on the Press, honestly, that 'I run my paper purely for the purpose of making propaganda and for no other purpose'. Yet his campaigns for Empire preference gained little political success.

The *Daily Mirror* based its success on being the spokesman of the working class. But a still more popular medium had come into existence even before the war. The BBC began regular television programmes on 2 November 1936, putting out two hours of programmes on six days a week, using an electronic system of transmission in preference to the mechanical system invented in Britain some years earlier by John Logie Baird. Regular programmes began in the USA on 30 April 1939. But sets were expensive and television was a luxury until the launching of a second, 'independent', channel financed by advertising (the first commercial programmes went out in the London area in September 1955); within two years 80 per cent of households in Britain owned or rented a TV set.

The impact on the failing newspapers in the 'middle-of-the-road' sector, neither quality nor popular, was swift. In the closing months of 1960 the *News Chronicle* and its companion evening paper, the *Star*, ceased publication. Daily News Ltd, their parent company, sold them to Associated Newspapers Ltd, Lord Rothermere's *Daily Mail group*, for £2½ millions. The circulation of the *News Chronicle* at that time was well over one million, and that of the *Star* 735,172; but in the battle for multi-million circulations that was not enough for them to survive and they 'merged' with the *Daily Mail* and London *Evening News* respectively. As a merger it was like that other described by A. J. Liebling, 'the merger between a cat and a canary'.

Shortly before, the Canadian radio and newspaper owner Roy Thomson (afterwards Lord Thomson of Fleet), who had earlier gained control of the *Scotsman* in Edinburgh, took over Kemsley Newspapers, publishers of the *Sunday Times* and a string of provincial papers. Subsequently he took a majority and controlling interest in *The Times*. Odhams Press gained control of the Newnes magazine empire at about the same time; Daily Mirror Newspapers took over Amalgamated Press, and later swallowed Odhams to become the International Publishing Corporation, by far the largest magazine publisher in Britain.

This last merger produced a conflict of newspapers. For as part of the Odhams deal the *Daily Mirror* inherited the failing *Daily Herald*. In 1964 an attempt was made to revive it by changing the name to the *Sun*, but after six poor years the paper was bought out by Rupert Murdoch. Mr Murdoch, an Oxford-educated Australian, had made his name in his family newspaper group in Australia partly with evening journalism but also by launching (in 1964) the first national daily paper in that country, the *Australian*. Coming to London, he had bought the *News of the World* in 1968. The Murdoch *Sun*, edited by Larry Lamb, only took a few years to challenge the *Daily Mirror* as the largest selling British daily. Soon Mr Murdoch was turning his sights to the American newspaper market.

Colour magazines, after a shaky start, proved a commercial success. Lord Thomson's innovation at the *Sunday Times* was soon followed at the *Observer* and the *Daily Telegraph*, though later the *Telegraph* colour magazine was transferred to Sunday.

The early 1970s threatened the survival of several Fleet Street newspapers. The advertising recession was rendered more acute in its effects by the introduction in 1971 of commercial local radio stations. Associated Newspapers closed down the *Daily Sketch*, and converted the *Daily Mail* into a 'quality tabloid'. Under the editorship of David English this at last turned the failing fortunes of that newspaper.

The success of two tabloids—the *Sun* and the *Daily Mail*—persuaded the *Daily Express* to change from broadsheet to tabloid early in 1977. The Beaverbrook papers had (with the exception of the *Sunday Express*) been suffering from the cold economic climate. This had obliged them to close down the printing of the *Scottish Daily Express* in Glasgow. The staff made a gallant effort to keep the newspaper going, but failed.

An analysis of Fleet Street had been made in 1966 by the Economist Intelligence Unit, but the stark facts it revealed were not heeded by managements or unions. Several newspapers seemed doomed, in particular the *Observer*, until in 1977 it was saved through the intervention of Atlantic Richfield, an American-based multinational oil company. In the same year Beaverbrook Newspapers were bought by Trafalgar House, predominantly a property company though with several other interests, and the old name of the group—Express Newspapers—restored.

Public concern at the condition of the British press led to the setting up of three Royal Commissions in 30 years (1947, 1961 and 1977). The first led to the creation of the Press Council as 'watchdog'; by the recommendation of the third, the Press Council was enlarged to 18 press and 18 lay members. But the latest Royal Commission came to no agreed conclusion about safeguards for the economic future of newspapers. The majority of members felt that there should be no government intervention; a minority believed that the political imbalance of the press could only be redressed by the provision of public funds, for an alternative.

However, the greatest threat to newspapers' survival was still the fear of a highly-paid workforce threatened with redundancy by the introduction of new technology, and expressing that fear through strikes and disruptions of production. Ironically, satellite communication and teletext systems of information retrieval through the domestic television receiver were developing while newspaper managements and unions haggled over a printing system not greatly changed since the days of Caxton.

(1) The World's Press

Britain is the only country in the world with so many newspapers circulating nationally. This is a practical matter of distribution: it has been possible, because the islands are so comparatively small and are networked by railways, to build up a distribution system that enables a paper produced in London in the evening to be delivered in the furthest cities (though not in the distant rural areas or to the Scottish offshore islands) at breakfast time.

This is changing. For technical advances have enabled newspaper pages and even whole newspapers to be transmitted from a central composing point to outlying cities—as *Asahi Shimbun* does in Japan, or *Pravda* in Russia.

But there are in fact more newspapers in the world today than there were twenty years ago, thanks to increased populations and technological change allowing wider distribution. In the rich countries of the West, while the larger distribution national and state newspapers decline and fold, the smaller local newspapers everywhere thrive. In the developing countries of Africa, Asia and South America, new local news sheets are still being started and the number of newspapers increases constantly—to feed the appetite of those newly literate populations for information.

In 1952 there were an estimated 7,000 daily newspapers in the world, with a total circulation of 230 million copies. In 1969 there were about 8,100 dailies, with a total circulation of 360 million copies. And these were only the *daily* papers. There are far more regional or provincial papers, mostly weeklies. In the United States alone there are 14,000 regional or provincial papers.

United States and Canada

In the 1960s the great city newspapers in America declined, and many small-town second newspapers closed or merged to give a near-monopoly situation. In Los Angeles, for instance, there were four city newspapers in 1957: ten years later, there were only two—but in the sprawling suburbs the number of local dailies had risen to twenty-eight.

The change in New York was no less dramatic, pivoting on the newspaper strike of 1966. Afterwards, the *New York Herald Tribune* closed (keeping alive its Paris edition, jointly with the *Washington Post*). That left New York with two general morning papers (the *New York Times* and the *Daily News*) and one evening (the *New York Post*), until in 1971 a new evening started— the *New York American*. (The *Wall Street Journal*, a specialised financial paper, continues to publish also in New York.) But there were some forty suburban dailies being published around New York.

In most small towns of the United States there used to be two morning papers, one Democrat, the other Republican. Today 96 per cent of America's small-town papers have a monopoly in their area. Where there are still two newspapers, in some cases supposed rivals have been allowed to merge printing plant and overheads through a special exemption from the anti-trust laws governing monopoly business operations.

The newspaper chains, with their greater capital resources and ability to invest in the latest plant, are increasingly gaining on the independent editor-proprietor. But in spite of the challenge of television, four out of five Americans still take at least one paper a day.

There is much the same situation in Canada, with a few distinguished big-city papers such as the *Toronto Globe and Mail* with its remarkable foreign coverage (for some years at the height of the Red Guard 'cultural revolution' it maintained a correspondent in Peking), but the large chains are increasingly capturing the small-town papers. The Thomson Group, for example, has thirty small daily papers in seven provinces from British Columbia to Newfoundland, and thirteen weeklies in four provinces. These include the happily named *Orillia Daily Packet and Times* of Ontario, the *Bathurst Northern Light* of New Brunswick, and the *Swift Current Sun* of Saskatchewan.

As in other countries, mergers and closures have inclined the Government to take notice and there has been a Senate inquiry into the state of the mass media in Canada.

Europe

Throughout Europe the press faces the same challenges: rising costs and limited advertising revenues for the larger papers, with the rewards going to the local press. In France, the Paris newspapers are in a critical economic position despite a Government subsidy on newsprint. The number of daily papers in Paris has decreased from twenty-eight in 1945 to thirteen in 1970, and observers predict that within a few years Paris—in common with other world capitals—will have two morning and two evening newspapers.

One of the evenings will certainly be *Le Monde*, edited and founded by Hubert Beuve-Mery and almost unique among the world's papers in its refusal to be concerned with trivialities (such as sport) and its refusal to print pictures (originally a technical decision, because the paper was started after the war on the ancient presses of *Le Temps* which could not cope adequately with picture-blocks). Yet for all its dullness of presentation *Le Monde*, written with high seriousness by a brilliantly well-qualified staff who own the paper through a worker-control scheme—maintains its reputation as one of the world's great newspapers.

There are no papers of equivalent authority in Italy, although *La Stampa* of Turin and *Corriere della Sera* of Milan approach it, as does the popular evening *Paese Sera*, and *L'Osservatore Romano*, the daily published by Vatican City and generally considered to be the voice of the Pope. Because so many Italian papers are owned by industrialists as strictly commercial concerns, they are regarded somewhat sceptically by their readers.

Much the same is true of the West German press, 40 per cent of which is controlled by one man—Herr Axel Springer, who starting as a young Hamburg publisher built up his massive newspaper and magazine empire. Herr Springer owns *Die Welt*, the lively right-wing Hamburg daily which circulates throughout West Germany. He also owns *Bild Zeitung* and its Sunday companion *Bild am Sonntag*, *Berliner Zeitung*, *Hamburger Abendblatt* and *Berliner Morgenpost*.

The *Frankfurter Allgemeine Zeitung* (Frankfurt General Newspaper) founded in 1949 after the licensing of newspapers was lifted by the allied post-war occupation authorities, is as solemn and serious in makeup as *Le Monde*, but carries a picture and feature section on Saturdays (in Germany, the type of contents of the British Sunday papers is to be found in Saturday supplements or in the weekly magazines such as *Der Spiegel* or *Stern*). In the south of Germany, *Die Suddeutsche Zeitung* has a wide circulation.

In other countries of Europe, governments have come to the aid of weakening newspapers. In Norway, for instance, the Government puts substantial advertisements in local papers, subsidises newsprint and allows cheap press rates for telephones. In Denmark the Government provides guarantees against the cost of newspaper plant. In Holland the newspapers receive subsidies based on a proportion of the revenue from advertising on broadcasting networks. But these are all symptoms of a basic weakness in newspaper economics, generally due to low pricing.

Press freedom has been restored in Portugal (since the 1974 revolution) and Spain. However, economic difficulties forced the closure of two of Portugal's oldest newspapers, *O Seculo* and *Jornal do Comercio*; and in Spain there has been violence against the media.

Soviet Union and Eastern Europe

Government control is also paramount in the Soviet Union and Eastern Europe, and while the Communist Party theory is that their newspapers are more free than those in the West (since they are controlled by the workers and not by capitalist proprietors) the world has observed in recent years what happens to journalists who in Russian-controlled countries express an independent view.

When the Prague newspaper *Rude Pravo* and the Czech television service supported the liberalising effects of the 1967–8 regime which abolished press censorship, they were ruthlessly suppressed by Russian intervention. The imprisonment or silencing of writers in the Soviet Union is another dismal aspect of communist ideology in action.

Nevertheless the Soviet Union produces two remarkable national newspapers, *Izvestia* and *Pravda*. *Izvestia* means 'news' and *Pravda* means 'truth': it is a traditional witticism that '*Izvestia* does not print the truth, and *Pravda* does not print the news'. The statement is false: both papers print a good deal of both news and truth, and in massive quantity.

Izvestia, with its head office in Moscow, is an evening paper printing in twenty-two cities of the USSR. Its circulation is thought to be between eight and ten million. Kruschev's son-in-law, Alexei Adzhubei, edited it from 1959 to 1964, raised its circulation, modernised its appearance, and brightened its presentation. *Izvestia* specialises in readers' letters and investigates many of them to produce follow-up news stories.

Pravda, the official paper of the Central Committee of the Soviet Communist Party, was founded in 1912 in St Petersburg by Lenin as an underground news sheet: it is therefore five years older than *Izvestia*. Somewhat more solemn, as befits a paper that prominently prints the official party line on all subjects, its head office is in Moscow. Pages are either flown or telegraphed to some thirty print works around the Soviet Union, and the circulation is about seven million copies a day.

China

Even more rigorous government control is imposed on *Jen-min Jih-pao*, the *People's Daily* of Peking, China's national newspaper. It is the official organ of the Chinese Communist Party and of the Government of Mao Tse-tung. It contains official pronouncements, occasional fiction and poems (always with a political slant), and many cartoons and caricatures. The *People's Daily* is said to have a circulation of around two million, but reaches far more readers since it is put up on the reading-walls in many public places.

The *People's Daily* has been an important tool in the modernisation of the highly complex Chinese ideogram-lettering, both by itself adopting a new and simplified system of ideograms, and by printing its headlines and text left-to-right and horizontally in the western fashion, instead of right-to-left and vertically, in the old Chinese style.

Japan and South-East Asia

Japan is unusual among 'developed' countries in having national newspapers with mass circulations that are read by the whole community. There is no division between 'quality' and 'popular' such as is found in Europe or America. Further, *Asahi Shimbun*, the largest-circulation paper, is both a morning and evening paper, printing in five cities—and also a radio and television company.

Asahi Shimbun also publishes magazines and books and has a substantial interest in property.

Asahi Shimbun prints around nine or ten million copies a day in Tokyo (the head office), Osaka (where the paper was founded in 1879), Seibu, Nagoya and Sapporo. Between these places, about 100 different editions are published each day: in Tokyo, there are eight morning editions and four evening editions.

Telephoto transmission has revolutionised production of *Asahi Shimbun*, where local copy (because of the 2,304 separate characters available) is still hand-written. The paper has also experimented with facsimile transmission by radio of whole editions to outlying sub-offices, and has moved on from this to experiment with the Teleview system where subscribers can rent or buy receiving sets for their own homes, printing-out whole newspapers at the touch of a button.

There are two other Japanese national papers that challenge *Asahi*. They are *Mainichi*, which tends to be middlebrow, and *Yomiuri*, which specialises in entertainment. Both have circulations above five million. But *Asahi* remains the leader, partly because of its comprehensive international news service, and partly through the number of sponsorships it takes up, from exploration and flight to competitions in the arts.

The newspaper situation in South-East Asia generally is more fluid, though the spread of education and prosperity has led to the foundation of a number of new papers (including the new papers in Singapore, the *Singapore Herald* and the *New Nation*). The largest newspaper in the region, however, remains the *Manila Times* with a circulation of a quarter of a million. A news agency for the region is being planned.

Australia and New Zealand

Australia has to date only one newspaper that aims at national coverage—the *Australian*, founded by Mr Rupert Murdoch in 1964. With a head office in Canberra, computer-typeset there and published in Sydney, it prints facsimile in Melbourne, Brisbane, Adelaide and Perth. Greeted with scepticism in some quarters, the *Australian* has proved a notable success, with a circulation around 150,000 in 1970. In 1971 it was joined by the *Sunday Australian*, a companion paper modelled somewhat on the London *Sunday Express*.

There are other Australian newspapers that are read outside their own regions. *The Age*, founded in Melbourne in 1854, is a serious liberal paper with a circulation of around 190,000, mostly in the State of Victoria. The *Sydney Morning Herald*, originally founded in 1831 and a daily from 1840, and controlled by the Fairfax family for a century, is a conservative paper, particularly strong on arts and literature. Its circulation is around 300,000 and its world record for small-ads enables it to publish editions of 128 pages, possibly to be increased to 144 pages.

Many new papers are in prospect for Australia, though after the attempt of *The Age* to start a companion evening in Melbourne as a rival to the successful *Herald* failed after a few months, proprietors are costing their ventures carefully.

In New Zealand the press is at present limited to one morning and one evening paper in each city: but the possibility of a national New Zealand newspaper is being explored by Mr Rupert Murdoch following his success with the *Australian*.

India and Pakistan

The circulations of the English-language city papers of both India and Pakistan are comparatively small for countries with such immense populations. The *Hindu*, with the *Statesman* and the *Times of India*, one of the leading organs of influence, has a circulation of around 136,000. *Jang*, the leading Urdu daily paper in West Pakistan, has a circulation of only around 200,000.

In part these restrictions are due to currency problems, since there is little locally produced newsprint and a strict limit on the quantities that may be imported. Though there are several papers that maintain high standards (such as *Dawn* of Karachi), development is restricted.

The same applies to the main local and regional papers throughout the Indian sub-continent. A further restriction in Pakistan is the Government control imposed by the military regime.

Africa

Similar controls apply to many if not all of the papers in the newly independent one-party states in Africa north of the Zambesi, though there are journalists who are working towards the day when a truly free press will be possible.

There are similar stumbling blocks to press freedom in South Africa, though technically the Afrikaans paper *Die Burger* of Cape Town is of a high standard. For many years Laurence Gandar has edited the *Rand Daily Mail* in Johannesburg, a powerful and distinguished voice of criticism.

Latin America

Political upheavals are nothing new in Latin America. They are often accompanied by changes in press freedom. In the past few years they have led to extreme changes in control for some newspapers and threats to others. In Peru the military junta expropriated the *Expreso*, the daily paper published in Lima, and turned it into a workers' co-operative. In Chile, following the re-establishment of a right-wing regime following the fall of the communist President Allende, there was continued harassment of the press, even of the country's chief paper, *El Mercurio.*

In Mexico, *Excelsior*—both a daily and a Sunday paper—is already a co-operative, and increasingly unpopular with politicians for its forthright criticism and vigorous expression of its independent position. In spite of this, *Excelsior* has a reputation for responsibility and a careful respect for facts. Mexico has two other important newspapers—*Novedades* and *El Universal.*

In Argentina and Brazil, right-wing military regimes lean heavily upon the freedom of the press. But *La Nacion* and *La Prensa* in Buenos Aires, and the *Jornal do Brasil* in Rio de Janeiro, uphold serious standards in a challenging situation.

(2) The Press in Britain

There are 135 daily (including Sunday) newspapers published in Britain, 1,174 weekly newspapers and around 5,000 periodicals and magazines (of which about 500 are house magazines). Of the daily newspapers, nine are national in circulation though published in London. There are seven national Sunday newspapers.*

Few countries have so many newspapers circulating nationally. The explanation lies in the geographical compactness of Britain, which enables newspapers printed in London to be distributed round the country and yet remain topical. Manchester has long been a subsidiary printing centre for many national newspapers. Other newspapers have other subsidiary printing points: the *Daily Mirror*, for example, also prints in Belfast.

Britain has the second highest figure for newspaper readership per head of the population in the world (the highest is Sweden). Because of their national coverage, British newspapers tend to have extremely high circulations compared with newspaper circulations in other countries (particularly the Sunday press).

* Figures from the *Newspaper Press Directory*, 1971.

National Daily Morning Newspapers

There are nine national daily morning newspapers in Britain. These are:

	Circulation*
Daily Mirror	3,844,592
Sun	3,722,731
Daily Express	2,432,075
Daily Mail	1,829,380
Daily Telegraph	1,310,011
The Times	306,115
Guardian	291,609
Financial Times	176,683
Morning Star	36,572

National Sunday Newspapers

There are seven national Sunday newspapers in Britain. These are:

	Circulation
News of the World	4,934,284
Sunday People	3,943,417
Sunday Mirror	3,967,947
Sunday Express	3,287,087
Sunday Times	1,373,534
Observer	656,242
Sunday Telegraph	796,407

London Evening Newspapers

There are two evening newspapers circulating in London and the densely populated South-East of England. These are:

	Circulation
Evening News	533,041
Evening Standard (Mon.–Fri. only)	411,538

Pricing

The comparative prices and circulation figures demonstrate how the quality newspapers make up for their lower circulations by charging a higher cover price. But it is generally accepted that the British press is substantially under-priced.

* Circulation figures quoted are those published by the Audit Bureau of Circulations and are the certified average daily net sales for the half-year ended June 1977 (later figures are significantly distorted by the effects of a series of industrial disputes in Fleet Street).

Newspaper Groups

Most national newspapers are owned by groups with interests in provincial newspapers, magazines, television, etc. The major groups (with their publishing subsidiaries) are:

Associated Newspapers Group Ltd
    Harmsworth Publications Ltd
        Daily Mail
        Evening News
    Northcliffe Newspapers Ltd
        13 provincial papers, including the *Western Morning News* (Plymouth)

Express Newspapers Ltd
    Daily Express
    Sunday Express
    Evening Standard
    Evening Citizen (Glasgow)

News International Ltd
    Sun
    News of the World
    provincial papers

Pearson-Longman Ltd
    Financial Times
    Financial News
    40 provincial papers

Mirror Group Newspapers Ltd
    Daily Mirror
    Sunday Mirror
    People
    Daily Record (Glasgow)
    provincial papers

The Thomson Organisation Ltd
    Times Newspapers Ltd
        The Times
        Sunday Times
    Thomson Group
        50 provincial papers including the *Scotsman* (Edinburgh) and the *Western Mail* (Cardiff)

United Newspapers Ltd
    30 provincial papers, including the *Yorkshire Post* (Leeds) and the *Morning Telegraph* (Sheffield)

The Regional Press

Twelve towns and cities outside London have morning newspapers. These are:

Birmingham Post
Western Daily Press (Bristol)
Northern Echo (Darlington)
East Anglian Daily Times (Ipswich)
Leamington Morning News
The Yorkshire Post (Leeds)
Liverpool Daily Post
The Journal (Newcastle)
Eastern Daily Press (Norwich)
Nottingham Guardian Journal
Western Morning News (Plymouth)
Morning Telegraph (Sheffield)

But the great majority of provincial newspapers are either evenings or weeklies (with a few bi-weeklies). There are more than 100 daily newspapers, 72 of them evenings, and 1,174 weeklies. The predominance of the evening paper in the provinces is explained by the general circulation of the national dailies in the morning, and by the concentration of local advertising in the profitable provincial evenings.

These have not been substantially hit by the introduction of commercial television as an advertising medium, since television advertising time is expensive, and the TV areas cover a much larger region than most local papers. The paper, therefore, has a continuing advantage as a local advertising medium. This may be challenged when commercial broadcasting is introduced, with its emphasis on local interests.

Specialised Newspapers

There are several newspapers produced to serve special sections of the community, such as the twenty-five religious weekly newspapers, and others devoted to sport, or commerce.

Periodicals

The weeklies giving radio and television programmes have the largest sale among British periodicals, closely followed by the women's magazines. Their circulations (*July–Dec. 1977*) are:

Radio Times	3,748,903
TV Times	3,658,176
Woman	1,537,973
Woman's Own	1,578,234
Woman's Weekly	1,641,101
Woman's Realm	763,540

Dailies: quality & popular
Weeklies: political & quality variety
52 *Journalism Made Simple*

Among other magazines are the popular 'variety' weeklies *Weekend* and *Reveille*, and the political weeklies such as the *Economist*, *New Statesman*, *Spectator*, *Tribune*, *New Scientist* and *New Society*. The majority of periodicals are trade, technical and of specialised interest. Many are produced by the large publishing groups.

Press Agencies

The principal press agencies, circulating news to many papers throughout Britain are:

Associated Press Ltd, 83 Farringdon St, London EC4. The British operating company of Associated Press of America.

The Exchange Telegraph Company Ltd, 1 East Harding St, London EC4. EXTEL is an independent news agency, founded in 1872, supplying financial, commercial and sporting news.

The Press Association Ltd, 85 Fleet St, London EC4. Owned by the major regional newspapers outside London, the PA was founded in 1868 and is joint owner of Reuters.

Reuters Ltd, 85 Fleet St, London EC4. The first news agency in London, Reuters was founded in 1850. It is owned by the newspapers of Britain, Australia and New Zealand through the Newspapers Proprietors' Association, the Press Association Ltd, the Australian Associated Press and the New Zealand Press Association. Reuters has about 1,000 correspondents in 180 countries, and it transmits to 120 countries.

United Press International, 8 Bouverie St, London EC4, is an international news agency operating from London.

Associations

(*a*) Employers

Newspaper Publishers' Association (formerly the Newspaper Proprietors' Association) is formed from the executives of the national newspaper publishing groups (in London and Manchester). It acts as the employers' association in negotiations with the unions.

The Newspaper Society is formed from the proprietors and managers of the regional and suburban newspapers, and similarly acts as the employers' association in union negotiations.

(*b*) Employees

National Union of Journalists. The NUJ was formed in 1907 to represent the interests of journalists on newspapers and magazines, and subsequently in radio, television, and public relations. The NUJ is affiliated to the Trades Union Congress

The pictures in this section are the winning shots in the British Press Pictures of the Year 1970, a competition organised by the Rank Organisation Limited and the Institute of Incorporated Photographers.

Above: The first prizewinner in the Royal Family section: Prince Charles and Princess Anne photographed informally in North-West Canada by Freddie Reed of the London *Daily Mirror*.

The boxer Henry Cooper leaves home to prepare for a fight.

This picture and those on the next three pages won the title of Press Photographer of the Year 1970 for Michael Brennan of the *Sun*, London.

A young man in Belfast lies dying after being hit by a Saracen tank during a riot: photographed by Michael Brennan.

Above: The sole survivor of a lifeboat disaster at Fraserburgh, Scotland, steps ashore after his rescue.

Below: The British Labour Party politician George Brown in an altercation at an election meeting.

Above: George Best of Manchester United in action.

Below: Model Kirsten Gille poses for a fashion picture near the Champs Elysée, Paris.

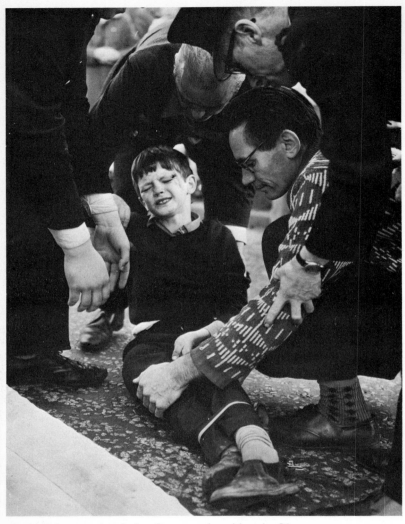

A small boy receives help after a road accident in Glasgow.

This picture and those on the next three pages won the title of British Regional Press Photographer of the year 1970 for James Robertson of the *Scottish Daily Record*.

A four-year-old approaches her first riding lesson : photographed by
James Robertson.

Cecil the swan stays on shore as Glasgow children take over his frozen pond: photographed by James Robertson.

Above: Scottish boxer Tom Imrie corners an opponent in the ring.

Below: The legs of a Clydesdale horse illustrate the inspiration of a new fur boot fashion: both pictures by James Robertson.

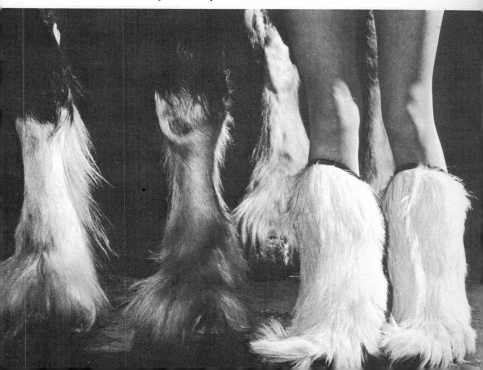

The pictures opposite and on the following page are from the sequence taken by Kenneth Lennox of the *Scottish Daily Express* during the rescue of the crew of the trawler *Summerside*, aground on rocks near Stonehaven. The sequence won first prize in the black-and-white sequence or picture story section of the British Press Pictures of the Year competition 1970.

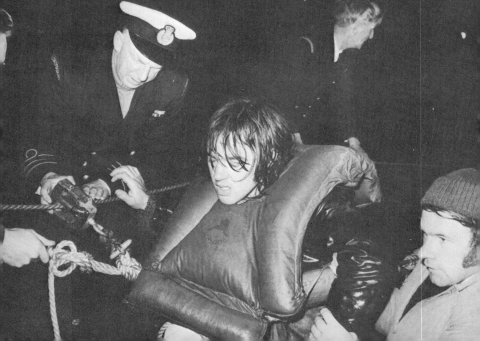

Winner of the Sport section of the British Press Pictures of the Year
competition 1970, this shot of Jockey T. Norman apparently whispering
instructions to his mount was caught by J. R. Macnee of the Sport and
General Press Agency.

A photographer with an observant eye can give life to such a static subject as a sculpture exhibition. First prize in the Feature category went to Tony Sapiano of Sport and General Press Agency for this composition seen in Holland Park, London.

Commercial photography is some of the most challenging since the subjects are generally unphotogenic by nature. This picture of angled steel being dipped into galvanising baths at a factory in East Lothian won Ian Brand of the *Scotsman* first prize in the Commercial and Industrial category.

News pictures cannot be posed and the photographer must be ready for the moment of drama. Canadian freelance photographer Franz Maier was on the spot when a Canadian policeman discovered a girl trapped but alive in the wreckage of a sports car. The picture won first prize in the News Category of the British Press Pictures of the Year competition 1970, organised by the Rank Organisation Limited and the Institute of Incorporated Photographers.

and to the Printing and Kindred Trades Federation, a federation of unions in the printing industry.

Institute of Journalists. The Institute was founded in 1884 and incorporated by Royal Charter. Despite efforts early in the 1970s to achieve some reconciliation with the NUJ, the two bodies now operate entirely separately, with some bitterness on both sides.

(c) Foreign Press

Foreign Press Association. Over 250 foreign journalists representing their papers in Britain belong to the FPA. An international press centre is now being built in Fleet Street.

(3) The Underground Press

If the conventional press and all who work for it are caught up in the mechanics of the operation (and much elsewhere in this book may suggest that) then the underground press is going back to grass roots.

Much of it uses the new technology to cut straight through from the writer to the reader, with the minimum of production technique. Where there is production technique, it is devoted to the use of colour and pattern that is more akin to the art print than to the ordinary newspaper.

The underground press has a strong group appeal. Generally it appeals to radical youth, often revolutionary youth, and its atmosphere is dictated by the world of popular music. Not, that is, the commercial 'pop' industry, but the rock and folk response that produced Woodstock and similar mass pop festivals.

In America, Greenwich Village was the origin of this pop press. The *Village Voice* was a local production but soon circulated internationally. San Francisco launched the *Rolling Stone*, which also appealed to a particular age-group and interest.

With the broaching of so many social taboos, in the theatre and film, a further sub-culture sprang up to voice this sexual licence—such papers as *Suck*, *Screw* and *Ball*.

In Britain, the development of the underground press followed that of America, but strongly under the influence of expatriate Americans.

Except, that is, for *Private Eye*. Started in the days of the 'satire' boom, the *Eye* under Richard Ingrams' editorship (and with Paul Foot writing 'Footnotes', superlative digging journalism) virtually emerged from the underground to take its place among conventional magazines of comment.

The British underground press has veered from the extreme left-wing political (*Friends*, *Black Dwarf*, *Red Mole*) to the intellectual

c

pop (*International Times, Oz*). Though these have also been taboo-breakers, they have given a voice to a culture that finds no expression in the conventional papers: *IT* was initially part-financed by the Beatles.

Paul Overy has suggested (*New Society*, 28 January 1971) that the vivid graphics and use of colour in *Oz* has a good deal in common with the spontaneous drawings of working-class children, and Mr Overy points to the relevant fact that many pop musicians have emerged from art schools.

Mr Overy finds the colour-on-colour printing of *Oz* easier to read than much fine-art printing: few would agree with him. The self-indulgent colour printing of much of the underground press is some-times interesting, but often virtually unreadable when the colours are out of register.

Most of these papers aim at a narrow readership with particular interests, and make no concessions whatever to older readers familiar with the conventional press. *Oz*, indeed, so offended convention that three members of its staff were convicted of publishing an 'obscene' issue, the notorious 'Schoolkids' ' issue No. 28.

But it begins to look as though there are moves to break out of the underground and challenge the conventional press on its own ground. *Time Out*, having built a success as a pocket-sized digest of events of interest to the young mixed with comment, has turned into a larger-sized weekly edited by its young founder, Tony Elliott. Meanwhile Richard Neville, the founder of *Oz*, has launched *Ink*, a weekly 'con-centrating on civil liberties, drugs, revolutionary movements and social problems as well as on clothes, records, books and films'.

In a number of cities in Britain local news sheets have been started, often with a strong political slant (see Ken Worpole and Roger Hudson: 'The Community Press', *New Society*, 24 September 1970).

CHAPTER THREE

FACTS ARE SACRED

'Comment is free; facts are sacred.' C. P. Scott, a great editor of the *Manchester Guardian*, made that much-quoted statement of a main principle of journalism. Like many epigrams, it is true in part. But it needs qualification, as Scott qualified it. 'A newspaper must have courage and fairness, and a sense of duty to the reader and community. Its primary office is the gathering of news: at the peril of its soul it must see that the supply is not tainted.'

These are admirable sentiments. But they suggest that there is some pure crystal spring of news, into which the journalist may dip his cupped hands. Every journalist sooner or later encounters the reader who passionately objects to something he has written. 'Why do you write lies?' he is asked. 'Why don't you tell the truth?'

The journalist's predicament in dealing with facts has been brilliantly described by Claud Cockburn:

> To hear people talking about the facts you would think that they lay about like pieces of gold ore in the Yukon days waiting to be picked up—arduously, it is true, but still definitely and visibly—by strenuous prospectors whose subsequent problem was only to get them to the market.
>
> Such a view is evidently and dangerously naive. There are no such facts. Or if there are, they are meaningless and entirely ineffective; they might, in fact, just as well not be lying about at all until the prospector—the journalist—puts them into relation with other facts: presents them, in other words. Then they become as much part of the pattern created by him as if he were writing a novel.
>
> In that sense all stories are written backwards—they are supposed to begin with the facts and develop from there, but in reality they begin with a journalist's point of view, a conception, and it is the point of view from which the facts are subsequently organised. Journalistically speaking, 'in the beginning is the word'. All this is difficult and even rather unwholesome to explain to the layman, because he gets the impression that you are saying that the truth does not matter and that you are publicly admitting

what he long ago suspected, that journalism is a way of 'cooking' the facts.

Really cunning journalists, realising this, and anxious to raise the status of journalism in the esteem of the general public, positively encourage the layman in his mistaken views. They like him to have the picture of these nuggety facts lying about on frozen ground, and a lot of noble and utterly unprejudiced journalists with no idea whatever of what they are looking for scrabbling in the iron-bound earth and presently bringing home the pure gold of Truth.

Is it not true [asks Cockburn], that ninety per cent of 'information received' by such serious persons as Ambassadors and Chiefs of Police really consists of significant rumours which can be interpreted by the person who knows enough rumours?

It is true.

It is important for the journalist because with so many facts, so much information reaching him by telephone and telex, radio and television without his even going out to look for it, the journalist becomes highly selective.

There is a strong temptation for journalists (in this case editors and news editors) to see what they expect to see. At the beginning of each day the executives of a newspaper, news agency, or radio or television newsroom sit down with the 'diary'.

This lists for them the predicted events of interest during the day. Parliament is discussing certain matters—what the MPs say may be interesting. There are some fascinating cases in court—a murder case, say, that has attracted public attention. There is a fashion show at a fashion house that has a reputation for producing outrageous clothes—a photographer will go there. The Minister of Transport is opening a new road and local residents have said they will stage a protest. All these events have to be 'covered'. Towards the end of the day, 60 per cent of the paper will be filling with items as a result of what was in the 'diary' at the beginning of the day.

So who compiles the facts in the 'diary'? Some derive from official announcements, such as proceedings in Parliament and the Courts. Others will come in public relations handouts, such as the fashion show and the Transport Minister's road-opening. One of the residents near the road may have telephoned in to say that they are going to make a protest.

(1) The Facts and How to Get Them

Persistence is a necessary quality for a good journalist. This does not mean offensiveness. Few stories are gained by bulldozing techniques, because a tough approach only raises the hackles of someone being questioned. There are occasions when a person feels like unburdening himself or herself to a total stranger, but seldom does anyone tell all spontaneously to a stranger taking it all down in a notebook.

Good journalism consists of the intelligent assembly of relevant facts. Often these can be got together before an interview, which then becomes a matter of confirming facts at first-hand. A journalist does not often go into a situation 'cold', or should not. He will be sent on a story because his news editor believes that there is a story to be obtained, which presupposes that certain facts are already known to him and will be given to the journalist before he sets out. This will be his 'brief'. It is not, and cannot be, comprehensive in the sense that *all* the story is known beforehand; and there are many occasions when the man on the spot finds and writes a story that is better than the one his news editor visualised, because the facts apparent on the spot reveal new implications that were not appreciated when the report was initiated in the office.

But many relevant facts can be discovered in cuttings (clippings) or reference books. It is the journalist's duty to arm himself with as much information as he can before setting out on a story. There may not always be much time, but the effort should be made.

(2) Cuttings (Clippings)

Many newspapers have a 'library' containing the principal reference books and also cuttings filed under people and subjects. If you ask for the cuttings about a person you will be given a file of the latest cuttings—the reference to him in the national press, and in some magazines. These will be filed in chronological order and should always be kept in order. Librarians are understandably annoyed with reporters who spray the cuttings around their desks like confetti and then jam them back into the folder in any order. Equally annoyed are other reporters who later may want to look through those cuttings in a hurry and discover that they are out of date-order.

The second heresy for users of cuttings is taking them out of the office. It is a strange quirk of fate that whenever someone takes the cuttings out of the office, those very cuttings are inevitably and urgently required within the office. Richer offices sometimes run to a photocopier to provide instant copies of cuttings for the use of reporters.

Cuttings are of great value in filling in the background about someone to be interviewed. They suggest lines of inquiry (if three months ago a film star said in an interview that he was looking forward to filming in Spain, or getting divorced, or buying an Alsatian, these facts provide pleasantly neutral talking-points with which to start an interview). But cuttings can provide too easy a crutch for journalists, since the temptation is always to retail the same anecdotes and incidents from past interviews. A girl barrister once agreed to escort a pop star to a film premiere, and she was photographed with him in the cinema foyer and written up by all the gossip columnists. For years afterwards she was branded, whenever she appeared in court, as the 'pop girl barrister'. Maybe she asked for it, but people can get unfairly typecast that way.

Always check with the cuttings for background information. But try not to rely on them too much, or to plagiarise other interviews too obviously.

Only experience will teach you precisely how a particular library files its subject cuttings. There is no point in asking for the cuttings on 'crime' if you are researching for a story about a burglary: the best course is to explain clearly and concisely to the library assistant what angle you are looking for, and let him advise you. At the same time, it is up to you to think of any sub-section that might throw light on your particular problem.

(3) Reference Books

Never ignore the obvious. Journalists have been known to search the most distant and abstruse byways when looking for an address that could be found in a fraction of a second by looking at the local telephone directory.

Keep a contacts book. Note down useful addresses and telephone numbers as they crop up from day to day. Some you will never have cause to use again. Others may prove vital at a key moment when you are working on a subsequent story.

The following pages list some of the most useful reference books. Some are specifically about Britain and British institutions, but most countries have similar books. Larger newspapers keep them in their libraries, and most may be found in town and city reference libraries.

(4) Who Is Who

Who's Who
Kelly's Handbook to the Titled, Landed and Official Classes
Whitaker's Almanack
The telephone directory
The electoral roll (at the town hall)
Local directories, e.g. Kelly's town and county directories
Dictionary of National Biography
Who Was Who (back to 1897)
Pear's Cyclopaedia
The New York Times Encyclopaedic Annual
International Year Book and Statesmen's Who's Who

Who's Who in America (most countries have a similar publication, e.g.
Reuter's *Guide to the New Africans* (Paul Hamlyn)
Penguin African Library, etc.

(5) Where

World Gazetteer
British Isles Gazetteer
Kelly's directories
Automobile Association and Royal Automobile Club handbooks
Post Office Guide
Bartholomew's Reference Handbook to Greater London

(6) Literary Background

Bible concordance
Shakespeare concordance
Oxford Dictionary of Quotations
Roget's Thesaurus
Brewer's *Dictionary of Phrase and Fable*
Partridge's *Dictionary of Slang and Unconventional English*
Fowler's *Modern English Usage*
Gowers' *Complete Plain Words*

(7) Proof Corrections

British Standards Institution proof corrections (see pp. 121–6)

(8) Sport

Guinness Book of Records
Football Association Year Book
Playfair's Football Annual
Playfair's Rugby Annual
Wisden's Cricketers' Almanack
Playfair's Cricket Annual
Cope's Racegoers' Encyclopaedia
Ruff's Guide to the Turf
Boxing News Annual
Amateur Athletics Association Official Handbook
Dunlop Lawn Tennis Annual and Almanack
The Golfing Year

(9) Who and What in the Professions, etc.

Accountants	Institute of Chartered Accountants List of Members
Antique Dealers	British Antique Dealers' Association List of Members
	The British Antiques Year Book

Architects	*Royal Institute of British Architects' Directory*
Army Officers	The Army List
Art	*Who's Who in Art*
Authors	*Authors' and Writers' Who's Who*
Aviation	The Air Force List (RAF officers)
	Jane's *All the World's Aircraft*
	'Flight' Directory of British Aviation
Business	*Directory of Directors* (company directors)
	The Stock Exchange Year Book (companies)
	Directory of Employers' Associations, Trade Unions and Joint Organisations
Charities	*The Charities Digest*
Churches	*Crockford's Clerical Directory* (Church of England)
	Church of England Year Book
	Catholic Directory
	Jewish Year Book
	Baptist Handbook
	Congregational Year Book
	Salvation Army Year Book, etc.
Civil Service	British Imperial Calendar and Civil Service List
Diplomacy	Diplomatic Service List
	Whitaker's Almanack
Education	*Municipal Year Book*
	Education Authorities Directory
	Public and Preparatory Schools Year Book (Independent boys' schools)
	Girls' Schools Year Book (Independent girls' schools)
	University Registers (Oxford, Cambridge, London, etc.)
	Commonwealth Universities Yearbook
	American Universities and Colleges (Washington)
	International Handbook of Universities and other Institutions (Paris)
Films, TV & radio	*British Film & TV Year Book*
	International Motion Picture Almanac (New York)
	International Television Almanac (New York)
	BBC Handbook (annually)
	Independent Television Year Book
Hovercraft & Hydrofoils	Jane's *Surface Skimmer Systems*

Law	The Law List (barristers and solicitors, England and Wales)
	The Scottish Law List (Scotland)
Local Government	*Municipal Year Book*
Medicine	*Medical Directory* (doctors)
	Medical Register (doctors)
	The Hospitals Year Book
Parliament and Politicians	*Vacher's Parliamentary Companion* (quarterly)
	Dod's Parliamentary Companion (annually)
	The Times Guide to the House of Commons (post-elections)
	The Statesman's Year Book
Peerage	*Burke's Peerage*
	Debrett's Peerage
Shipping	The Navy List (Royal Navy officers)
	Lloyd's Register of Shipping
	Lloyd's Register of Yachts
	Jane's *Fighting Ships*
Theatre	*Who's Who in the Theatre*
	Spotlight (casting directory)

(10) Picture Agencies

Besides the press agencies, there are picture agencies which circulate press photographs, and maintain their own files and libraries from which newspapers obtain pictures (for instance) of people who suddenly come into the news.

The principal agencies in Fleet St are:

AP—Associated Press Ltd, 83 Farringdon St, London EC4

Central Press Photos Ltd, 6 Gough Square, London EC4

Fox Photos Ltd, 69 Farringdon Road, London EC1

Keystone Press Agency Ltd, 4 Red Lion St, London EC4

PA—Press Association Ltd, 85 Fleet St, London EC4

Sport & General Press Agency Ltd, 2 Gough Square, London EC4

UPI—United Press International, 8 Bouverie St, London EC4

For historical pictures, the principal agency is

Radio Times–Hulton Picture Library, 35 Marylebone High St, London W1

There are several international picture agencies, the most famous of which is Magnum, with its headquarters in Paris. The London agency is

Magnum Photos, 145 Fleet St, London EC4

(11) Deduction and Investigation

Some people think of facts (in the phrase of Claud Cockburn previously quoted) as 'pieces of gold ore in the Yukon waiting to be picked up'. The reference books listed at the beginning of this chapter contain such facts: in a sense, each of those books is a goldmine of information. But maybe you are looking for diamonds. The analogy does not, of course, bear pressing too far. But supposing you are looking for diamonds. What do you do?

First of all, you have a mental image of what you are looking for. You have done a certain amount of research into diamonds and you know that they are mined in certain countries and not in others. So you go to one of those countries, and you find where other prospectors are mining. You look on a map and discover that the present workings lead in a certain direction, and that there is unmined land beyond. That is where you start digging.

Investigative journalism works like that. You check with the reference books. You read what has been written previously on the subject. You analyse the problem in various contexts, and then start digging—sometimes on foot, sometimes by telephone. You come up with dozens of rough, crude facts. Some are wholly irrelevant. You put those to one side, but do not forget them. You concentrate on the signposts that point you in the direction you think you want to go. It may be that the signposts start to lead off in a totally different direction. Then you have to decide whether that is a more important direction, and more likely to lead you to your goal. Maybe some new fact reminds you about one of those earlier-discovered facts that you put on one side, which now suddenly clicks into place in the directional jig-saw puzzle.

This is where the 'nose for news' of the good reporter comes in handy. But there is always the temptation to put two and two together and make five. This is how you tell the interpretative reporter from the expert. This has been well defined by A. J. Liebling:

There are three kinds of writers of news in our generation. In inverse order of wordly consideration, they are:
1. The reporter, who writes what he sees.
2. The interpretative reporter, who writes what he sees and what he construes to be its meaning.
3. The expert, who writes what he construes to be the meaning of what he hasn't seen.

To combat an old human prejudice in favor of eyewitness testimony, which is losing ground even in our courts of law, the expert must intimate that he has access to some occult source or science not available to either reporter or reader. All is manifest to him, since his conclusions are not limited by his powers of observation. Logistics, to borrow a word from the military species of the genus, favor him, since it is possible not to see many things at the same time. For example, a correspondent cannot cover a front and the Pentagon simultaneously. An expert can, and from an office in New York, at that (A. J. Liebling, *New Yorker*).

Liebling went on to analyse American press coverage of the fatal stroke and subsequently the death of Josef Stalin, the Russian leader. Unfortunately there were few American correspondents in Moscow, and their sources of information were severely limited. This did not prevent the American press (and indeed, to be fair to them, the world's press) from speculating at length whether the death of Stalin would make war more or less likely (this was, of course, at the period of greatest tension between Russia and the US).

No doubt to his great delight, Liebling discovered one paper in which the editor was reporting on the front page that Stalin's death would make war less likely, while the foreign editor on an inside page was asserting that the death of Stalin would make war more likely. It is a sobering study for all experts.

Never get so far from the basic facts that you cannot, at the last resort, grasp at something solid if you feel your deductions slipping.

The problem is that the reporter in words is doomed today to move further and further into the field of interpretation and deduction, because the few basic facts in any situation are often covered adequately by the moving pictures of television and the word-reporter has to 'go behind the news'. Too often that is an uncharted land.

The 'expert', in Liebling's sense, may sometimes be driven to guesswork—which he calls intelligent deduction—in order to sustain his own reputation for expertise. It is a tightrope that the plain journalist should not tackle. No one, in any case, wants to know what he thinks. They want to know 'the facts', and his skill will lie in selecting the right ones.

The facts, as we have seen earlier, may be a mixture of what he can discover and what he deduces. That must not mean what he *invents*. A reporter tends to get the story he asks for. This is partly because the average human being, who is kindly towards individual reporters however much he may dislike the press in general, is prepared to help a nice young man asking civil questions. Many are prepared to help to the extent of giving the answers that they think the reporter wants.

'Did you see a blue car driving away?' may thus extract the answer: 'Oh, yes, well, now you mention it—I think there was a car. . . . Well, I'm not sure of the colour, but now you say it was blue. . . . Yes, I think it was blue. . . . Yes, it was blue, that's right.'

People are not particularly observant, and if suggestions are put to them, they are likely to grasp at the suggestions because they realise subconsciously it may please the questioner if they throw the answers back—like a volley in a game of tennis. So the reporter has to weigh the validity of the answers that are given to his questions when he is making an inquiry. If an interviewee pauses before answering a difficult question, does it mean that he is fabricating a false answer, or that he is truly searching for the precise words in which to phrase an answer that is crystal-clear and true?

What the reporter deduces from this may be accurate or false, depending on his acuteness and experience. But he must learn how to think ahead. Like the successful lawyer in court, he must learn to build up his questioning in definite directions so as to arrive at the subjects and controversies he wishes to examine in detail. If the interviewee digresses from the main line of questioning, there may be some reason for this. Again, the reporter must work out the reason, and discover whether it has any relevance to the matter he is investigating.

But always make the distinction between deduction and assumption. The reporter (unlike the 'expert') must not assume anything. He must test even the most basic assumptions on which the story rests. For there is not much point in interviewing a centenarian on her secrets for living to be 100 if later you open a rival paper and find that afterwards she looked at her birth certificate, discovered that after all she was only 99, and died of shock.

CHAPTER FOUR

ON THE NEWSPAPER

(1) News Reporting

Get the facts. That is the key to news reporting. But which facts? In any situation, there are so many. Good reporting is the discovery of as many important facts as possible, and their selection and presentation so that they make a comprehensible story.

The reporter must be equipped to report. He must carry a note-book, two ballpoint pens (so that he is never left without writing materials in mid-assignment), a selection of coins for telephoning (or a telephone card: though he can reverse charges), and a press card to identify himself to the police and other authorities. If working overseas he will also carry a cable card authorising him to use cable facilities at press rates.

Most reporters begin in the district office of a local newspaper. There they will be put, as juniors, to do the rounds of police and fire stations, hospitals and town halls, looking for stories. These can seem boring chores. But the good reporter is always looking out for the significant fact that is going to make a news story. It may not be obvious to the people who are giving him information, and so it is never enough to ask 'Anything interesting happening?' Ask to be given a run-down on what is happening, and then you decide whether there is anything interesting.

A local reporter should learn all he can about his district. He should know his way around it—every street, every square, every café. There is no way to learn a town better than by walking round it.

The reporter must know something of the town's history, its principal industries, the ways it has changed in recent years, the planning proposals for the future. The churches and clergy are invaluable because they meet families at moments of greatest stress and even today, when religious observance is waning, often know their parishioners well.

Junior reporters often have to cover the regular events in a town—the meetings of the Women's Institute, the annual flower show. Never despise these. Reports of them help to sell local papers. But beyond that, a casual conversation may often lead to some other human story; social events are where people meet each other and exchange gossip, the sort of gossip that is news.

Always be aware of change, and the prospect of change. The first news of a rehousing scheme may come in a formal statement from the Town Hall, couched in planning jargon and with an architect's drawing of the supposed improvement. But behind that scheme there may be half a dozen poignant stories of old people who will have to leave the homes they have lived in all their lives, and whose predicament is of considerable human interest.

Good shorthand is never wasted—particularly today, when so many press statements may be repeated on radio or television, and the newspaper reader knows whether what is printed in his morning paper is precisely accurate or not, because he has heard the public figure concerned making the statement on radio or TV the night before.

The art of interviewing is best learned by experience. But there are certain skills that can be studied. First, never go into an interview 'cold' if you can help it. Nothing is more annoying than a reporter who asks obvious questions the answers to which are readily available in a reference book. Prepare for an interview as well as possible.

If you are to interview an industrialist, look him up in *Who's Who* and the *Directory of Directors*. Look up his company and note the salient facts about it. See if the cuttings library can produce any background information on developments in that industry.

Important people are often surprisingly tolerant of silly questioning, because they realise that unless the facts are given to the reporter, he will probably produce an ignorant and untrue interview. One Lord Mayor of London, well known for his interests as an amateur musician, was once asked by a reporter from a famous national daily in my presence: 'Lord Mayor, are you interested in music at all?' He did not flinch. 'Yes,' he said patiently, 'I do enjoy music'— and he went on to explain that he attended concerts, played the piano, and so on. At least the reporter was able to get the facts right.

Having briefed yourself on the background for an interview, plot the questions you want to ask. You may not follow the script as the interview proceeds. One line of questioning may suggest another, and the person being interviewed may go off along lines of interest of his own.

Do not try to curb an interviewee unless it is obvious that he is evading the questions. After all, it is what he has to say that is interesting, and it may be more interesting than your questions. But before an interview ends, check with your original list of questions to see whether any vital area has been left unexplored: the interviewee may deliberately be avoiding it.

The tough questioning of some television interviewers gives some young journalists the impression that interviewing should be brusque and sharp. Remember that the television interviewer plots his interview in advance, often with the person being interviewed. The television interviewer has a very limited amount of time at his disposal, and must make the most of the time available on camera. Such techniques do not always work effectively in newspaper interviewing.

Look at yourself. Imagine what your reactions would be if someone came up to you, or came into your office, and started asking the questions you plan to ask. And re-phrase your questions accordingly.

Imagine what the people you are questioning were doing before you came along, and what they would probably be doing if you were not taking up their time. Try always to get a sense of the time-factor in their lives, to assess whether you have to extract information fast, or have time to work up to the relevant questions.

Early in the course of an interview the journalist must decide whether his questioning should be direct or indirect, soft or hard. Some people respond well to being asked hard direct questions. Others respond better if the interviewer leads up gently to the main point. The journalist must work out within the first few minutes of meeting someone which approach is likely to be more fruitful.

Always try to go to the man at the top. You may be (and in these days of public relations, often will be) diverted to the firm's public relations officer—but then you should ask to see the man at the top.

Never be frightened to talk to the important and the influential. Remember that they probably need good newspaper publicity as much as you need an interview with them; and if you are courteous and have good questions to ask, they will give good answers.

If you are interviewing a particularly busy man, get clear at the beginning how much time he proposes to give you. Ask his secretary while you are waiting to go into his office. If you are there at 3 pm and she knows he has a meeting of the works committee at 3.30 pm, she will tell you—and you will then know that you have got to get through the interview within half an hour, or have the tycoon tapping the desk and the secretary buzzing to remind him of his next appointment, when you are just about to ask the key question.

Some reporters find that people talk more easily if the interviewer does not flourish a notebook and ballpoint too ostentatiously under their noses. A small notebook is often preferable to a large one, and if you can safely balance it on your knee, it distracts the interviewee less. Some reporters use tape recorders, but they too can be inhibiting to a free interview.

But if an interviewee produces detailed figures and statistics, take them down deliberately and slowly. If necessary, ask the interviewee to pause while you do: and then read them over to him to make absolutely certain that you have got them correctly. No one minds the checking of vital facts: indeed, it adds to the mood of confidence the reporter must build up.

If during an interview the subject makes some startling assertion or comment, it is as well to ask: 'May I quote you on that?' This makes absolutely certain that he knows that he is likely to be quoted, and can hardly complain afterwards that he said no such thing.

It is surprising how many people say things when questioned which they subsequently swear they have never uttered. It is for this reason that the reporter should always keep his notebook for at least three months after an interview, so that if a statement is challenged, he can produce the note made at the time.

A reporter should always identify himself: 'I work for the *Bugle*, and my name is Smith—can you tell me, please, if . . .' This should act as an intimation to the person being questioned that what is said may be published in the paper. If you work out a set form of introduction and get into the habit of using it to preface every interview and telephone call, you are guarding against the possibility that you will forget to warn someone that he may be quoted in print.

If an interviewee says that he is talking 'off the record', then the reporter must preserve this confidence. Sometimes people talk 'off the record' and then make statements that seem innocuous and quotable. In that case, ask whether such statements are still 'off the record', or whether you may quote the interviewee on those statements and those statements only. Sometimes statements are made to the press that are 'non-attributable'. This means that they may be published, but the source may not be named—and that he may subsequently deny having said any such thing. Such statements are published at the reporter's and the paper's risk.

When a reporter has got his information, he then has to write it. This is often the point of greatest conflict between those who are interviewed, and those who interview. For the reporter must write something that will be read. What is interesting to the person interviewed may not be interesting in the same way to the readers of the paper. This does not mean that the reporter must sensationalise, though some will: but it does mean that he will often pick out some statement or fact to lead his story, which the interviewee will not consider the most important statement or fact.

Thus if an industrialist gives an interview to explain that the production of a new dishwasher is to be transferred to another town, and that this will enable the company to double its production, he may add that unfortunately a thousand people in this town will have to be made redundant. He may, and probably does, regard the doubling of production of his dishwashers as the most important fact. The local newspaper would certainly regard a thousand people being put out of work in the district as the most important fact, and lead the story with that fact.

When a reporter has obtained as many facts as he can, he must assemble the story. He may do this either by returning to his office to write it, or by telephoning it back to his office. In either case, if there is a news relevance he will first of all telephone his office for instructions. Always keep in touch with the office (and on going out, leave a list of the places you may be contacted at specific times, with telephone numbers—even if one of them is the local pub).

The opening sentence of a news story must always be short, and should generally contain the main fact. Remember that a news story is about news, and so never start: 'In 1760 there were ten thousand people making boots in Blackpool. Over the years things have changed. For years they made clogs, and today they make slippers for astronauts.' Better would be: 'Slippers from Blackpool trod the moon today. For Blackpool shod the astronauts.' (That is a fictional example, I hasten to add.)

When beginning, it may be helpful to note down the most important facts in a story, and then check to see that those facts are in the first few paragraphs. Always check when you have finished a story to see that you have got the facts right, that names are correctly spelt, that quotations are accurate, that technical terms are explained, and that no vital link is left out. Always check.

(2) Feature Writing

The feature article is usually by a named author (as distinct from the general anonymity of news reports) giving background information on events or personalities in the news. A feature may be written by a general author or by one of the paper's specialists (the medical correspondent on the correlation between smoking and lung cancer, or the music correspondent on the season's prospectus of concerts by the local orchestra).

Sometimes feature articles are written by personalities who are themselves newsworthy and have something particular to say (a Member of Parliament writing about a Bill he is sponsoring, or the captain of the local football team airing his views about violence on and off the field). For many years newspapers paid 'big names' in sport large sums of money to allow their names to be put above articles that were in fact 'ghosted' or written by journalists: the National Union of Journalists has in recent years stood out against this practice.

Features are often written at a more considered pace than news reports. The writer may have more time to research facts, to draw conclusions, and to point significance. This especially applies if the feature is planned in advance, to be published simultaneously with some predictable event, such as a Government White Paper or the election of a new Mayor. Half the skill of feature editing lies in forward planning—identifying what is going to be interesting, important and relevant on a certain day or in a certain week in the future—finding the right 'peg' and hanging the right feature on it.

Other features are written in greater haste. The 'instant feature' may be put together from facts drawn from reference books, cuttings, or whatever personal reminiscences can be dug up in the available time. Thus if a revolution in some foreign country brings to power a man virtually unknown to the general public in this country, a feature writer will be detailed to put together all discoverable information about him. There is often a distinct flavour of scissors-and-paste about such features, but if they give interesting and relevant information in a palatable form, they are none the worse for that.

Such feature articles are valuable when they answer the questions that readers are likely to be asking, and one or two more that they won't have thought of. How has the new head of state come to power? Why has he been chosen, and who is backing him? Has he any experience of government or administration? Is he a strong man or a compromise candidate? Is he likely to favour one power-block or another? Has he travelled or lived outside his own country, or is he a narrowly nationalistic figure? Is he likely to change the social and economic structure of his own country, and his country's place in world affairs? And basically—is his arrival likely to have any impact, in the short term or the long term, on the life of the ordinary reader of the paper?

The second type of feature article is the 'human interest' article, a never-failing source of fillers for the popular press. Such articles are based on the timeless subjects of sex, money and the battle between the generations. The sex features, in recent years an expanding business in the British and American press, are often initiated by comment on court cases, divorces, or the public–private lives of 'personalities' in show business, television or sport.

A doctor was brought before the General Medical Council charged with breaking a professional confidence by telling the parents of one of his girl patients that she was taking a contraceptive pill at the age of sixteen. This story combined two important factors —sex and the generation-gap—and stimulated many thousands of words on these subjects.

If you were the girl's parents, would you want to know whether she was on the pill? Should a girl of sixteen be allowed to take the pill? Should doctors tell? Such features represent an expression of public view and debate that is a valid function of newspapers, particularly at times of rapid social change. They may well help, by airing conflicting views, to establish a new platform of social convention.

There is often a dreadful predictability about such features. When a woman gets a divorce complaining that her husband snores, it can be guaranteed that many thousands of words will be written and published answering such profound questions as: How do you stop your husband snoring? Would you move into separate beds if your husband snored? Features of this sort in the popular press are probably a distillation of the conversations held over a million breakfast tables, in a million train compartments and through a million coffee-breaks. They are a vital constituent of what I have called the 'familiarity factor'.

A third type of feature is the personality profile. Based on an interview with some important or interesting (or important *and* interesting) figure in the news, the profile is sometimes used as an exercise in revealing the character of the subject through the established and recognisable character of the interviewer.

Let us take as an example of this third type one of the interviews by Terry Coleman in the *Guardian*, since it happens to display several of the clues to good feature-writing in general.

First, start off with a lively and attractive phrase that will require the reader's attention. Then keep steam up until the reader is well and truly hooked. And then filter in the essential facts that give the feature a reason and topicality. Mr Coleman was interviewing Lord George-Brown, the politician and former Labour Minister, on the eve of publication of Lord George-Brown's book of political memoirs.

This is the opening:

> 'If I were advising God,' said Lord George-Brown, adding quickly that this was blasphemous, 'on how to make me the second time, there are parts of my temperament which I would suggest he left out.'
>
> Which parts? Well, this volatility, this capacity to say his own mind without first stopping and asking himself if he wouldn't achieve his purpose better if he did things another way. And that, he said, was what was going to happen to his damned book: he thought there were some parts which, if he'd said them a little less pertly, might have got me to pay attention to the other parts of the book. From the book he went back to himself: 'It would have been better, could I have kept the other nice things, to have been a quieter, politer individual. But if I were that, I suppose I wouldn't be the other things either.'
>
> Mr Brown's damned book—and he still encourages you to call him Mister, and prefers it—is 'In My Way', a volume of political memoirs to be published next Monday. . . .

This is a copybook example of how it should be done. First, the explosive opening quotation (and it should be added that this demonstrates that the old rule about never opening a story with a quotation can, sometimes, be broken successfully—but make sure the setting requirements permit it before doing it).

The rules may say, also, that you should never start a news report with a conditional clause; but any reader with the usual amount of curiosity could hardly fail to be caught by this one. Then follows a paragraph in which Mr Coleman allows his subject, being highly articulate and self-aware, to sketch out his own character as vividly and as well as it could be done. It also demonstrates Lord George-Brown's aversion to journalists and their nasty habit of highlighting the petty irrelevancies of life, instead of concentrating on the major issues that really matter.

By the end of the second paragraph Mr Coleman has established the character of his subject, demonstrated the edgy and awkward relationship between interviewer and interviewee that is likely to lead to a rocky ride, and shown—in the reference to the 'damned book'—that he proposes to be as ironically forthright as his subject. Then in the third paragraph he slips in the vital fact that justifies the feature and gives it topicality: 'Mr Brown' has written a book, it is a book of political memoirs, and it is to be published next Monday. Mr Coleman places these facts skilfully. He has also by this time established his own attitude towards Lord George-Brown, and goes on to spell it out:

> He is a very friendly man. The first time I met him many years ago, was at a dairy festival in the City of London, when he turned up saying it was only right and proper a dairy festival should be held in the City, seeing how Dick Whittington's cat had been a heavy milk-drinker.

After this, Mr Coleman can go on to deal seriously with the points raised by Lord George-Brown in his book about politics and about personalities. He can even dare to cross swords with him:

> Mr Brown is a strong Common Market man. . . . Europe was our continent, the one we lived in, the one we'd always been in. I suggested that in modern history, Europe had been the continent we had always been out of, at which Mr Brown said he didn't want a history lesson from me (*Guardian*, 27 March 1971).

A feature writer and interviewer of Mr Coleman's assurance and experience can get away with that. Less experienced journalists are wise to remember that it is the subject of the interview who is interesting, and not their own personalities. In this instance Terry Coleman uses himself as a chopping-block for a sharp blade, but it is a dangerous technique unless and until you are very sure of yourself.

The Lord George-Brown interview is a good example of forward planning. Books go to press many months before publication;

review copies are sent out a month or so before; the official publication date is established in advance. So such an interview can be done ahead of publication, and is certain to be topical on or around the book's publication date when it can be certain that the publisher will be drumming up interest anyway. But check that no factual statement in the interview has been overtaken by events, and check that the subject hasn't died in the meantime.

A useful device for such feature interviews is to intersperse paragraphs of description with direct quotations. These lighten the look of the article on the page, since the dialogue provides irregular lines of type between the slab-paragraphs of description. They also break up the pace of the article for the reader, giving him a change of mental gears.

How do you become a feature writer? Most feature writers are reporters who have proved that they are good at creating atmosphere and at lively descriptive writing. Often such writing must be cut out of news reports—the adjectives and adverbs are slashed out by the sub-editors. But editors and news editors are always on the lookout for journalists who can do more than report the plain facts (though that is the essential skill, and the staple of journalism). A good feature writer should also be a good reporter, but there are good reporters who cannot construct a feature article.

The fourth type of feature is the personality column. Most newspapers have two or three of these, usually weekly, written by men and women who filter the news through the mesh (finer or thicker) of their own personalities to give it an individual and often idiosyncratic slant. Because of the local character of the American press, many of its personality columns—such as those of Walter Lippman—are concerned with the hard material of politics. In Britain, most personality columns tend to be the expression of one vivid offbeat mind.

The most successful columnist of recent years was 'Cassandra' (Sir William Connor) who wrote a daily column for the London *Daily Mirror* from 1935 to 1967. 'Cassandra' was a former advertising copywriter who day after day gave his passions and prejudices free rein to the delight of *Mirror* readers. His style was tough and astringent, softening only when he wrote about cats, gardens or bad puns. He was never self-indulgent as a writer and his genius lay in the sharpness of his vision and the precision of his use of words. For example:

An extraordinary large part of my life is spent holding a black plastic object that stretches from my mouth to my ear.
I talk, shout and whisper down it for hundreds of hours a year.
Much of the time when I do this I am in a small red room that is usually filthy, always uncomfortable and frequently ill-lit.
This constricted house of pain is called a telephone kiosk.

Even that brief extract demonstrates the clarity, pace and exhilaration (and frustrated irony) of 'Cassandra's' journalism.

Newspapers are depressing enough at the best of times and the columnist with 'the light touch' is eagerly sought. He need not be where the news is happening: Patrick Campbell of the *Sunday Times* crafts an entertaining column out of the domestic problems of living in the south of France. Katharine Whitehorn of the *Observer* writes incisively about the perpetual personal crises of humanity: Marjorie Proops of the *Daily Mirror* is a universal aunt to generation upon generation of adolescents and young-marrieds whose problems are always new to them and always deserve to be treated with the affectionate high-seriousness she accords them.

The best feature-writing is good journalism. A good feature merits its length, justifies its prominent display in the paper, and gives interesting and accurate facts readably. It should be well constructed, it should have a beginning, a middle, and an end.

(3) Specialisation

The ambition of many journalists is to become a specialist. It seems enviable to have a niche of one's own, to be able to plan the day and the week without being under constant pressure from a demanding news editor. It does not always work out like that. Only the quality papers and the larger popular nationals can afford to delegate specialists full-time to many subjects, and even they are always subject to the overriding control of the news desk. So often general reporters are given the task of covering certain special subjects in which they are interested.

Two specialisations carry special prestige. These are Parliament and the City. Reporters working in these fields are operating in particularly important areas, and they are areas in which experience counts. The parliamentary and City correspondents operate physically away from the office, in Whitehall and the City finance centres, and often they have the editor's ear and act as editorial advisers.

As society is constantly changing, so specialisations are constantly changing. Compare the divisions of government. In Britain now those government departments concerned with industry, trade and technology have been combined in the Department of Trade and Industry. The government departments concerned with local authorities, transport, housing and planning are combined in the Department of the Environment. This is because government has recognised that industrial research and development, manufacturing and exporting are all interrelated. Roads, housing and planning are all interrelated. Similarly in newspapers the old specialisations are becoming outdated and being replaced by new spheres of reportage similar to those of the new government departments.

Thus the old-fashioned motoring correspondent used to be concerned with motoring as a leisure pursuit, and the car as a status symbol. Most of his readers would be weekend motorists, and on the popular papers many of his readers would read eagerly his reports of new cars in the hope that one day they might be able to afford to buy one. Today many more families in the western world own a car. Their problems are those of congested roads and lack of parking space. These are problems of town planning, the provision of new roads, and the conflict between motorways and housing.

So specialisations can change, and must change. The specialist must no longer be narrowly concerned with his own world, but be prepared to link it with other subjects.

There is another important division between newspaper specialisations. Some of them are important to the reader because they affect his personal and social life (politics, national and local, industrial topics, medicine). A newspaper will treat these subjects seriously because they are matters of reader-interest: people will buy the paper to read about them. But there are other specialisations that have a double concern for newspapers. Among these are entertainment, property, motoring and travel. These matters interest the reader. But they also attract lucrative advertising to the paper. These are rich-spending worlds, and the reporter dealing with them will feel more than most reporters the pressures of publicity and advertising; and the editor will be aware that if he treats these subjects fully and in detail in his editorial columns, the paper's advertising revenue will benefit. No editor can ignore this, and many papers today arrange advertising supplements to take advantage of it. The various specialists may be involved in the editorial preparation of these supplements, in addition to their other work.

Politics

There are three types of parliamentary reporter in Britain. All belong to the Parliamentary Press Gallery, which has about 300 members. First there are the parliamentary reporters who take down verbatim the proceedings of Parliament for *Hansard* (the official record), the Press Association news agency, and a few newspapers who publish detailed parliamentary reports (such as *The Times*, the *Guardian* and the *Daily Telegraph*). Secondly there are the parliamentary sketch-writers who write descriptions of what goes on from a personal viewpoint, selecting events they consider most important or amusing, and creating a personal pen-picture of the main events of the day. Thirdly there are the Lobby correspondents.

The *Hansard* verbatim report is published daily during the parliamentary session (for both the House of Commons and the House of Lords). It is an official record, published by Her Majesty's Stationery

Office, and contains every word spoken in debates. The Press Association report is edited into a more selective report of the most important exchanges of the day and circulated to the country's newspapers by teleprinter.

The Lobby correspondents are a smaller group. A recent study of them by Jeremy Tunstall* shows that there are rather more than a hundred of them, authorised by the Serjeant-at-Arms (the disciplinary officer of Parliament) to enter the Lobby leading to the parliamentary debating chamber, and talk there to Ministers and Members of Parliament. The national and provincial morning and evening newspapers, the BBC and ITN, and the Press Association and Reuters news agencies have one or two Lobby correspondents each.

Their job is to obtain political information. They attend press conferences given by the Prime Minister's staff twice a day, by the Leader of the House of Commons (who prepares the agenda for parliamentary proceedings) and the Leader of the Opposition once a week, and other press conferences as they may be called by Ministers or MPs.

The job of the Lobby correspondent has been compared with that in America of the White House correspondent (who attends press conferences given by the President of the United States, and briefings by his staff) and the reporters of Congress.

The Lobby correspondent has a peculiarly difficult job since many of the things he is told are 'off the record' or 'non-attributable'. This is why so may reports in the British press by political correspondents begin: 'The Prime Minister, I believe, will shortly do . . .' this or that. This indicates that the Prime Minister's press secretary has told the Lobby correspondents unattributably what the Prime Minister intends to do.

The difficulty for the Lobby correspondent is that he cannot break out of this wholly artificial convention by writing what is actually happening, because if he does he could be expelled from the Lobby. Mr Jeremy Tunstall quotes the 'Lobby rules' laid down in 1956, which state that the Lobby correspondent's primary duty is 'to protect his informants'. Because of this, the situation arises in which the Lobby correspondent relies for information on people who can withhold information from him unless he obeys the convention. Understandably it takes time for a new correspondent to attain the position of trust between informant and correspondent on which the Lobby system is based. The national newspapers tend therefore to recruit their senior Lobby men from among the Lobby correspondents of the provincial press, who know the ropes.

* *The Westminster Lobby Correspondents*, Jeremy Tunstall (Routledge & Kegan Paul, 1970).

Juniors are usually recruited from reporters with political interests or experience, who have an awareness of the way Parliament works.

Political sketch-writers are closer to feature writers than straight reporters. They inherit the tradition going back to the eighteenth century when the press had to fight to be allowed to report Parliament at all. Perhaps one of the greatest of them in this century was Harry Boardman of the *Manchester Guardian*. However, from 1978 the BBC was allowed to transmit edited radio selections of the proceedings of Parliament.

For the past few years there has been a continuing battle to obtain the direct televising of Parliament (led skilfully by television commentator Robin Day). As a move towards this, the television journalists would like to see a selective programme rather on the lines of the 'Today in Parliament' programme presented by the BBC on sound radio. This has not been permitted so far: and with the increasing acerbity in Britain and America between politicians and the media, the prospect looks unpromising.

Both the BBC and ITN give reports direct to camera from their own parliamentary reporters and Lobby journalists.

The number of reporters of Parliament has increased in recent years (particularly when the Sunday newspapers were allowed representation in the Lobby). Now there is pressure from several magazines and weeklies, who are at present unrepresented.

One chore of parliamentary reporters is to analyse and report on the contents of government reports—White Papers, which set out decisions, Green Papers which set out proposals for public discussion, and Blue Books which are the official reports of Royal Commissions and Parliamentary Committees of Inquiry. So that these may be read carefully, reporters receive them some days in advance of publication, until when they are 'embargoed' and may not be published or quoted.

Finance

Financial journalism is a most distinct branch of the profession: for this there are four main reasons. The first is that the financial or City journalist's skills are more saleable outside journalism than those of other reporters. Not only can he go into public relations (financial PR is the fastest-growing sector of a fast-growing industry) but he can also switch into investment analysis or management with stockbrokers, merchant bankers and finance houses. This has the corollary that financial journalists as a group earn more than other specialists.

The second reason is that pure financial journalism, untainted by economic or industrial journalism, is restricted almost entirely to the national dailies and Sundays, the London evenings and a few of the biggest provincial papers.

The third is that financial journalists have an out-of-house office in the financial area of the City, which accentuates their strong sense of independence.

The fourth is the power wielded by financial journalists in money terms. A good City story can move the price of a share by 10 or 15 per cent and the total market value of the equity by several million pounds. Such stories can not only make or break important deals but can, on occasions, make or break companies (and journalists).

Qualifications. There are two qualities that matter in a City journalist. The first is that he must be approved by his City Editor. The second is that he should produce stories that are justified by events.

Style hardly matters to start with: the City Editor will probably rewrite your copy anyway.

City journalists have this in common with racing tipsters—their predictions not only affect the pockets of their readers but also their track record can be accurately observed. Paper qualifications in banking, economics, accountancy and the stock exchange are virtually meaningless. People with high 'qualifications' have failed to make good City journalists and people without them have often made the top jobs.

City Stories. In any really big news story affecting the country the stock market is certain to figure. To this extent anything that affects shares is a City story but, more narrowly, a City story is one about a company or group of companies quoted on a stock exchange. More narrowly still, a successful City story is one that not only moves the price of the share or shares discussed (any fool can do that), but after that movement, such a price change is held. Lastly, an important City story is concerned with a share in which there is a free market: and this means only the biggest 100 or so of Britain's quoted companies.

However, within that framework one can go all the way from embroidering the merest wisp of a Stock Exchange rumour to the serious analysis done by the Lex column of the *Financial Times* or the simple explanatory documentaries which—at present—fill most of the television time given to financial reporting.

With this wide variation of tempo in mind we can divide City stories into four main categories: straight reporting, analysis, following leads and comment.

Straight Reporting. Straight reporting is mostly concerned with announcements from companies (usually of annual or interim results) but also from such bodies as the Treasury, other Ministries, trade associations, etc. These will, of course, be available to every City journalist.

The first point which (curiously) is sometimes forgotten is to give the name of the company the story is about. You must also mention (*a*) what the company does (unless this is obvious from its name), (*b*) the period covered, (*c*) the dividend, (*d*) pre-tax profits, and (*e*) the comparative figures in each case for the previous account-ing period, with an indication of whether these are strictly compar-able and if not, why not. On serious papers you will be concerned with calculating earnings-per-share and projected earnings-per-share.

On annual accounts you must check that the auditors have not qualified their report. You can say little further, except by quoting some stockbroker's opinion, until you have some knowledge of analysis.

Analysis. Like financial journalism itself, analysis is a combination of art and science. Too few City journalists ever bother to learn more than the rudiments of it. More is demanded of the good financial journalist, though one well-known City Editor who cannot read a balance sheet has achieved the same effect by employing people who can.

It is only after analysing company announcements that you can put rumours, tips, market gossip and other people's views into perspective and form a sound judgement of the situation. The first point in analysis is to check more carefully than is possible in straight reporting (where there is only the company's statement to go on) that the results are truly comparable. Within the framework of the various Companies Acts it is possible to have quite wide variations in accounting methods without having to say so, although since the 1967 Act it is no longer possible to change the method of valuing stocks without disclosing the fact.

Apart from any announced differences between one set of ac-counts and another—the most common are mergers and rights issues—check the following points:

Any change in depreciation as a percentage of fixed assets;
Any change in research and development as a percentage of sales;
Any revaluation of fixed assets;
Any expenditure, special or not, capitalised rather than set against profits, or vice versa;
Any change in the method of taking profits on long-term contracts which span the company's year end. For example, changing from taking profits on completion to taking them *pro rata* on the proportion of the contract completed;
Any change in the tax charge as a percentage of pre-tax profits.

If a change appears that looks significant, the reason may well yield the key to a good story. Remember that companies try to hide good news as often as bad.

When you are sure that the accounts are truly comparable it is possible to see how the company has done, calculate earnings per share, extrapolate the results forward, calculate profit ratios and trends, and apply many other factors, from government statistics to common sense.

From this analysis it is possible to draw conclusions. Too often there will not be time to go into much detail. Phone calls to two or three stockbrokers to get the views of their analysts will help—but only if you are a sufficiently skilled analyst to be able to interpret their views.

Following Leads. In all kinds of markets, but especially in bull markets (those when share prices are rising), there are more rumours going round the Stock Exchange than any man or any City office can investigate. One test of a good City journalist is when his nose leads him three times out of five (about the best one can ever hope for) to rumours that have something in them. Once you have a lead that seems to be worth following, you act on it as any good reporter would do.

For example, a story on a property development that could transform the fortunes of a company might easily involve—apart from research work on the clippings—telephone calls to

1 The Greater London Council Planning Department;
2 One or more GLC members;
3 One or more of the London boroughs Town Planning departments;
4 One or more borough councillors;
5 Two stockjobbers dealing in the share;
6 The analysts of any stockbrokers who specialise in that stock or sector;
7 A couple of estate agents;
8 Directors of the company;
9 The companies' competitors;
10 People to get you contacts with any of the above.

Remember: very few good stories ever came out of stock market gossip in a Throgmorton Street bar—but useful leads have done. You have to do the work.

Comment. City journalists have this advantage: when there is no hard news, they can always fall back on comment. When company reports are thin on the ground, space can be filled with a leader on where the market is going from here, which sectors are performing best and why, or worst and why, and so on.

Ethics. Any City journalist can make money on the side by buying or selling shares about which he is going to write. But if the story is not valid, though the price moves, the change will not be held. The City soon realises when this is happening. The rule is therefore publish first, deal afterwards. It may be professionally acceptable to deal on a story you have in confidence and cannot use in the paper; but when a story is given to you for publication and not for private use, then your first duty is to publish.

Television and Radio. It is only recently that television and radio have made much use of stock market news (other than giving the closing prices) but there are signs that this is changing. As the number of channels increases, so will stock market coverage. But so far television has hardly explored (except in the 'Money Programme' on BBC 2) the visual possibilities of companies. Television has not yet challenged the newspapers on the City Editors' most cherished preserve—share tipping.

Power. The City journalist has considerable power in money terms. He is in more danger of being conned or bribed than other reporters.

Shady brokers and public relations men will try to feed him doubtful stories or to persuade him to tone down bad results. The only criterion of judgement is the best interest of the newspaper-reading investor, who relies on the City journalist to advise him honestly and accurately.

Local Authorities

The 'Town Hall' reporter is responsible for reporting the meetings of the local authority, and will also analyse and report on matters of local administration—such as development plans, rehousing schemes and the like. He will often get to know the local councillors personally, and be advised in advance when any particularly controversial subject is to be raised.

But he has to maintain the independence of his newspaper. He will not give more attention to one side than the other, and though he is always liable to charges of bias and partisanship (the local councillor has not been born who does not believe that he is under-reported in the local paper) he must beware of becoming too personally committed.

Local papers are the public watchdog against maladministration in local government. A reporter who works feverishly to construct a 'scandal' story where none exists does his paper no good. But the reporter who winks at some administrative sleight-of-hand because the councillor is a friend of his is betraying his profession. The local authority reporter must read through the minutes of councils and committees with scrupulous care, and learn the complexities of procedure.*

* The best explanation is in the study-notes prepared for their correspondence course by the National Association of Local Government Officers (NALGO House, 8 Harewood Place, London W1) and available

The Town Hall reporter is a key figure on a local paper because so many local government decisions directly affect the town's residents and ratepayers, and are seen to do so. Though much of his job may be tedious and time-consuming, his vigilance is vital to the success of the paper.

Industrial

The Industrial Correspondent is concerned with industry, both management and workers. He will report the arrival of a new company in the town, the number of people it will employ and the skills required. He will get to know the local trades union leaders and the Trades Council, and when there is an industrial dispute he will discover what it is all about and try to present a fair account.

The Industrial Correspondent on a national newspaper does the same thing on a larger scale. He will probably report the annual conference of the Trades Union Congress, interview union leaders, and if a major government decision is made affecting union matters, he will get comments from the union side and from the employers' associations.

Trade union matters are extremely complex. Wage rates and conditions of employment, productivity agreements and the introduction of automation are often delicate and intricate negotiations. Reporting them in popular newspaper terms so that the report does not distort the details is a challenging assignment. The popular press likes to present the news briefly and clearly: industrial matters are seldom brief or clear, their contracts and agreements peppered with important sub-clauses and qualifications. The industrial correspondent needs a keen eye to pick out the essential facts from masses of verbiage.

Confederation of British Industry, 21 Tothill St, London SW1.
Trades Union Congress, Congress House, Gt Russell St, London WC1.

Medical/Science

Medicine has taken over as the new religion. In the old days the squire, the parson and the doctor were the authorities in any small village. Today the squire has probably sold the big house to an industrial tycoon, the parson preaches to a congregation of six, and the doctor alone carries the worries of the world.

Therefore medical subjects are of perpetual interest to newspaper readers. Many newspapers either pay a local doctor to write a weekly column on medical matters and to be available to advise on news

from the National Council for the Training of Journalists (Harp House, 179 High Street, Epping, Essex), price 65p.

stories with a medical slant, or they buy one of the syndicated columns from a larger newspaper or feature agency.

But many medical stories these days are not strictly medical: they are sociological. They are concerned with human relations, with mental attitudes and with differing attitudes in personal relations, particularly where sex or 'permissiveness' are involved.

Some newspapers recruit a scientifically qualified reporter on to the staff; others allow a general reporter to specialise in this field and to read through the medical and scientific journals (such as the *BMA Journal*, the *Lancet* and the *New Scientist*) which are a mine of potential news stories.

The General Medical Council is the disciplinary body of the medical profession. Its proceedings are conducted publicly before a court of senior doctors, and as the cases before it are often the results of complaints from the public, they too receive wide publicity.

British Medical Association: BMA House, Tavistock Square, London WC1.

General Medical Council: 44 Hallam St, London W1.

Space Exploration

Television has become the principal medium for reporting space exploration. Since the American astronauts became their own reporters—the first example in history of an explorer actually reporting his own achievements visually and aurally to millions, at the moment of achievement—the news reporter has been cut out of space exploration. He has been reduced to a mere 'expert', a feature writer of television, sitting safely on earth and pontificating about the background of the endeavour.

National newspapers still send their correspondents to the Space Center to do 'I-was-there' reportage, but this only becomes a relevant activity when disaster strikes. It is difficult to see the crowd round the launching-pad as more highly motivated than the crowd at a circus watching a high-wire act. Thus the near-disaster of the Apollo 13 flight became a running story on the front pages of nearly every newspaper in the world, as readers projected themselves into the predicament of the astronauts in their damaged craft.

The reporter of space exploration is therefore a historian, recording what has been done in the past, and a herald, announcing what is to be done in the future. The present is covered, now, by the astronauts themselves.

National Aeronautical and Space Administration; Space Center, Houston, Texas, USA.

Entertainment

The entertainment reporter is bombarded with handouts and invitations for interviews from all the publicists whose job it is to get entertainers into the papers. Few industries have the public relations aspect of their work so comprehensively organised as the entertainment industry. This is when the theatre, film company or orchestra want publicity. When there is some news story in their field that could embarrass them, no industries are so well armoured against intrusion or resentful of it.

So the entertainment reporter has to keep a cool head among the seductive delights of meeting the famous actors and actresses of stage, screen and television. Often they are among the most difficult people to interview because their trade involves speaking other people's lines. There are comedians who are funny and articulate away from the footlights but they are comparatively few.

Publicity handouts are therefore useful since they give a basis for a news story and it can be personalised and filled out with a few quotations from the leading actor. The important thing is to get the facts right—the name of the show, the author and producer, the date it opens.

The newspaper reader has an insatiable appetite for gossip about the public figures of the entertainment world. Most of those figures learn that supplying such information is part of their job, and an important part. Managements that are eager to publicise the opening of a show are happy to see a show die without publicity: so the reporter must keep an independent eye on the theatre lists.

(See the chapter on Criticism, below.)

Motoring

New cars fascinate people and the motoring correspondent reports the launching of new cars. He will usually have been invited by the manufacturer to try out one of the cars. The problem is that while such 'press cars' are no doubt tuned normally, and are in every way similar to the production car that the manufacturer is producing, the mass-production system means that 'rogue' cars do come off the production line. This can rebound on the motoring correspondent who has given the car an enthusiastic welcome.

Though the motoring reporter is in close contact with the motor industry, he also keeps an eye on the consumer organisations (such as 'Motoring Which?') who do a Ralph Nader operation on the motor industry. The motoring correspondent must, however, keep on friendly terms with the leaders of the industry, and not only because that industry is a substantial newspaper advertiser.

Thanks largely to the work of the consumer organisations, motoring reporting has now become much more forthright than it was only a few years ago, and correspondents feel free to criticise adversely if this is called for.

Some newspapers make a feature of motor sport and motor racing. Some of them sponsor race meetings. In such cases the motoring correspondent will cover motor racing in considerable detail, and may become involved in the preparation and even the administration of such meetings, together with the paper's advertising and promotion department.

Travel and Holidays

Now that more people are taking holidays abroad, most newspapers publish travel and holiday articles. These have a particular economic advantage in the period immediately after Christmas when normally advertising falls off except for the January sales. It is at this time of year that many people sit down with the glossy brochures produced by the travel agents—brochures obtained from replies to newspaper ads—to plan their summer holiday.

Most newspapers publish advertising supplements or pages, lavishly filled out with advertising from travel agents and foreign tourist boards. The travel correspondent on a national newspaper may be thought to have an enviable life, travelling round the world as he does at the expense of holiday firms and airlines. The job is rather less exotic in practice, since on such trips the travel writer is rushed from tourist town to tourist beach, usually in the off-season when the weather is bad and a freezing wind blows the breakers over the sand.

He is then taken on tours of new hotels (with the tourist boom, there is hardly a resort in the world that cannot boast a dozen new hotels which it is eager for travel writers to inspect). One new hotel room is almost invariably identical with another, so the travel writer will be busily trying to extract from the hotel manager whether he welcomes children, and if so at what price, whether his restaurant serves English or exclusively local food, whether there are lifts to all floors for the benefit of the elderly, and whether the staff speak reasonable English.

He will be working out whether the local coinage will be easy or difficult for the visitor to get used to, whether the hotels are really a stone's throw from the beach, whether that beach is public or private and if it is private whether there is a supplementary charge for using it, and whether this charge is included in the quoted all-in rate.

He will look round the hotel and try to work out whether it is on the direct flight-path to the local airport, and whether there are pegs in the ground nearby—which could suggest that an extension is about to be built, probably during the height of the summer and with

D

deafening building works twenty-four hours of the day and night. He will look everywhere to see whether there are clean sheets in the beds and adequate clean towels in the bathrooms.

Then, before he has had time to sit down or laze in the comparatively warm beams of the fitful sun, if any, he will be swept off to the other end of the town to see yet another new hotel and listen to promises that a golf course and a swimming pool are to be built before the summer season starts. It is a wearing life.

Television has now taken up holiday and travel journalism, with programmes that examine the advantages and disadvantages of certain resorts. These can have a devastating effect: one group of holiday villas in the Portuguese Algarve mentioned favourably by Cliff Michelmore on BBC 1 was a few days later booked solid for the next two years.

The Leader

The leading article, or 'leader', is the newspaper's official view of the events of the day. It is personally supervised by the editor even if he does not write the column himself. The quality papers keep a staff of leaderwriters, and on occasion (for example if a political election or coup leads to the establishment of a new government in a distant country) the expert on a country or subject may write a leader about it.

Generally the editor will hold a 'leader conference' following the main editorial conference of the day. At this, the line to be taken will be discussed and the editor may talk through the development of the leader's argument. When the writer has completed his leader he takes it directly to the editor, who if he has time will correct or amend it himself. Some 'writing editors' (editors who have achieved their eminence as writing journalists rather than—as is more common in Fleet Street these days—as sub-editors or administrators) will substantially rewrite the leader: it is, after all, the column of the paper for whose opinions the editor is held personally responsible.

As with all columns of comment, it is important first to state the facts of the case being argued. Never assume that all readers have read all the news or watched all the TV bulletins or programmes. Sometimes a leader may be a comment about a matter that is an important news story of the day, and then the facts will be on the front page of the same issue of the paper and merely need summarising or given a cross-reference in the leader itself.

But even then the leaderwriter must remember that his column may be locked up inside the paper while the main news pages may change more often. So if the facts of the case are liable to be brought up to date during the run of the paper's editions, it would be rash to tie the leader to early facts.

Thus if there is a bad accident on the M1 motorway and the leader-writer is commenting on the low standard of motorway driving, it would be dangerous to begin: 'Three people have been killed on the M1 today . . .' An updated front page story might later give the news that five people had been killed. It is always foolhardy to comment too precipitately on such hard news stories, anyway—an updated news story might reveal that the accident was caused by a cow straying on to the motorway, and the police on the spot might issue a statement saying that only the high standard of driving by motorists avoided much more terrible carnage.

Newspaper leaders often fall into the trap of assuming that the facts are truly stated in a brief news report. The facts, briefly told, may all be true: but there may be other facts that materially change the implications. A leaderwriter must read all available reports. Even then he will be wary. If all the papers give a nearly identical form of wording, it can be reasonably deduced that one 'stringer' or local reporter has telephoned it to all the national papers. Perhaps the report is full and accurate: but always check.

The great 'Cassandra', columnist of the *Daily Mirror*, used to tell how once he read that a man in South Wales had been sent to prison for stealing a bottle of milk. He said in court he did it for the sake of his starving children. 'Cassandra' wrote one of his most scorching columns, tearing the magistrates apart for their inhumanity. Then he discovered that the man was a liar, had no children, and was a notorious thief of milk bottles from doorsteps.

Leaders should give a single view. As they are usually (even in the quality papers) comparatively brief comments, there can be no room for the detailed academic thesis.

Beware the liberal syndrome, the awful ability to see—and give—both sides of a question. A. J. Liebling calls these 'Ademonai-kodemonai' articles, someone having told him that these words are Japanese for 'On the one hand . . . on the other hand.' A good leaderwriter chooses only one side to every question, and hammers it home for all it is worth.

Leaderwriters are more prone to cliché than most journalists, because their column is devoted to pointing out whether in the paper's opinion a certain event is a Good Thing or a Bad Thing.

The leader works best when it looks behind the facts of a news story to point out relevancies and significance that may not be immediately apparent. Thus a local council's decision to license the building of a supermarket may have dramatic impact on people who live on the site now, and will have to be rehoused—has the council indicated that it will rehouse them, and if not, why not?

The new supermarket may attract new traffic into the town: can the streets cope with the increase, and is the council requiring the

supermarket chain to provide car-parking space off the street?
Will mothers with prams and pushchairs have safe access to the
site on foot, or must they cross a busy road?

Is the supermarket going to have an effect on neighbouring shops,
and does this matter to the town? There may be political implications in the town: do any councillors have a business interest in the
scheme—as shopkeepers, property owners, builders, etc.—they have
not declared?

All these are matters a leader could reasonably deal with, within
the legal rules governing the publication of 'fair comment on a
matter of public interest'.

Sports Reporting

The best sports reporting captures the atmosphere as well as the
facts of the game. But remember that the reader wants to know the
facts first. The skill of the Brian Glanvilles and Michael Parkinsons
lies in weaving the essential facts into prose that can captivate readers
with little interest in sport.

Big sporting events today are rituals. Like all rituals, they have
rules and conventions. The reporter must learn those conventions.
He must find out which players are on form, and which have not
done well in the past few games. He must brief himself on the past
performance of the teams and the individual players (or horses)—
because the significant fact about a game may be the emergence of
one participant in a way that has not happened before. This may be
the most newsworthy aspect of the game.

The sports reporter must therefore do as much research as he
can before the game starts. Like a good news reporter, he must
anticipate the physical problems of reporting. If he is working for
an evening paper it will be essential to know how his report is to
be got out of the ground. He will have discovered which telephone he
is going to use (or his runner, if he has someone helping him by telephoning his story in separate 'takes' while he goes on watching the
game). He will have found an alternative telephone; local shopkeepers
are often willing to help—particularly newsagents, since they have a
vested interest in the reporter getting his story back to his office.

Time is vital in sports reporting; not only the time at which the
report must be back in the office to catch a certain edition of the
paper, but as a means of measuring what happens in a game. Have
a reliable watch, and remember to check precisely what time a
game starts.

Identify the players at the earliest stage—if possible check as soon
as the players come on to the field whether the names are as given
on the programme, or whether someone has changed numbers (if,
as usually happens in football, the players are numbered). There

will often be a friendly reporter covering the game for a paper from the visiting team's town who will be glad to check the identities of his team in exchange for yours, if there is any doubt.

An evening paper reporter working on an afternoon game will be writing his report as he goes along. He will start off with a provisional lead—it may have something to do with the size of the crowd, the state of the ground or the weather conditions. This may well be torn up in favour of a stronger lead as the game progresses: a quick goal, a dramatic run, or a fine performance by one player may provide something better. But it is as well to get a passable opening on to paper as soon as possible.

The reporter for a weekly or a morning paper has a slightly easier time since he does not have to telephone his report in separate 'takes'. Unless, that is, he is reporting from a foreign capital, when the time-scale may require him to do just this. It is a skill that is worth practising.

Sometimes journalists are criticised for making too much of isolated incidents in sports, building them up into significant dramas when they were in fact minor and soon forgotten. Remember to keep a balance between the general pattern of the game and such dramatic incidents. Because it is difficult to report the same team week after week without seeing the same moves being attempted time and again, the same pattern of strength and weakness recurring, it is tempting to concentrate on the unusual at the expense of the familiar.

Regular fans of that particular team may understand this; but the report has to be read by people who do not follow that team, and cannot be assumed to know the characters of the players and the style in which they play.

Get to know the manager and the officials. This becomes more important as football (in particular) becomes more personalised, and individual players have their own devoted following. Know your way around the ground: you may want to get a quote from the manager, the players or the referee in a hurry, and there will be no time to argue then your accreditation with some obstructive doorkeeper. The personal lives of sportsmen are now matters of great public interest, especially since their earnings put them among the big spenders whose homes, families and cars are regarded as of public concern.

The sports writer is different from the general reporter in one respect: he is at the same time reporter and critic. He is giving his opinion about the game at the same time as he is describing the facts of it. He judges the quality and skill of the players, who in this sense are actors in a public spectacle. But opinion must be authoritative to be effective. The young reporter who delivers a devastating and witty broadside about the lamentable performance of some local team will not be forgiven if he gets the names of the goal-scorers wrong, mis-spells the name of the striker and generally falls down on the facts.

Avoid the floral prose and the prettily turned phrase until you have the essentials of the game firmly down on paper. Make sure you give the names of the teams, the ground the game takes place, and the score. Then by all means add the adjectives.

Do not try to build up a sporting event more than its quality justifies, in an attempt to enlarge your own reputation. Remember that the people who saw the game with you saw what happened as well as you did, and many of them will read your account.

But watch out for the news event that is more important than the game itself. It may not happen within the field of play: at the Celtic–Rangers match when sixty-six spectators died as a crowd barrier collapsed in the last moment, few reporters were aware of what was happening. To be fair to them, they were not in a position to be aware of it. Yet that dreadful scene in Glasgow was on the front page of nearly all the world's Sunday newspapers.

Each sport has its own following, and its own jargon and special terms. Avoid using jargon without explaining it for the benefit of readers who may not be familiar with the game. Most readers of the sports pages will probably be familiar with the rules and jargon of the major sports, such as football and cricket—but never assume that they are.

But sporting events are dramatic contests, and the reporter may justifiably accent the drama. Like the theatre critic, he may usefully comment on how an effect is achieved, how a successful goal may be tracked back to a skilful piece of play some minutes earlier. The crowd may have missed it: the sports writer who observed it is entitled to point it out and praise those responsible.

Amateur sport is very important to local newspapers, since news of amateur events widens the paper's readership. But like amateur theatre it must be judged on its own level, and that may well be some distance below professionalism.

It is frustrating for the keen reporter of minor sports, battling to get a few lines into the paper, to find that his sport is only newsworthy when some extraordinary event happens—as when the English women's table-tennis team beat the Russian champions in an international match in Japan. A sporting event that had until that point been barely mentioned in the British press then suddenly graduated to the news pages. That, unfortunately, is life. You must expect a sport to be judged more on its news value than on its quality as a sport.

Televised Sport. Television commentary on sport basically follows the rules for newspaper sports reporting, but with a few extra hazards. The commentator must be aware always of what the viewers are seeing. The temptation—particularly for reporters trained in newspapers and sound radio—is to describe the obvious.

Commentaries on team games should concentrate on a 'who's who' approach. The viewer can see what is happening, and what moves are being made—he wants to be told who the players are making those moves. It is legitimate to recall how an aggressive series of moves was started, particularly if it led to a goal (and the introduction of slow-motion replays, that can be run immediately after the incident, has made this a commonplace of TV journalism).

There are incidents in sport that the camera fails to catch. The camera's eye can only be in one place at once; the commentator tries to watch the monitor set and the game simultaneously. So if the viewer misses something important, the commentator can fill in the facts.

Foreign Reporting

Many newspapers, radio and television stations have their own correspondents based in the great cities of the world. The foreign correspondent gives a personal view of what he sees: he tries to obtain a 'beat' on the reports from the international news agencies such as Reuters. Alternatively or in addition, special correspondents are sent abroad from time to time to cover specific assignments. As international air travel becomes faster, there tend to be fewer resident correspondents and more 'visiting firemen'. All newspapers keep lists of local journalists in many foreign cities who can be relied on to cover important events in an emergency. These are the local 'stringers'. They have the advantage of being on the spot, and therefore know their way around: but most of them earn their living by supplying information to a variety of newspapers and agencies. The media can be compared in this with the changing pattern of international diplomacy. There was a time when the ambassador was the most important representative of his country in a foreign capital. Today, when there is a really important international negotiation, it will be conducted not by the ambassador but by the country's Prime Minister or Foreign Secretary, flying in to look after things personally. The emergence of the star-name 'foreign correspondent' of the twentieth century is owed to fast transport.

The Time Factor. The reporter abroad is hounded by time. Few foreign editors ever fully come to grips with the fact that New York is five or six hours behind London, and that midday in London is dawn in New York. The New York correspondent is therefore accustomed to being woken at dawn and asked to ring up everyone from the President of the United States down.

There is a Standard Time system throughout the world, dividing the world into time zones. Since 1883 this has been based on the Mean Time of the Greenwich meridian (which runs approximately through London). The international Date Line, across which the date changes, is approximately down the 180th meridian. There are four time zones coast-to-coast across the United States (and a three-hour time difference East to West), and several across the USSR. The full list of time zones is in *Whitaker's Almanac*, but the following list gives an indication of it:

Ahead of London:		
	12 hours	New Zealand
	11 hours	Solomon Islands
	10 hours	Victoria, Queensland (Australia)
	9½ hours	South Australia
	9 hours	Japan, Korea
	8 hours	Coastal China, Hong Kong, Philippines, South Vietnam, Western Australia
	7½ hours	Singapore
	7 hours	Thailand, North Vietnam
	6½ hours	Burma
	6 hours	East Pakistan
	5½ hours	India, Ceylon
	5 hours	West Pakistan
	4 hours	Central USSR, Seychelles
	3½ hours	Iran
	3 hours	West USSR, Iraq, East Africa
	2 hours	(East European Time) Finland, Eastern Europe, Middle East, Central and South Africa
	1 hour	(Central European Time) Britain (in summer*), Scandinavia, Europe (incl. Poland and Czechoslovakia), Nigeria, Angola
Greenwich Time		Britain (in winter), Iceland, Algeria, Morocco, Tangier, Ghana
Behind London:		
	1 hour	Azores
	2 hours	Cape Verde Islands

* After a three-year experiment with British Standard Time, Britain reverted on 31 October 1971 to Greenwich Mean Time in the winter and Central European Time (British Summer Time) in summer (April–October).

3 hours	Greenland, E. Brazil, Argentina
3½ hours	Newfoundland, Labrador, Uruguay
4 hours	(Atlantic Time) E. Canada, Bermuda, Puerto Rico, C. Brazil, Falkland Is., Bolivia, Chile, Venezuela
5 hours	(Eastern Time) Canada, E. states of USA, Bahamas, Cuba, Jamaica, Peru, Panama, W. Brazil
6 hours	(Central Time) C. Canada, C. states of USA, part Mexico, Guatemala, Nicaragua
7 hours	(Mountain Time) Canada, M. states of USA, part Mexico
8 hours	(Pacific Time) W. Canada, Alaska, W. states of USA, part Mexico
9 hours	part Alaska
10 hours	W. Alaska, Hawaii, Christmas Island
11 hours	W. coast Alaska, Samoa, Midway Island

Resident correspondents of daily or evening papers find it useful to keep two clocks in their offices and homes, one set to local time and the other to London time. They learn to live to a curious time-schedule governed from London.

The Visiting Correspondent. The visiting correspondent has one main problem: how does he get the story back? Ironically, with the improvement in communications that enables him to get to a trouble-centre, it becomes more difficult to transmit copy out. If a major world crisis happens—as it sometimes does—in a comparatively small town, the world's press will descend by air within a matter of hours. The telephone system and the cable station will probably be subject to many hours' delay (if it has not been taken over as part of a political coup or revolution). The hotels will be full, the few hire cars all booked, and the unfortunate reporter is left to his own ingenuity.

Keeping in touch with the office then becomes a major challenge. The local 'stringer' is usually helpful, particularly if he wants to maintain his future links with London. In a war situation the reporter is out on his own, and has to travel, observe and communicate as best he can. Usually reporters from media that are not in rivalry will band together to exchange what shreds of information they can glean: for one pair of eyes is meagre equipment with which to survey the condition of a country.

There are a few obvious keys. Are the shops open, and full of goods? Are there any signs of food shortages? Are there people on the streets? Are the buses and trains working? And the other services—water, electricity, telephones? Are the police around—and in obtrusive numbers?

The foreign correspondent learns a healthy scepticism. There are often plenty of people who will tell him dramatic stories—the difficulty is in checking and verifying them. And if the official sources deny everything—which unofficial sources can be trusted? The correspondent must discover, and use his intuition to assess what is reliable information and what is propaganda.

But in the end the evidence of his eyes is what he must rely on, interpreted by an intelligent judgement of whether what he sees is typical or unusual, if not unique. But the first rule for a foreign correspondent is to correspond—to keep in touch with his office. Great stories have been written out of the experience of being thrown into some foreign gaol, but they are not immediately useful to the paper, and foreign editors, though profligate in sending their men into the firing line, tend to get nervous and distraught when those men are actually being fired on.

The Equipment. A knowledge of languages is useful but rare among foreign correspondents. It is difficult to learn enough to get by colloquially in more than two or three countries. But a knowledge of English, French and German will take you round most of the world. Today some would add Russian and Chinese, but by the time you have learnt enough you may well be too old for the job.

There are some elementary pieces of equipment and preparation:

Passport	Keep a current passport (in Britain it takes 21 days to get one, price £5, from the Passport Office in London: a standard passport lasts 10 years).
Visas	Certain countries require the traveller to obtain a visa before entry. Particulars of cost may be obtained from Embassies and Consulates. Some countries require passport photographs: keep a small stock of these.
Medical	Different countries have different requirements. Most require a valid certificate for typhoid and smallpox, and (for tropical countries) yellow fever and cholera. Check with a doctor or vaccination centre how far ahead of departure the vaccination must be done. These are valid for the following periods:

Smallpox	3 years
Typhoid	1 year
Cholera	6 months
Yellow fever	10 years

Currency	Take money in Travellers' Cheques. Within the Sterling Area* there is no limit on the spending of British currency. Outside the Sterling Area permission to spend over £300 must be obtained from the Treasury; special business allowances are permitted. Observe the rules and regulations governing the export and import of currency, breaching which is a serious offence in some countries (e.g. it is illegal to bring roubles out of the USSR).
Insurance	All newspaper and radio and TV networks insure their employees who go abroad. If travelling independently take out personal insurance against sickness or accident, to cover any possible medical or hospital costs.
Transport	The foreign correspondent uses what transport he can find—planes, trains, cars, horses, mules or his own two feet. He learns a healthy disregard of timetables and schedules. It can usually be guaranteed that whatever form of transport he uses, it will be late, miss some vital connection, and require him to use his ingenuity and guile to complete the next leg of the journey.
	On long air journeys it is necessary to confirm forward bookings: on landing at one airport for overnight stay, the first duty of the traveller is to confirm with the relevant airline that he is there, and will be travelling on. Where there is no advance reservation, do not accept assurances that the aircraft is fully booked ahead. There are more often than not empty seats on incoming flights and the persistent traveller who hangs round the desk in some foreign airport usually gets away sooner or later by sheer persistence.
Car hire	It is useful to be able to travel around independently by hiring a car. Though British driving licences are valid in some countries, other require the visitor to take out a local licence. On the other hand, the Automobile Association issues an International Driving Permit (price 53p—it requires a

---

* The Sterling Area consists of the British Commonwealth countries (except Canada and Rhodesia), the Irish Republic, British Trust Territories, British Protectorates and Protected States, Iceland, Jordan, Kuwait, Libya, South Africa and South West Africa, Southern Yemen, Western Samoa.

passport photograph) valid for one year in almost any country in the world except China.

Credit cards — International credit cards are useful as a means of paying for services (including car hire) without a large initial deposit. These include club cards (Diners, American Express, Carte Blanche), transport system cards (Pan-Am, TWA, Canadian Pacific) or international hire company cards (Hertz, Avis).

Customs — Be careful of the customs regulations governing the import and export of goods (including currency) from one country to another. Certain countries have unusual restrictions—e.g. those limiting the import of certain plants to prevent the carrying of agricultural pests and diseases. Consulates and Embassies provide particulars of these restrictions.

Cameras — If you carry a camera, carry the purchase receipt with you. British Customs (for instance) are strict on the import of cameras and watches and often ask for evidence that the goods were not bought abroad. Be wary of photographing military installations, ships, etc.—in many countries this is a serious offence.

Clothes — There are as many ways of travelling as there are correspondents. Some travel with little more than the clothes they stand up in, and a lightweight portable typewriter (preferably housed in a lightweight case that is nevertheless strong enough to stand a good many knocks).

The correspondent who will be interviewing prime ministers and presidents will probably take at least one formal lightweight suit, with at least one white shirt and a dark tie. The foreign correspondent is preferably inconspicuous, not a walking clothes-horse for the King's Road.

Some dress for war, with boots and a denim or battledress outfit that has the advantage of many pockets (no journalist can have too many pockets) and of looking reasonably presentable even when crumpled after a long flight. It gives the impression that you are looking for the nearest gunfire, if not actually *en route* to interview some guerilla leader in a forest fastness.

Drip-dry shirts, and underclothes, are the essential constituents of a correspondent's wardrobe. It

used to be said that you should take an adjustable
bath-plug to Russia, together with a supply of
toilet paper; but Russian hotels in general are now
coming round to the conclusion that these are
provided with a hotel room, as once they were not.
(Notwithstanding that business about lightweight
suits above, a fur coat and thick gloves are advisable for Russia in winter.) If you want to soften
up British Embassies abroad (who sometimes greet
British correspondents as harbingers of gloom and
disaster—as, of course, they often are), English
expatriate wives and secretaries are often disarmed
by one quarter-pound of any familiar British tea.

Travellers going abroad for a comparatively short period find it an
advantage to pack everything into one small suitcase. Suitcases are
now sold of a size that will fit beneath an aircraft seat, and which
qualify as 'hand luggage'. The advantage of this is that the traveller
can walk straight out of the airport (after passing through immigration and customs) on landing and does not have to wait, sometimes
for many minutes, while the unaccompanied luggage is unloaded
from the aircraft hold.

Include in your kit the elements of a first-aid outfit: Codeine,
antiseptic cream, a few adhesive plasters and (if you are going to
that sort of situation) a tin of anti-bug powder. Not much use
against gunfire but useful at other times.

Pens and ballpoints tend to leak in the pressurised cabins of aircraft and they are best carried wrapped in a paper towel in your
hand luggage (but accessibly—on many air journeys immigration
cards are handed out for filling in during the flight).

Communications. Many novels written by foreign correspondents
contain a chapter in which the hero takes the phone off the hook,
abandons his flat, ignores all his office's cabled requests for urgent
copy, and flies up-country to some Shangri-la for a languid affair
with a ravishing blonde (or sloe-eyed beauty, depending on the
country in which the novel is set). Aspiring correspondents should be
warned that this is the wishful thinking to which journalists are
prone; and that if they fail to keep in touch with their offices, the
next communication they will get from home will be a dismissal notice.

'Keep in touch' are the final words said by every foreign editor
on the departure of a correspondent abroad. He means it. By whatever method—telephone, cable, cleft stick and runner, or carrier
pigeon, keep in touch: otherwise you might as well not be there.

Use the long-distance telephone sparingly, and have your report
written out (if time allows) before making the call. But remember

that there may be many hours' time-lag in telephone calls from your outpost to your office (check, on arrival, how long).

Unless there is some subtle reason for secrecy, and if time permits, call on your national Embassy or Consulate. They like to know which of their nationals are in the area, and you might need their help if you are slung into gaol.

Telephone calls to your office may usually be paid for by reversing the charges. In many countries (e.g. America) you ask for this service by saying that the call is to be 'collect'.

Cabling is sometimes more reliable. Journalists abroad usually carry a cable card entitling them to send cables at press rates, and to charge them to their home offices. Cables are charged by the number of words, and correspondents therefore use a bastard form of language known as 'Cablese' in which some words are run together and articles ('the, a') omitted. Thus 'Go west, young man' would be cabled as 'Youngman westwards', which would cost the rate for two words as against four. But beware that you compress in such a way that only one possible meaning results. Cablese can lead to unhappy ambiguities.

The Single View. The foreign correspondent can give only one man's view. Some of his value to his paper or radio or TV network comes from the prestige of his being there at all—certainly if he is represented there when the paper's opposition is not. The world of foreign correspondents does remain one in which old-fashioned 'scoops' are still possible.

But the foreign correspondent still has only one pair of eyes. There is a fraternal friendship among journalists abroad: if one is injured or falls ill, his bitterest rival will often cable a covering story to the sick man's paper. But in reporting, he is on his own.

He can go to a great deal of trouble to find a reliable local source of information, to recruit a local interpreter who seems to be giving him honest translations of what people are telling him. He can trust the evidence of his own eyes.

Yet even then he must be wary. Remember the final sentences of Alexander Solzhenitzyn's novel *The First Circle*. Political prisoners are being carried round Moscow in brightly painted vans labelled 'Meat'. A French newspaper correspondent sees one of these vans, remembers he has seen several others, and writes a story about the admirably well-organised food delivery service in Moscow.

Things are not always what they seem. A foreign correspondent, more than most, must look behind the facade of the news.

(4) Fashion Reporting

James Laver, the writer on social history, has a theory that women's fashion is based on the seduction principle, while men's fashion is based on the hierarchical principle. This theory has caused amusement in the City but not much in the world of fashion, which takes itself far more seriously than (superficially at least) the money market does. Fashion is an expression of those perennial fascinations of humanity, sex and snobbery and money. High fashion is very expensive and therefore attracts the interest of those who have money and want visible ways of flaunting the fact, and those who do not have money but dream of what they would wear if they had.

Fashion is big business. Fortunes are made and lost on the subtle change of a skirt-length, a line or a fabric. The mini-skirt, the midi and hot pants are news, a talking-point, and the communications media latch on to them—particularly because so much news is by contrast concerned with crisis and disaster. The picture tabloids sell on pretty pictures of pretty girls; fashion models are sometimes pretty (or at least dramatically effective). The sub-editor who knows nothing about fashion and cares less will give a lot of space to a subject that calls for lavish illustration with 'girlie-pictures'.

The world of fashion is divided into two parts. There is 'high fashion', with its concentration on the salons of the named designers of Paris and Rome (and to a lesser extent London and New York). And there is the ready-to-wear market, which provides the millions of ordinary women with something that is recognisably fashionable, but at prices that they can afford to pay.

The pace is still set by the twice-yearly fashion shows in Paris and Rome, organised by the Chambre Syndicale de la Couture Parisienne (100 Faubourg St Honoré, Paris 8e) and the Camera Nazionale della Moda Italiana (Via Lombardia 44, Rome). The decisions of such houses as Cardin, Christian Dior and Yves St Laurent in Paris, and Valentino, Laug or Mila Schon in Italy have worldwide implications. So the fashion editors of most of the world's press attend their new season fashion shows.

These used to be closely guarded until the moment of the show itself—and afterwards, because the fashion house imposed a strict embargo on photography, allowing only outline sketches by artists. So the fashion artist capable of producing an effective and accurate quick sketch is much valued. Today some of the tension has gone out of these occasions, since prestige and commercial success is as likely to come from the names who are dressed by certain houses—Mrs Jacqueline Onassis, Madame Pompidou or Elizabeth Taylor—as from sales achieved in the week of the show itself.

The ready-to-wear market is now of equal importance to the fashion writer. Women, and particularly young women, are prepared to set their own fashions rather than be dictated to by some high authority in Paris or Rome. The mini, the midi and the hot pants fashion were all, significantly, mass-movements which arrived suddenly and were taken up by many millions of women. Mainly young women, since the young now have a greater amount of spending-power in the western world than ever before, and are eager to indulge it. They buy pop records, and they buy clothes, but they buy what they like, not what someone tells them they must like.

The fashion writer has to be on the lookout for spontaneous fashions that are apparently self-generating and 'catch on'—such as the gipsy fashion, based often on shawls and long skirts discovered in second-hand shops and a thousand trunks in attics. Or the fashions stimulated by and encouraged by the film world, such as the Bonnie-and-Clyde fashion for 1920s gear or the fad for fringed coats in suede appropriate to the shanty towns of a thousand Westerns.

The message used to be brought down from Paris and Rome as tribal writ after the great fashion shows, and be adapted and translated into cheaper cuts and fabrics for the masses. Today the masses—boys as well as girls—create their own fashions and it is part of the fashion writer's job to observe them and write about them for the benefit of readers who will then decide whether or not to follow them.

The media are the means whereby the retail stores inform their potential customers what is available. So the fashion writer is often concerned with promotions that link paid advertising with editorial mentions. This does not mean that the stores control editorial decisions: but it is in the paper's interest that its readers should be able to buy the clothes that are written about.

(5) The Women's Page

Despite the arguments of the women's liberation movement which would release women from what they regard as the tyranny of domesticity, the majority of women newspaper readers eagerly turn to anything in a newspaper that is concerned with the home. Most papers therefore provide one page—if not daily, then several times a week—that is concerned with information about the home. This tends to be seasonal in its approach. In spring there will be features about wedding preparations, and about spring-cleaning; in the early summer there will be features about preparing for holidays, how to get a suntan without sunburn, and the best way to pack for air travel; and in the weeks before Christmas there are regular features about buying presents, recipes for Christmas foods, and the best antidotes to overeating.

Though there are commercial interests here—the local stores are often involved in specific promotions that can be reflected in the pages of the local paper—such features rely on the dedication of the woman to home-making. New fabrics, furniture and furnishings are always coming on to the market. The women's page can point out their advantages and disadvantages, but first of all provide the important information that they are available. In anyone year many millions of young women are making their first home, and simultaneously their parents are often refurnishing for their retirement. So such articles are always topical and valuable to several sections of the readership. The difficulty is in writing them each time with an appropriate freshness and novelty. Promotions and exhibitions such as the *Daily Mail* Ideal Home Exhibition often provide good new ideas.

The women's pages frequently have a column listing and illustrating new items on the market. These are often provided by the public relations department of a local store or stores, but you should go out and around looking for appropriate items and not rely on the handouts from a store that has bought a quantity of left-handed electric carving-knives and wants to sell them.

Household hints are sometimes included in the women's pages, rather like gardening, on the probable supposition that women will nag their husbands into doing something. How do you replace a fuse? Carpenter a cupboard? Remove stains from a loose cover of a man-made fibre? The do-it-yourself approach has now become general, and householders are prepared to tackle more and more adventurous jobs. The popularity of Barry Bucknell's programmes about household repairs on television indicated how receptive the public is to this sort of information.

The Consumers' Association (14 Buckingham St, London WC2), publishers of *Which?*, have many local groups in different towns. A local paper could give publicity to the excellent reports many of them produce on local goods and services. The Council of Industrial Design (28 Haymarket, London SW1) has a Design Index of well-designed British goods (mainly consumer goods such as furniture, pottery, tableware, electrical and household goods, fabrics and carpets) and a press office that also issues photographs. Design Index is available for public inspection in London, Manchester, Liverpool and Glasgow.

Increasingly the women's pages are concerned with social problems. The National Council of Social Service (26 Bedford Square, London WC1) can give information about voluntary social services, and the local branches of the Women's Royal Voluntary Service are usually glad to get publicity for their services to the elderly and the handicapped. Every town and city has its local authority welfare services and these, too, can often provide worthwhile stories.

There are many recurring personal problems that can be dealt with helpfully in an answers-to-readers column. Here a newspaper must be careful not to stray too far into the worlds of the doctor or the psychiatrist. Many of these columns wisely use the phrase: 'See your doctor'. Nevertheless many people in trouble and distress are more willing to write to a pseudonymous newspaper columnist than to face a real doctor in his consulting room. It remains important that the columnist should not try, as an amateur, to cure sicknesses that need professional treatment.

However, local newspapers took up valuably the cause of the provision of cervical cancer examination clinics for women, as the *Sun* published a praiseworthy series of illustrated features on the detection of breast cancer. There are other basic facts—such as that babies can asphyxiate themselves if provided with too soft pillows—that can usefully be put across in newspaper articles, and this publicity could prevent tragedy. Such articles, serious treatments of important social problems, are well worth their space.

(6) Criticism

All newspaper criticism of the arts looks two ways. It looks outwards at the audience and the prospective audience, telling people who may want to go to the theatre or cinema what is new; and it looks inwards, measuring new shows against the individual critic's standard of excellence. So the critic explains first of all what a show is about, what it is like, what sort of a show it is; and then he says whether in his opinion, from his experience, it is good of its kind.

The Theatre

There was a time when the New York critics, the 'butchers of Broadway', could make or break a new show on the day after it opened. The cast would rush for the first editions of the morning papers knowing that the notices would be immediately reflected in the box-office bookings. That power is possessed by few other critics in few other cities. In Britain the block-bookings of the ticket agencies have more commercial influence than the benevolence or otherwise of the critical notices. Yet the critic does have considerable power.

He must remember the audience for whom he writes. That does not mean that he must lower his sights or his standards of what is good or bad, if he is writing for a popular newspaper. But if he is writing for a popular newspaper he must remember what the majority of his readers are likely to enjoy. He must explain the character of a new show in terms that make it abundantly clear to the reader whether or not he is likely to enjoy it. The critic may personally enjoy experimental theatre, audience-participation and the rest. He is fully entitled to say so. But he should also be able to recognise the pleasures of a light drawing-room comedy if it is well crafted, well staged and well performed.

Young reporters are sometimes given the tickets for an amateur performance by some local operatic society, and this is their first experience of reviewing. The show may be terrible, but no one is going to thank the novice critic for saying so in cruel terms, even if his notice is the wittiest piece of invective ever penned. It is always tactful to discover whether the leading soprano—so consistently off-key and poor on cues—is the managing director's wife before slaughtering her performance in a few well-chosen words. Apart from such matters of personal research, the young critic must remember that amateurs are not professionals, that they are performing largely for their own pleasure and that of their friends, and that they will be quite happy to see their names in the paper without any judgement on their performances at all.

Nor is it good or profitable for the critic to indulge his own capacity for word-spinning at the expense of the actors. The actors have put a great deal of work into the preparation of the show; actors are notoriously bad judges of theatre. So while the deliberately bad deserves to be castigated, the innocently mediocre is best ignored.

The national newspaper critic operates by more stringent standards. He needs immense stamina, for a start. He must sit through an enormous number of different performances, perhaps one each night of the week in the height of the season, and then rush to telephone or typewriter after it is over and within minutes (if he is to catch the main editions of a morning paper) produce several hundred words of supposedly considered comment. He must answer those two questions: What is it about? Is it good of its kind? And only then does he ask a third question: Did I enjoy it, and would my readers enjoy it?

The London critic has a further handicap—the first-night audience. The London first-night audience is like no other audience in any theatre. It is composed of 'first-nighters', in the stalls and the gallery, and of friends of the cast who sometimes give themselves away by cheering the most unimpressive performance with enthusiasm. It is difficult for the critic to insulate himself from audience reaction of this sort; indeed, every performance in the theatre is in some degree a dialogue between players and audience, and it is the critics' misfortune that they form part of the least representative audience of all.

For this reason the London theatre managers have in recent years adopted the system familiar in other cities of the world; they launch new productions with 'public previews' at reduced prices for a few nights before the official premiere. These enable the cast to play themselves in before the critics see the show.

Even so, the sensitive critic becomes aware that some actors react well to first nights, while others temperamentally do not. This does not mean that the critic makes allowances for first-night nerves, or is tolerant of anything that goes wrong. But he remembers that the circumstances in which he sees a performance are bound to be unusual, simply because he and his colleagues are in the audience.

The British theatre is today predominantly London-based, and economics have forced managements to abandon the provincial tours that used to precede and follow a London run. The National Theatre and the Royal Shakespeare Theatre at the Aldwych run repertory tours of the major provincial cities (and the Royal Shakespeare Theatre has its main company performing from spring to autumn at Stratford-on-Avon). Some provincial cities have their own repertory companies of a high standard (for example, Nottingham, Liverpool and the Bristol Old Vic).

These, with such out-of-London theatres as those at Guildford and Chichester, sometimes act as try-out stages for new plays. There are also increasingly important experimental theatres in London, such as the Open Space run by Charles Marowitz. The English Stage Company at the Royal Court and the Mermaid, Puddle Dock, in the City of London have also started many shows that have graduated to the commercial managements of the West End.

This pattern of theatre affects the character of theatre criticism, since the critic must be aware if he is reviewing a play in the West End that comparatively few of his readers will ever see it. The London critic of a provincial paper will remember that a proportion of his readers will probably be noting down any show that he particularly recommends, in order to see it on an occasional visit to the capital.

The Film

The film critic has a different work schedule. Generally he views the forthcoming new films at specially organised press shows, often held in the morning (the audiences filled out with nurses and other night-workers). Most film critics on national papers, and the London critics for the provincial press, produce a column once a week. On the rare occasion when a film of special newsworthiness is screened, a critic may be asked to write a faster notice for the news pages.

Theatre and film criticism is different in kind—for this reason. The theatre critic sees one live performance. The next performance, with a different audience, may be very different in mood and effect. The performance a few months later may be even more different because the leading players may have left the cast and been replaced by their understudies.

But the film is a fixed product, finished and complete (unless, as too often happens, the distributors scissor lengths out of it before sending it on the circuit of local cinemas). The critic may change his mind about it, because he is happy or sad when he sees it, well-fed or hungry. But the film itself does not change. It will be the same film in twenty, thirty, forty years' time when shown on television, and the film critic is asked to produce a thumbnail description and rating for the television column of the paper.

Film is the director's medium. The critic need not be a director or cameraman, any more than the theatre critic has to be a competent playwright or actor. But he must be able to assess the technique of film-making, and understand how different effects are achieved. The film is a visual medium using light and shade as well as words and music to create an effect: the critic must measure how the director uses these factors, and decide whether he has made new and impressive developments. He must study the way D. W. Griffith used spectacle and crowds, the sensuality of Valentino in the silent days; the comedy of Charlie Chaplin, Harold Lloyd and Buster Keaton; the spine-chilling drama of Alfred Hitchcock; the great days of the Hollywood star system (well described by Alexander Walker); the atmospherics of the Swede Ingmar Bergman. The critic need not be historian, but he learns enough about the development of the cinema to be able to recognise how the director is getting his effects, and from what sources he is deriving his inspiration.

The Book

Authors believe that most book critics only read the 'blurb'— the few descriptive words inside the dust jacket. This is not always true, though some reviewers give that impression. There are basically three types of book review in newspapers (and always be sure which is expected of you, if offered a book for review). The first is the essay—a comparatively long article written by a reviewer who knows something about the subject and can judge it from a standpoint of authority. The second is the column in which a general reviewer gives an account of one or more books week by week, using his own taste as a microcosm of the taste of general readers. The third, not strictly a review but a feature article, is the piece put together from the contents of the book, but not offering a detailed judgement on it. This last is often written by a reporter who will treat the story told by the book as he would treat any other news story.

The essay-review generally expresses a personal reaction. Sometimes the reviewer may use the book as a peg on which to hang some individual experience or argument. He may build up his own thesis during the course of the essay, and then point out in the last few paragraphs how far the book itself comes up to the elevated standard of the reviewer's thesis. This may be fascinating journalism when it is done by someone of superior scholarship, though it often says more about the reviewer than the book. 'Tonstant weader fwowed up', as Dorothy Parker wrote in a review of *The House at Pooh Corner*.

Several hundred books are published each week and authors are glad to get even the cursory mention they may be given in the second type of review, the book-column. If one book is outstanding the regular reviewer will usually lead the column with it, and relegate the others to a few lines at the end. The reviewer has to make an implicit comparative judgement of the books he has been given by the space he allots them, before he begins to make any verbal comment.

Young journalists may occasionally be given a book and told to 'de-gut' it for the third type of notice, the book feature. It is helpful to read the book first. Then look for any newsworthy point or local reference: 'Mr Blimp does not think much of Halifax. He stood for Parliament here in 1906 and in his autobiography he describes Halifax people as thick-headed nincompoops. They failed to elect him.' Once you have dealt with any specific point such as this, describe what the book is about, give a summary of the author's views if any, and then say whether in your opinion it is good of its kind.

Reviewers are usually given the books they review. The books come into the office perhaps a month before publication date, accompanied by a review slip giving the title of the book, the name of the author, the price, and the publication date. Always type these at the head of your review, since it is customary not to publish a review before the official date of publication (though this convention is broken from time to time with bitter recriminations from publishers).

A specialised paper may require a review that points out the relevance of the book to its particular readership. But it is not necessary to go quite as far in this direction as the American magazine *Field and Stream*, which some years ago published this review:

> Although written many years ago, *Lady Chatterley's Lover* has just been re-issued by Grove Press, and this fictional account of the day-to-day life of an English gamekeeper is still of considerable interest to outdoor-minded readers, as it contains many passages on pheasant-raising, the apprehending of poachers, ways to control vermin, and other chores and duties of the professional gamekeeper.
>
> Unfortunately, one is obliged to wade through many pages of extraneous material in order to discover and savour these side-

lights on the management of a Midland shooting estate, and in this reviewer's opinion the book cannot take the place of J. R. Miller's *Practical Gamekeeping*.

Music and Art

Unlike other forms of criticism, music and art require a total process of translation. The critic has to find words to express something that is of its essence wordless. This is difficult, since if the composer or the artist had wanted to say in words what he wants to express, he would no doubt have used words. This may be why musicians and artists, among those criticised, regard critics as insensitive idiots.

On local papers the performances of the local musical society and the shows of the local art club are usually more important for their social than their artistic content. The readers will be interested to know that Mrs Smith sang Carmen with vigour and enthusiasm; they will not be much interested to learn that the young critic thought her performance inadequate. A decent restraint is often kinder when criticising local arts. There are several well-worn ambiguities that can be employed to give a fair and accurate criticism without compromising the journalist's critical standards. You could say that she 'obviously gave the audience great pleasure', for example. True, no doubt, and it does carry the passing innuendo that she didn't please the critic much.

Television and Radio

Television and radio criticism can have no impact on the show itself (they share this situation with film criticism) because the show is dead by the time the criticism appears. It is a response to something seen or heard, and can only therefore influence the producer or director to do differently next time.

TV and radio columns are for this reason more often a general study of the medium (such as the weekly column written by Milton Shulman in the London *Evening Standard*) or else an anticipation of something remarkable that ought to be watched. The television companies sometimes give the critics previews of unusual or newsworthy programmes in the hope that this will be done.

Certainly television and radio criticism can be valuable when (for example) a critic of wide experience can bring a lifetime's judgement to bear on an ephemeral medium, as the late T. C. Worsley did in the *Financial Times*. But a critic must always justify the space given to him by being readable even if the reader has not seen the programme. This can usually be said of Nancy Banks-Smith in the *Guardian*.

How to Become a Critic

The good critic is read by many who are not particularly interested in his subject, as well as those who are. A concert review by Sir Neville Cardus in the *Guardian* often gave as much pleasure to those who would never think of going to the Royal Festival Hall as to those who shared the experience with him. So a good critic must be an interpreter to the wide world, not merely to those who are familiar with what he is writing about.

At this point good criticism becomes good journalism. But the beginner must be prepared for many rebuffs if he wants to join the tiny circle of national newspaper critics. He may be a general reporter who lets it be known that he is interested in the arts. He may be asked from time to time to help the paper's critic by reviewing some suburban repertory or a second show on those nights when there are two premieres on the same evening.

Few critics start their careers in criticism. Two famous journalists who came to Fleet Street hoping to become theatre critics finished their days in wholly different jobs—one as his paper's Industrial Correspondent, and the other as the doyen of Sports Editors. There is a strong element of luck, and even more of the fortuitousness of dead men's shoes, in being in the right place at the right time. So don't bank on it.

The essential is that you should be able to write readably. Few theatre critics know in detail what goes on behind the footlights. Not many film critics could tell one end of a camera from the other. A music critic who could coax a note out of an oboe would be a rarity. But the best of them can write readable prose fast.

(7) Magazine Writing

Magazines have a specialised readership. They are bought for the specialised information they contain. Because of the conditions of their production (often using colour) their contents cannot be as topical as those of a newspaper. They go to press weeks or even months before publication, and one essential of magazine writing is therefore that nothing shall be included that can clearly be overtaken by events. Fleet Street well remembers the woman's magazine that published a vivid account of the Queen at one year's Trooping the Colour ceremony on Horse Guards Parade: unfortunately between the magazine going to press and its publication the Queen was ill, and did not attend. The reputation of both writer and magazine suffered.

Because magazines are specialised, they mostly attract readers from a narrower cross-section of the population than newspapers. A magazine editor can therefore define the interests of his readers with greater certainty: and if some magazines are produced to a formula that seems to change little month by month, provided the magazine holds its readership the formula is obviously correct. The would-be magazine writer must assess the market he or she intends to write for, and then decide whether the subject he or she would like to write about is likely to be acceptable.

Magazines are produced on comparatively tight budgets and editors must be sure of what they are getting. They are always looking out for new writers and new ideas that will appeal to their particular readership, but ideas are not enough without the skill to make them effective in words. An editor will want to see a completed article, or evidence of a writer's capability, before he commissions him to complete another article from a good idea.

Despite the dreadful warning of the Trooping the Colour anecdote, magazines try to be topical by linking their contents to some certain topical peg—such as seasonal feasts: Easter, Christmas, the New Year.

Many magazines have a small staff and rely for contributions on freelance authors and journalists. Once this panel has been established, the routine of production is greatly eased. It sometimes seems to hopeful writers that the magazine market is unduly difficult to break into, but this is because the reliability of established authors is greatly valued by editors.

They also value the specialists who can write readably and authoritatively about their specialisations—for instance, the bank manager who writes brightly about coins.

It is difficult to make a reasonable living exclusively from writing for magazines. Many magazine journalists are also book-authors. In one sense the magazine article is more like a book than a newspaper article in form. It may be around 1,500 to 2,000 words long, and this allows the writer to plot its development with greater breadth than is possible in the brisk world of newspapers.

A magazine article needs an attractive and if possible startling opening sentence, like a good newspaper article. But there is often room to adduce more facts, to use more descriptive detail, to draw detailed parallels and even to go into entertaining digressions, which are scarcely possible in the 600-word newspaper feature. But the article must have shape, and its shape must be clearly defined.

If the article is an interview with a personality, there is room for tangential interviews with his friends which throw light on the subject.

But the magazine article must be complete in itself. If it has a relevance to some news story or topical event, then the facts must be spelt out in detail. This is partly because it is bound to be read some time after the event, when the readers will have forgotten the detail.

And the magazine reader cannot turn back to the news pages to check up on the facts which the article is developing.

Unless the magazine article is a personality column—a regular column by some named personality, such as the late Godfrey Winn, whose whims and interests became familiar to his readers over the years—the author should generally remain impersonally in the background (unless, of course, the piece is a direct first-person narrative relying for its primary interest on the author's being able to say: 'I was there').

The magazine article must be carefully researched, and should give the impression that there is a great deal of research which has not been included in the precise and methodical report the author is presenting. At 2,000 words, an author has an opportunity to state a case, to produce relevant evidence in the appropriate order, and then to formulate a conclusion, rather like a lawyer presenting a case in court.

There must be much craftsmanship in magazine writing; but the tool-marks, the evidence of detailed labour, should never be allowed to show.

(8) The Periodical Magazines

The periodical magazines appeal also to a specialised market but being produced faster are interesting principally because they are topical: they are commenting on the events of the day, and their virtue lies in their topicality.

Among the periodical magazines in Britain are three political weeklies (the *New Statesman*, the *Spectator* and *Tribune*), a politico-economic journal (the *Economist*), a weekly devoted to sociology (*New Society*) and one devoted to popular science (the *New Scientist*) and the humorous weekly *Punch*. Among the fortnightlies is the bravely irreverent *Private Eye*.

The weeklies accept articles from outside contributors, but the main body of the papers consist of articles invited by the editors from established journalists who are expert in their fields, or from political figures with a particular point of view to put.

Many of these papers have strong book pages, reviewing the important new books of the day authoritatively and at some length. In each case the main book-review generally consists of a page-long essay of some academic seriousness, generally with a political, social or literary relevance. These magazines have considerable influence in their criticisms of the arts.

The market is, however, extremely limited. It is possible that the university journalist may be discovered and invited to write for the weeklies, but there can never be more than one or two such opportunities a year.

(9) Technical Journalism

There are innumerable technical journals catering for specialised interests from bee-keeping to heavy engineering. These generally have small editorial staffs, mainly concerned with the production of the journal; an editor or an editorial advisory board knowledgeable about the subject and well informed about newsworthy developments; and a panel of contributors working in the particular field, and able to write informatively about it.

Technical journals are often indigestible to the uninitiated since their sale (often a limited sale, by post or special order) is to those working in that industry, trade or profession.

Such journals are extremely important since they are one of the main influences for change and modernisation. Writing for them requires clarity and accuracy, since they are read by experts who are quick to point out errors.

Many journalists working on such magazines also act as freelance contributors to national newspapers and general magazines, since the specialised information that comes their way is often of more general interest if it can be rewritten in a popular and palatable form. But the ethics of such freelancing require that the journal must always have first claim on the journalist's loyalty, and popular stories must not be generally published until the magazine has itself reached the bookstalls.

(10) House Journalism

Many companies, nationalised industries, banks and other organisations publish their own house magazines—either internally, for the enlightenment of their staffs, or both internally and externally, as a public relations exercise.

As companies grow to vast proportions, many of them employing thousands of workers, it is difficult for internal communications to remain good. Workers in one factory do not know what workers in another factory in the same group are doing. The house journal fills that gap.

It may consist of a number of general articles describing certain aspects of the firm's products—perhaps that some item made by the firm went to the Moon, or was carried up Annapurna by the climbers. It will also list births, marriages and deaths among the employees; many house magazines carry wedding photographs.

Such magazines and news sheets (for an increasing number of them is being produced in a newspaper format) make a valuable contribution to the wellbeing of any company and humanise what is often a discouragingly impersonal organisation. This can best be achieved when the editor and his staff are allowed a considerable degree of independence, and perhaps even allowed to comment adversely on conditions in a factory. Most such magazines are produced within the public relations department of a company, and so are regarded by the directors as an aspect of the company's public face. It is not good journalism when that public face appears to be too bland and flawless.

CHAPTER FIVE

HOW TO PRODUCE A NEWSPAPER

(1) Newspaper Design and Type Balance

A newspaper is tailored to its market. The same news is available to the editors of *The Times* and the *Daily Mirror*. They treat it very differently because the majority of readers of each paper require different presentations of the news (otherwise, clearly, one or other paper would go out of business).

The editor of a 'quality' paper knows that his readers will be interested in reading lengthy articles, because most of those readers have been educated to use the printed word as a principal means of communication. The editor of a 'popular' tabloid, on the other hand, knows that the majority of his readers get their information from visual impressions and the spoken word. So the look of a tabloid page, with its headlines and pictures often taking more space than the body text, is intended to tell a story at a glance. A bold big-letter headline shouts 'This is important!' or 'This is interesting!' The type face and layout of a newspaper are therefore as important as the information content.

(2) Type Faces

The study of letter-forms is an education in itself, and a brief description must leave out many details. The reporter is not concerned with typography, but it is the basic tool of the sub-editor.

We are so accustomed to letter-forms from the beginning of our education when we learn our ABC that familiarity breeds contempt. Our minds interpret letter-forms without thinking about them: we group these odd shapes together to make words without stopping to consider why they should be the shapes they are.

There are about 5,000 different type faces in the world, in the various alphabets used by man. They can be divided into many different categories.

A fount of type is a collection of letters, numbers and other devices such as punctuation marks, all of the same character and belonging to the same family.

A series of type faces consists of several founts in different sizes.

113

A family of type is a collection of founts and series all of the same basic design, but in different sizes and weights or widths.

The weight of a type face is referred to by its x-height. In each family of type there are certain letters that project upwards from the main body of the letter (for example, b, d and h). There are certain letters that project downwards (g, j and p). Other letters are shaped entirely within the main body (a, e and x), and the height of these letters is known as the x-height.

The variations between the x-height and the height and depth of the ascenders and descenders, as the projecting pieces of the letters are known, makes a considerable difference to the impact of a type face on the page.

In general, a letter-form with a small x-height and long ascender and descenders will give a more spindly and weak appearance than a letter-form with a large x-height and small ascenders and descenders. This is because a larger amount of the face of the letter will be printing on the paper, and there will be less beard. (Beard is the space on the metal stamp above and below the x-height, to allow for the ascenders and descenders.)

Type faces are measured in points. A point, in the system used in most English-speaking countries, is 0·0138 inches or one-twelfth of a pica (0·166 inches). There are approximately 72 points to the inch. The point sizes refer to the measurement of the body of a letter (that is, from the top of an ascender to the bottom of a descender, not the x-height). The text sizes most commonly used in newspapers are $4\frac{3}{4}$, 5, $5\frac{1}{2}$, 6, $6\frac{1}{2}$, $6\frac{3}{4}$, 7, $7\frac{1}{2}$, 8, 9, 10 and 12 pt. For headlines 14 pt to 96 pt are used.

In Europe the Didot system is used, where one point is 0·38 millimetres (0·148 inches).

In British newspaper offices old English names are used for these sizes, though they do not correspond exactly. The names used are Pearl (5 pt), Ruby ($5\frac{1}{2}$ pt), Nonpareil (6 pt), Minion or Min. (7 pt), Brevier or Brev. (8 pt), Bourgeois (9 pt), Long Primer or LP (10 pt) and Pica (12 pt).

The column width or page size of a newspaper is measured in ems. A pica em is 12 pts, since in Pica type the letter 'm' forms a square— the body of metal on which that letter would be cast in single-letter casting would measure 12 pts in height and 12 pts in width. The pica em is commonly known as a mutton to distinguish it from a different sort of em.

Frequently typesetters want to start a line of type so as to leave a small space between the margin and the beginning of the first letter of type. This space is an indent, and the instruction for it will be 'Indent one em'. In that case, the em to be used is the em of the particular type being employed in the line. Thus an 8 pt type will have an 8 pt em. A common print instruction is 'Nut each side', which provides a narrow space between the type and the column rule at either side. An en is half an em.

Broadly, type faces used in newspapers may be divided into Serifs and Sans Serifs (or Sans for short). The serif is the fine cross-line at the end of the limbs of any letter. It derived originally from the custom of Roman stonemasons who, when cutting the lettering of inscriptions, would finish off the end of each letter's limb with a cross-stroke of the chisel, for neatness. The early printers took the capital letters of the Roman monuments to be the highest standard and copied them in metal.

Most newspapers use serif type faces for the main body text (that is, the parts of the news and features pages other than the headlines). There are experiments going on in Britain with the use of sans type faces for body type (the *News of the World* has tried it) and some European papers have adopted sans faces almost entirely.

Some people maintain that serif faces are easier to read when assembled in tight-packed text, but perception experiments by the Applied Psychology Research Unit at Cambridge have suggested that there is little difference between the two. It is natural to assume that serif faces are more legible, because they are more familiar, from book production as well as newspapers.

The general method of laying out newspapers is to fill the line edge to edge to a predetermined measure, and the Linotype machine does this automatically be allowing for wider spaces between words than would normally be used. A line set in this way is said to be 'justified'. But as the length of words varies (as, of course, do the widths of individual letters), if a regular space were left between each word in a line, the length of line as printed would vary. If the left-hand margin were aligned vertically, the right-hand edge would have a wavy effect (as the right-hand edge of a page of typescript does). A line set in this way is said to be 'unjustified'. Unjustified measure is sometimes used for variety, or for special display purposes (for example, when setting a picture caption in half-column or other narrow measure down one side of a picture). Experiments have been carried out in setting some European papers entirely in unjustified setting.

Many newspapers have now adopted a sans type face for their classified advertisements, since the words used in such ads are generally short or abbreviated and interspersed with numerals and points. These give visual variety while the sans serif letter-forms provide clarity even at $4\frac{3}{4}$ pt.

Further variety can be given within body type by using a contrasting type face within the same family—usually either bold or italic.

A selection of newspaper headline types, showing the variations of different types in the same point size. From the top, in pairs of capitals and upper-and-lower-case: Times Bold, Century Bold, Bodoni Bold, Headline Bold.

JOURNALISM MADE SIMPLE SOME TYPEFACES

Journalism made simple some typefaces

JOURNALISM MADE SIMPLE SOME TYPEFACES

Journalism made simple some typefaces

JOURNALISM MADE SIMPLE

SOME TYPEFACES

Journalism made simple

some typefaces

JOURNALISM MADE SIMPLE

SOME TYPEFACES

Journalism made simple

some typefaces

Two further headline faces—Placard Bold Condensed and Univers Bold—showing the contrasting weight and width in the same point size.

JOURNALISM MADE SIMPLE
SOME TYPEFACES

Journalism made simple
some typefaces

JOURNALISM MADE SIMPLE
SOME TYPEFACES

Journalism made simple
some typefaces

Slabs of body text will also be broken up visually by the use of minor headlines, called crossheads.

Some papers begin stories or sections of stories with a larger letter, usually two or three lines deep (after the fashion of the mediaeval manuscript illuminators) known as a drop-letter. This must be cast separately and the lines into which it fits must be cut by hand. This time-consuming fashion is now going out of use except in magazines where the preparation time is less significant.

(3) Introductions

One way of giving impact to the beginning of a news story is to set the opening lines across two or three columns, and in a larger point size than the story that follows it. Many papers use a contrasting type for these introductions or intros: if the body type is serif, the intro may be set in a bold sans face.

Though it is possible to start a story in single-column measure beneath a double-column headline by various layout techniques this always looks unbalanced. The disadvantage of setting across two or three columns is that it takes longer, and so (particularly on evening newspapers where speed is essential) must be kept to a minimum—usually six or seven lines are enough.

If a bold sans type is used for the first two or three sentences of the intro, the story would then go into an intermediate point size of the standard body type for the next few sentences—set across either two columns or a single column, depending on the page layout (for example, existing pictures may restrict the freedom within which type changes may be made in different editions at speed).

(4) Newspaper Character

Type faces determine a newspaper's character. Few have the definite character of, say, *The Times* in the typeface specially designed for it by Stanley Morison. Most newspapers do have a planned series of type faces which are available to the sub-editors. These are set out in a printbook that gives samples of the various faces, the key numbers by which they are identified within the office, and sample word-lengths across one, two and three columns.

The newcomer must therefore study the type faces in use, the office's printbook, and work within those limitations. The speed of newspaper production requires that everyone shall know quickly what is intended, so figures are used to identify type faces rather than their proper names.

(5) Newspaper Design

A newspaper's type faces must be restricted enough for people to be able to handle them in a hurry, and yet flexible enough to achieve a variety of effects. Large and bold faces are needed for those special occasions when a really big story demands grandiose treatment; more modest faces are needed to headline the general run of reports.

Newspapers have in general been sceptical of developments in modern graphic design. Except for the *Daily Express* and London *Evening Standard*, who used Raymond Hawkey to design decorative headings in the early 1960s, there has been little experimentation of the sort that has enlivened the underground press.

What experimentation there has been has come from the world of advertising. But newsprint is a poor surface on which to print, and so much clean modern design is based on the contrast between slabs of type and the white surface of paper. A newspaper cannot afford to leave blank spaces, since the thin and grubby texture of newsprint too often produces 'showthrough', the impression on the reverse of the sheet coming through to the front.

The standardisation imposed by computer typesetting and computer-based layout is, however, leading towards more rigid forms of layout design. Many newspapers now divide their pages into 'grids' which are in effect boxes (usually rectangular, and either vertical or horizontal) into which text can be cut. Variety and contrast are achieved by variations in headline size and weight, and by the use of picture blocks.

B.S. 1219 : 1958

NOTES ON THE USE OF SYMBOLS FOR CORRECTING PROOFS

All corrections should be distinct and made in ink in the margins; marks made in the text should be those indicating the place to which the correction refers.

Where several corrections occur in one line, they should be divided between the left and right margins, the order being from left to right in both margins, and the individual marks should be separated by a concluding mark.

When an alteration is desired in a character, word or words, the existing character, word or words should be struck through, and the character to be substituted written in the margin followed by a /.

Where it is desired to change one character only to a capital letter, the word 'cap' should be written in the margin. Where, however, it is desired to change more than one character, or a word or words, in a particular line to capitals, then one marginal reference, 'caps', should suffice, with the appropriate symbols made in the text as required.

Three periods or full stops (constituting an ellipsis, see No. 61) should be used to indicate an omission, except where the preceding sentence has been concluded, in which case *four* full stops should be inserted, the first of which should be close up to the preceding word.

Normally, only matter actually to be inserted or added to the existing text should be written on the proof. If, however, any comments or instructions are written on the proof, they should be encircled, and preceded by the word PRINTER (in capitals and underlined).

(Words printed in italics in the marginal marks column below are instructions and not part of the marks).

SYMBOLS FOR CORRECTING PROOFS

No.	Instruction	Textual mark	Marginal mark
1	Correction is concluded	None	/
2	Insert in text the matter indicated in margin	⋀	*New matter* / *followed by* /
3	Delete	Strike through characters to be deleted	ℐ
4	Delete and close up	Strike through characters to be deleted and use mark 21	ℐ
5	Leave as printed	. . . . under characters to remain	*stet*
6	Change to italic	——— under characters to be altered	*ital*

No.	Instruction	Textual mark	Marginal mark
7	Change to even small capitals	===== under characters to be altered	*s.c.*
8	Change to capital letters	==== under characters to be altered	*caps*
9	Use capital letters for initial letters and small capitals for rest of words	=== under initial letters and ____ under the rest of the words	*c. & s.c.*
10	Change to bold type	∿∿ under characters to be altered	*bold*
11	Change to lower case	Encircle characters to be altered	*l.c.*
12	Change to roman type	Encircle characters to be altered	*rom*
13	Wrong fount. Replace by letter of correct fount	Encircle character to be altered	*w.f.*
14	Invert type	Encircle character to be altered	↺
15	Change damaged character(s)	Encircle character(s) to be altered	✗
16	Substitute or insert character(s) under which this mark is placed, in 'superior' position	/ through character or ⋏ where required	⋎ *under character (e.g.*)
17	Substitute or insert character(s) over which this mark is placed, in 'inferior' position	/ through character or ⋏ where required	⋀ *over character (e.g.*)
18	Underline word or words	_____ under words affected	*underline*
19	Use ligature (e.g. ffi) or diphthong (e.g. œ)	⌒ enclosing letters to be altered	⌒ *enclosing ligature or diphthong required*

No.	Instruction	Textual mark	Marginal mark
20	Substitute separate letters for ligature or diphthong	/ through ligature or diphthong to be altered	*write out separate letters followed by* /
21	Close up—delete space between characters	⌒ linking characters	⌒
22	Insert space*	⅄	#
23	Insert space between lines or paragraphs*	> between lines to be spaced	#
24	Reduce space between lines*	(connecting lines to be closed up	*less* #
25	Make space appear equal between words	| between words	*eq* #
26	Reduce space between words*	| between words	*less* #
27	Add space between letters*	/ / / / / / between tops of letters requiring space	*letter* #
28	Transpose	⌐⌐ between characters or words, numbered when necessary	*trs*
29	Place in centre of line	Indicate position with ⌐ ⌐	*centre*
30	Indent one em	⌐	□
31	Indent two ems	⌐	▭
32	Move matter to right	⌐ at left side of group to be moved	⌐
33	Move matter to left	⌐ at right side of group to be moved	⌐

* Amount of space and/or length of re-spaced line may be indicated.

No.	Instruction	Textual mark		Marginal mark
34	Move matter to position indicated	[ ]	at limits of required position	*move*
35	Take over character(s) or line to next line, column or page	⊏		*take over*
36	Take back character(s) or line to previous line, column or page	⊐		*take back*
37	Raise lines*	↑	over lines to be moved	*raise*
			under lines to be moved	
38	Lower lines*		over lines to be moved	*lower*
		↓	under lines to be moved	
39	Correct the vertical alignment	‖		‖
40	Straighten lines	═	through lines to be straightened	═
41	Push down space	Encircle space affected		⊥
42	Begin a new paragraph	[	before first word of new paragraph	*n.p.*
43	No fresh paragraph here	⌒	between paragraphs	*run on*
44	Spell out the abbreviation or figure in full	Encircle words or figures to be altered		*spell out*
45	Insert omitted portion of copy NOTE. The relevant section of the copy should be returned with the proof, the omitted portion being clearly indicated.	⋏		*out see copy*
46	Substitute or insert comma	/ through character or ⋏ where required		*,/*
47	Substitute or insert semi-colon	/ through character or ⋏ where required		*;/*

*Amount of space and/or length of line may be included.

No.	Instruction	Textual mark	Marginal mark
48	Substitute or insert full stop	/ through character or ⋏ where required	⊙
49	Substitute or insert colon	/ through character or ⋏ where required	⊙
50	Substitute or insert interrogation mark	/ through character or ⋏ where required	?/
51	Substitute or insert exclamation mark	/ through character or ⋏ where required	!/
52	Insert parentheses	⋏ or ⋏ ⋏	(/)/
53	Insert (square) brackets	⋏ or ⋏ ⋏	[/]/
54	Insert hyphen	⋏	|-|
55	Insert en (half-em) rule	⋏	en
56	Insert one-em rule	⋏	em
57	Insert two-em rule	⋏	2 em
58	Insert apostrophe	⋏	ʾ/
59	Insert single quotation marks	⋏ or ⋏ ⋏	ʿ/ ʾ/
60	Insert double quotation marks	⋏ or ⋏ ⋏	ʿʿ/ ʾʾ/
61	Insert ellipsis*	⋏	.../
62	Insert leader	⋏	⊙⊙⊙
63	Insert shilling stroke	⋏	Ⓞ
64	Refer to appropriate authority anything of doubtful accuracy	Encircle words, etc. affected	⊘

* See notes on use of symbols.

125

MARKS TO BE MADE ON PROOF, OR PROOFS, AFTER READING

Mark	Meaning
' Revise ' (and signature)	Correct and submit another proof.
' Revise and make-up ' (and signature)	Submit another proof in page form.
' Revise, make-up and impose ' (and signature)	Submit another proof in page form and imposed.
' Clean proof ' (and signature)	Submit clean proof to reader. If a specific number of proofs is required, this shall be stated.
	NOTE. This mark is intended for use only by printers' readers.
' Press ' (and signature)	Print off.

Where the printer has drawn the author's attention to any particular point by means of a query (see No. 64), it is desirable that the author should settle the query or, if the text is already correct, strike through the query.

Extract from B.S. 1219 : 1958, *Recommendations for Proof Correction and Copy Preparation*. Reproduced by permission of the British Standards Institution, 2 Park Street, London W1A 2BS, from whom copies of the complete Standard may be obtained.

(7) Layout of a Page

The skill of page makeup lies in putting the greatest amount of information into the page to produce variety without confusion. Every paper has its own style. Many, particularly the quality papers, have moved from a vertical makeup—where the main story is at the top, and reads down the page—to a horizontal style.

The horizontal style is useful when a limited number of lengthy articles have to be put on the page, and may usefully be given lengthy headlines across four, five or six columns. The style may be seen often in the feature pages of the *Guardian* and the *Sunday Times*.

The peril of vertical makeup is that the bottom of the page becomes a mish-mash of small filler-stories, looking like dregs at the bottom of a bottle of wine. Ideally the good newspaper page should be clean and neat from top to bottom.

In broadsheet papers it is best to avoid placing photographs—particularly portraits—across the fold.

But the heaviest challenge to page makeup is presented by the advertisement department, who have first bite at the untouched planning sheet which is then offered to the sub with the ads marked in. Making a decent page with three down-column ads is virtually impossible.

(8) Sub-editing

The sub-editor prepares copy for the printers. Copy may come from a variety of sources: from the reporters (through the news editor), from the telephone copy-takers (again, through the news editor), from the paper's own correspondents abroad (through the foreign editor) and from news agency tapes.

Some stories arrive from a single source and the sub-editor's task is simply to mark it up for setting. But it will seldom be the required length. The chief sub-editor may think it worth four inches of space, when the reporter has written ten or twelve inches. The sub-editor must then cut it down, making sure that none of the essential facts is lost.

A sub-editor can seldom spare the time to 'cast-off' or measure every piece of copy precisely. He must learn to gauge how much space a story will take, and he does this by examining the basic text sizes that his paper uses, and counting up how many words may be allowed to various lengths. This is a matter of experience, and is soon learned.

How much work a sub has to do on a story depends on the reporter. It may be that the reporter has 'sunk' the most interesting point of the story low down on the second folio of his copy. In that

MAKE-UP SHEET

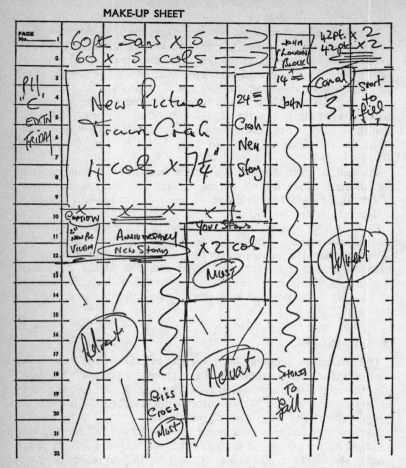

A news page roughed-out by the sub for the printer, giving indications of
the placing of pictures and stories.

case the sub will turn the story round to make the most interesting
point the intro.

There is a perpetual battle between reporters and subs. Reporters
can never understand why their superlative prose cannot go into the
paper as they write it. Subs are aware that if they did not catch the
mis-spellings, libel risks and plain errors of fact in reporters' stories,
there would be a bigger turnover in newsrooms than there is.

The sub must be accurate. He must check the facts of a story,
look out for errors, and if there are obvious missing facts he must go

The news page made up from the instructions, with 'filler' stories added on the stone

back to the reporter and ask him to fill in the gaps. The sub represents the newspaper reader. He must read every story 'cold', as the person buying the paper would do, and he must contrive to make the story interesting.

Sometimes a number of versions of a story are running at the same time. The paper may have its own reporter present; news agencies may be adding their accounts on the tapes; and finally there may be yet another reporter in the newsroom adding further background as a result of telephone calls. The sub then has to put together these various and sometimes conflicting accounts into one coherent whole. Where the reports conflict, the sub takes the paper's own reporter's account.

Essentially it is his job to make the story clear. Reporters sometimes indulge in poetic flights and convoluted prose: the sub must curb such indulgence. The story must be factual, must be as complete as possible, and must flow clearly from one point to the next.

Avoid linking phrases that tie one paragraph to the last. They cause endless trouble on the stone, when the story cannot be cut without making nonsense of it. Ingenious and experienced reporters are prone to such linking phrases, which if the sub does not excise them tie up far too much time and energy at a later stage when there is neither time nor energy to spare.

If we take a single piece of copy, the sub first of all reads it through, then puts his own name on it, and rings it (to indicate that it is not to be printed). Then he adds a catchline if the reporter has not already provided a suitable one. The same instruction applies to subs as to reporters—choose a catchline that is not likely to appear elsewhere in the paper (e.g. crash, crisis, death, date, or any other too-familiar word).

Many subs write a headline before they sub the copy, as the business of headline-writing is perhaps the most difficult. Then the sub goes through the copy, cutting out superfluous matter, trimming it to length, and preparing it to fit whatever space has been allocated to it.

He looks to see that the most vital information is in the story (and checks again when he has finished subbing to make sure that he has not inadvertently taken it out)—such as the names of the people involved, the result of a court case, the place where an incident happened.

The sub checks the spelling of names and places (which is not to say that the reporter should have failed to do so earlier: a double check never did a newspaper any harm). He checks, too, with the house style book, if there is one. Many newspapers have curious spellings, particularly of foreign place-names, that are honoured by custom (such as Irak for Iraq). It doesn't really matter which way

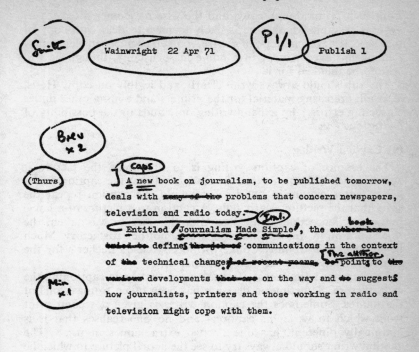

A new book on journalism, to be published tomorrow, deals with ~~many of the~~ problems that concern newspapers, television and radio today. Entitled *Journalism Made Simple*, the ~~author has tried to~~ define ~~the job of~~ communications in the context of ~~the~~ technical change ~~of recent years,~~ points to ~~the various~~ developments ~~that are~~ on the way and ~~to~~ suggests how journalists, printers and those working in radio and television might cope with them.

A page of copy after the sub-editor has prepared it for the printer. He puts his name at the top left, rings everything that is NOT to be printed, indicates type sizes, and removes the quotes from the book-title, putting the words into italic instead, since that is his paper's style. In practice, the final sentence should be sent to the printer on a separate sheet, as it is in a different type face

they are spelt, but if one sub fails to follow the house style and lets Iraq by when Irak is the house style, you can be sure that on the same page there will be two other references to the place, spelt in house style. At least house styles make for consistency.

Every paper has some writers who are so authoritative and venerable that they have persuaded the editor that the words they transmit are holy writ and cannot be under any circumstances improved. Sub's heads have rolled for so much as removing a comma from such prima donna copy, and the wise newcomer discovers as soon as possible whether he is likely to have to deal with copy of that sort. It never matters, of course, if a sub corrects an elementary spelling mistake or error in a name in such copy, though he will seldom be thanked for it.

The sub should always write clearly and legibly on copy. He is, after all, preparing material for the printers and among other duties correcting errors.* Poor handwriting only adds to the possibility of confusion.

(9) Caption Writing

The essence of caption writing is to illuminate the picture it accompanies without making the reader feel that the caption writer has a better picture in mind. Nor should the caption repeat the story that the picture clearly tells. A caption to a picture of a horse jumping a fence that said: 'Just after this picture was taken, the rider went on to win the National' would not be satisfactory. Much better would be 'Johnny Cooke on Specify clears Becher's for the second time as they near their National win.'

The caption writer must always beware that he is captioning the right picture. Sometimes a decision has been taken to mask one of the figures. Sometimes the caption writer is given a second print from which to write his caption—and no one realises that it is marginally different, has one or two extra names in it. . . . The caption writer should always try to see the actual picture to which he is adding words.

(10) Headlines

The first requirement of a headline is that it should fit. The paper's typebook indicates how many letters a headline may hold across one, two or three columns—but only loosely. The width of letters varies considerably in headline types, and the sub must learn the variations.

There is no space in headlines for literary flair. The headline must be brisk, attractive, and must give the guts of the story. Now and again the offbeat teaser headline is permissible, but generally only on offbeat stories (most papers like to have one light story of this sort on the front page if they can find one, particularly on a day when the rest of the page is concerned with death and disaster, as newspapers frequently are).

The basic headline should contain significant words and the minimum of definite or indefinite articles: yet it must make sense.

* Avoid whimsical ambiguities and (unless the editor likes them) puns. For excellent guidance around the pitfalls of subbing see the excellent *Simple Sub's Book* by Leslie Sellers (Pergamon Press, 1968).

The headline may easily degenerate into ambiguity: a good headline can be read in only one sense.

Because headlines must be short, there is a temptation to use such newspaper words as 'probe', 'row', 'quits'. Avoid these.

Crossheads, which are set as breakers in a long story, should be recognisably subsidiary to the main heading, and have some association with it.

(11) On the Stone

The sub working on the stone, as makeup or revise sub, is on the printers' territory. He is wise to take their advice. Often the stone sub is (at least initially) chivvied by the printers and required to show that he understands their problems. The sub who tries to work too rigorously 'by the book' will soon find that his life is not pleasant. If, on the other hand, he shows some sensitivity to the printers' problems—which are always considerable—he will find metal appearing by magic.

When making corrections on the stone to galleys or page proofs, it saves time to replace a wrong word or phrase with another word or phrase of precisely the same length. In machine setting this means that the correction can be made in one or two lines; but if the sub deletes a word, or writes in an extra word, this may mean that a whole paragraph of several lines needs to be reset.

The sub is the link between the editorial department and the printers. Both sides are vital to the efficiency and success of the newspaper, which depends on their good relations. The more a sub knows about the printing of the newspaper, the better he gets on with the individual printers, the better the paper will run. Particularly is this true at those moments of crisis when changes have to be made quickly, new copy subbed and set rapidly, and there is no time for the formalities. It is at those times that the good relations between subs and printers are tested.

(12) Managerial Problems

Editorial and Advertising. A newspaper is a business. Most newspapers or newspaper groups therefore have a managing director, whose function is that of a managing director in any business—to see that the business is run efficiently, to see that it makes the most economic use of its resources to manufacture a saleable product, and to see that the business makes a profit.

Conventional newspapers obtain their revenue from the sale of newspapers to the public, and from the sale of advertising space in the papers. The balance between the one and the other is difficult to strike. While a paper such as the *Daily Mirror*, with its enormous circulation, can usually balance the paging between advertisements and editorial, few newspapers anywhere in the world are in that happy situation.

Advertisements are divided into two kinds—Display and Small Ads. Display Ads are the large advertisements, often spread across several columns or whole pages. Small Ads or 'classifieds' are the few lines of small type announcing births, marriages and deaths; house and car sales; personal announcements and the like. National newspapers tend to obtain a predominance of display ads; provincial papers often thrive on smalls.

The job of the Advertisement Manager is to obtain such advertisements. From time to time he may, in association with the editorial department, organise an advertisement supplement—several pages devoted to one subject, with the advertisements sold to a variety of companies with an interest in that subject, and the editorial content similarly associated with it. Sometimes advertisers choose to produce their copy in a style or typeface that makes it look like editorial matter. Where this is done, the advertisement must be clearly identified as such.

Contrary to general belief, there is seldom undue pressure on editorial writers to 'plug' advertisers or their products, and few editors would countenance any such influence. Faced with a situation where a journalist is reminded by an advertiser of the value of his financial contribution to the paper, most editors would prefer to risk losing the advertiser rather than their independence, and rightly.

The Managing Director is concerned with the overall position of the company as a business. He is concerned above all with costs: with the costs of newsprint and ink, of wages and salaries, of distribution and publicity. The newsprint costs of the average newspaper are the largest single item in the budget (around 30 per cent); editorial and production costs each account for some 20 per cent.

In any other business, the product can be programmed over a long period. The company may plan an advertising campaign, and be reasonably certain of the quantities they will produce and to whom they will sell. None of this is certain in newspapers. On a day when there is a dramatic news story, the paper may sell every copy it can print. On other days, there may be poor sales. For there is a significant 'impulse' sale in newspapers (which is one of the reasons why so many papers have adopted large banner headlines that can be read more easily across a newsagent's counter than in the hand).

The management of a newspaper must also be vitally concerned with staff relations. Here again, the problem is a difficult one. Most employees will be paid regular salaries and wages. They must be paid whether the employees are fully used (when, for example, the paper has many pages because it has attracted heavy advertising) or whether they are under-employed (when there are no dramatic news stories, there is an advertising recession, and the paper is thin). Other employees—particularly printers—may be paid by piece-rates, which means that they are paid for the work they do. When there is plenty of work they are well paid, but when work is scarce they are poorly paid and understandably resent it.

Good managements try to bring their employees as fully into the picture as they can, providing them with targets and incentives. Once again, because of the vagaries of the newspaper industry this is not easy, but it must be attempted.

Finally the Managing Director has to plan for the future. He must know the working life of his printing plant, and study the complicated developments within the industry to work out what will be the best investment for his company in the future. Do we adopt computer-setting? The capital cost would be huge; would there be an adequate return on that capital? Are the Japanese right in developing home-printouts for newspapers? Is this going to be the pattern of newspaper printing in the near future? Would we sell more newspapers if we invested in expensive colour equipment? Would the advertising revenues cover the investment cost and provide a reasonable profit?

The Managing Director investigates the possibilities in such uncertain fields, and must then—with his Board of Directors—come to a decision. The difficulties of the newspaper industry, more than most, are due to the fact that in today's circumstances all these vital decisions are so hugely expensive.

'Giveaway' Papers

Most newspapers earn between two-thirds and three-fifths of their income from advertisements. So it was a logical development that papers would be produced drawing *all* their revenue from advertisements, and giving them away to the public.

Estimates of the number of 'giveaway' groups in Britain vary between 30 and 100. Some of the biggest newspaper firms—the News of the World, Westminster Press and Associated Newspapers—have moved into this field.

The principle is that a paper is built round local advertising, with a greater or lesser amount of editorial matter, and then distributed free to homes in the area. Advertisers know that their message is being put through the letter-boxes of the people they are trying to contact: but they do not know what impact such advertising can have.

The News of the World Organisation, stimulated by Mr Rupert Murdoch's success with 'giveaways' in Australia, is now operating in Liverpool, Blackpool, Cardiff and London. Some 100,000 copies are distributed in Liverpool and Blackpool, 60,000 in Cardiff and a quoted 770,000 in London. These figures are a serious challenge to local newspapers, though so far it does not seem that many local papers have materially suffered from the emergence of this new form of publication.

The key to the success of the 'giveaway' papers must be the efficiency of their distribution. They employ part-time distributors and check carefully to see that the papers are in fact being delivered. But the success or failure of the 'giveaway' revolution depends on whether the papers are interesting to the people who receive them. If a housewife finds a bargain in the advertising columns, or a fascinating news item or piece of local gossip in the editorial columns, then the local paper will be in jeopardy. But as in other forms of journalism, the 'giveaway' must be professional and interesting on its own account, as well as an advertising money-spinner, if it is to survive.

Circulation and Distribution

However good a newspaper may be, if its potential readers cannot obtain it, the staff are wasting their time. Not so many years ago small tattered boys used to wait outside newspaper offices for the latest editions of the paper, and then carry off their pile of papers to sell them in the streets. We are assured that every millionaire started by selling newspapers on the street corner, though it is improbable that every small boy who sold newspapers became a millionaire.

Today few small boys in the western world care to do this (even if the juvenile employment laws and the union agreements would permit them to). So newspapers have a problem of distribution.

The newspaper reader expects his newspaper to be on the doormat when he walks downstairs in the morning. To achieve this, newspaper distribution staffs work through the night and thousands of newsagents get up at four o'clock in the morning to divide the papers and mark them into the various delivery rounds—and hope that the delivery boys are still saving up to buy that new bicycle and will arrive to take the papers round before they go to school.

Like the morning postal delivery service and the daily milk round, it is a fast-dying operation. But it is still the way in which Britain's morning papers are delivered.

London evening newspapers are sold on a 'sale-or-return' basis, partly because they have a substantially greater impulse sale—for instance, on the London main-line railway stations to home-bound commuters—than morning papers. Only 18 per cent of London evening paper sales are by home delivery, and 15 per cent are sold from station bookstalls.

Papers that sell in this way naturally rely considerably on 'bills'—

the sales-point sheet announcing some item of news that the newspaper hopes will tempt buyers. These are often ingenious, but can be too ingenious if the bill sounds far more exciting than the product delivers—if, for instance, the bill announces 'Famous Film Star Dies' and the reader buys a paper with trembling fingers and discovers (on page 5) that a minor bit-player in Hollywood second-features is no more.

The traffic congestion in large cities is also a problem for the distributors of newspapers. Each day more than 15 million national dailies and nearly 2 million London evening papers are handled by the wholesalers and retailers. There are 20 newspaper wholesalers in London, and some 40,000 retailers in Britain.

Outside London, most newspapers are distributed in bulk by train, and the distribution operation is a complex one. A journalist who produces his copy late—if the story is of sufficient importance—can wreck the whole finely tuned delivery process.

CHAPTER SIX

PRINTING

For nearly 500 years printing has been the basic tool of communications, education and scholarship. Only in this century has it been challenged effectively by the telephone, by radio and by television. But in spite of these rivals in the distribution of the basic facts of news, the printed word is still the best method of collating information for reference and historical record.

This is because the printed word can be assimilated at whatever speed the reader's mind selects, while the spoken word and the visual image move onwards at a virtually unalterable speed. The eye can refer back, in printed text, to recall or check a fact or a statement. Few listeners or television watchers possess a video recorder, the electronic machinery to enable them to do the same with spoken or visual images.

(1) The Process

The principle of printing has changed little until this century. If you take an embossed (raised) or engraved (cut below the surface) image, and coat it with a pigment or ink, the image when paper is pressed upon it will be transferred to the paper. One of the simplest applications of printing in general use is the adjustable rubber date-stamp. You set the stamp to the appropriate date, press it upon an ink-pad, and then press it upon paper.

A new method of transferring images to paper was invented in the nineteenth century—photography. The computer has now produced a yet faster method of printing and of page composition. Newspaper printing is now in a transitional phase which uses some or all of these modern technologies.

In its ultimate form, the journalist sits in front of a visual display unit (VDU) and types his story into the computer, correcting it as he goes along. The sub-editor calls the text up on his VDU to edit it. The make-up sub can plan his page on another page-size VDU, calling up slabs of text, editing and shaping them at will (or changing them from single- to double-column setting) by pressing buttons. The text exists only on the computer tape until it is fed into the printing process. Portable VDUs may now be carried by journalists, which in effect link them directly to the printing press.

The introduction of such technology is not being achieved without immense changes to work routines, and often at the cost of redundancies in the old printing trades. Already there are many newspapers in the United States produced by these modern methods. In Britain the adoption of this new technology has been slowed by the understandable reluctance of print workers to see their traditional skills superseded.

(2) Hot Metal Setting

The traditional method of printing employs metal type which is arranged in a frame or 'chase'. There are three methods of producing this type.

FOUNDRY TYPE is type that is cast in single letters, numbers and symbols, and stored in cases for use as required. The cases are usually stored in racks one above the other, and because of this, capital letters are known as Upper Case and small letters as Lower Case.

SLUG-CAST TYPE is type cast within a machine (a Linotype or Intertype) which manufactures a slug, or line of type, from molten metal as the operator types a keyboard somewhat like that of a typewriter. One important advantage of slug-casting is its speed, and the other the fact that the metal lines so produced can be melted down after use and the metal used again.

SINGLE-TYPE is produced on a Monotype machine. Like a Linotype, this has a keyboard, but the operator produces a spool of perforated tape. This is fed into the caster which produces individual characters in the order required: these too can be melted down after use.

Material to be set is divided into headlines, which are generally set in the case-room by hand, and body text, which is set on Linotype or Intertype machines. This is because the headline will contain comparatively few words, and those in large letters which can economically be put together and spaced out by hand. Body text, in contrast, will contain many more words but will generally be set across a fixed column-width that can be pre-selected by the 'Lino' operator.

(3) Headlines

The case-hand is given an instruction showing the wording of the headline, the size and character of the type face required, and the width of space to which it is to be set. He takes a composing-stick, which is a small metal tray, to the appropriate case of type, picks out the correct letters and assembles them in the correct order, filling out any gaps with blank metal spacers to bring the whole to the correct width.

If the headline is for a main streamer (up to 96 pt) the actual metal, as selected and arranged by the case-hand (if set in 'founders' type') may then be taken to the page and be placed in position.

Most smaller headlines are usually cast on a Ludlow machine which produces a single slug of metal from the founders' type. This single slug is rather easier to handle than the assemblage of founders' type, which can accidentally fall apart as it is placed into the page, particularly if it contains a number of small pieces.

(4) Body Text

A page of typescript is sent from the sub-editors to the composing-room desk. The overseer may cut it up with scissors into two or three takes, each of four to six lines. He identifies each take with a catchline and a number in sequence. The Linotype operator comes to the desk and is given the next take to be set. Therefore one operator may set only one small section of a story, particularly if it is arriving just before an edition. For this reason, reporters must write clear sentences so that each by itself makes sense.

The Linotype machine has three sections: the keyboard, the magazine and the mould wheel. The keyboard controls its overall operation, governing the width of slug to be set, and the size and character of type face. As the operator presses the keys, metal matrices of individual letters drop from the magazine into an assembler. When the line is complete, the assembler moves into the casting position, and the letters are spaced out to complete a full line. Behind the machine is a vat of molten metal, electrically heated, and the mould wheel then releases sufficient metal to cast the line which drops into a tray beside the operator. The matrices are then carried upwards to the magazine and redistributed automatically into their correct places for further use.

When the Linotype operator has completed his task he carries the metal, with the original typescript, to the 'random'. This is a desk on which complete stories are assembled from the various takes that are being simultaneously set. When the random operator finds that he has a complete story, from take one to the end, he assembles it in a galley—a narrow tray that will hold about four inches of type, sometimes more, up to a column—and hands it over to be proofed and taken to the stone.

The proof is a rough imprint of the contents of the galley, and several copies are rolled off at this stage. One is sent with the original typescript to the readers. The readers are correctors whose duty is first to see that what has been written by the journalist is accurately reproduced in type, and secondly to pick out any apparent errors of fact, spelling or house style that need correction. The galleys of body text are then assembled, with the headlines and illustration blocks, on the stone.

(5) Illustrations

In letterpress printing, illustrations must be converted into relief surfaces that will print effectively beside type. A drawing (such as a cartoon) is made into a line block, a photograph into a half-tone block.

A line block is made from a negative image of the original drawing. This negative image is printed on to a zinc plate covered with photographic film and etched, leaving the image standing out. A half-tone block is made by photographing the original image through a fine mesh screen. The effect of this is to produce an image made up of a great many small dots of varying intensity. Where there are many dots the picture will be dark, where there are few it will be light. This dot-image is then transferred to a metal plate and etched. The usual screen for newspaper half-tones has between 55 and 65 dots to the square inch. Web-offset printing can reproduce much finer variation and pictures printed by this process do not show the dots so clearly, and so seem more true to life.

There are two electronic engraving machines now in use—the Scan-a-Graver and the Klishograph, which pick up the image by means of a photoelectric cell and simultaneously engrave a plate with an identical image.

The thin metal plate carrying the line or half-tone illustration is sent to the foundry to be attached by fine pins to a metal base the precise height of the base of a piece of type, thus raising the surface of the illustration to the exact level of the other surfaces to be printed in the page. Sometimes the plate may be attached to the base with double-sided adhesive tape.

The production of blocks has been further speeded-up by the introduction of powderless etching processes, and by photosensitive plastic plates. Both innovations have cut down the block-making process—formerly one of the most time-consuming in newspapers—to a matter of a few minutes.

(6) The Stone

On the stone, newspaper pages are assembled. It is so called from the fact that in old print works, this bench was made of stone (usually marble). Today it is a waist-high workbench covered with steel, usually two feet six inches across and of varying lengths. When the preparation of a page is due to begin, a chase is placed on the stone. This is a steel frame, the same thickness as the base of a piece of type but rather larger than a newspaper page since it incorporates locking devices on two sides to hold the contents firmly.

The stonehands assemble sections of type in the chase on the instructions of stone sub-editors. The makeup—a sheet indicating where each item is to go—is sent across from the editorial department in advance, but usually there is one stone sub who spends his time on the stone overseeing the makeup of the news pages. The makeup of specialised pages—features, advertisements, etc.—will be controlled by the sub-editors who have planned them. The stonehand is an extremely valuable member of the newspaper team, since type when it arrives at the stone on galleys seldom exactly fits the space provided for it. The stone sub and the stonehand between them must then, in whatever time is left to them before the page is due to leave the stone, rearrange this complicated jig-saw by the use of spaces, rules and layout changes. While the page is being assembled, corrections will be arriving from the readers, accompanied by corrected lines which must be inserted and erroneous lines thrown away.

The half-tone blocks for illustrations and line blocks for drawings including cartoons also come to the stone and are put in place. Sometimes the bases arrive before the shells or plates of the half-tones; but in this case the base, giving a solid measure of size, enables the rest of the page to be made up.

A hand metal guillotine and a mitring machine are available to the stonehand for cutting leads (spacing metal) and rules to length, and for mitring the joints of rules and borders.

When the page has been completed, it is locked up. Some chases have their own inbuilt locking keys, others are locked with quoins, or bent keys. The page is beaten by the stonehand with a mallet and planer. The planer is a block of wood with a leather back, and it is moved regularly across the surface of type and tapped with the mallet to ensure that the type surface is perfectly flat for printing.

The page is then inked by hand and proofed by means of a roller —either a hand roller rather like a domestic rolling-pin or a metal-core roller built on to the stone for the purpose. The page proofs are checked by the printer or his assistants, and by the stone sub. If the proofs are passed as correct the page is then sent 'off the stone'.

(7) Moulding

The completed chase, which is known as a forme at this stage when it is full of type and blocks, is transferred from the stone on a trolley and placed beneath a moulding press. This hydraulic press moulds the image of the completed page on to papier-mâché cards, known as flongs.

(8) The Foundry

The moulded papier-mâché flongs are now spoken of as matrices. These matrices are taken to the foundry, for casting. A modern newspaper running at speed will probably need several identical plates cast from the same matrix, so that several machines may print simultaneously. The matrix is placed in a curved casting box and hot metal—usually a lead base with 6 to 8 per cent tin and 13 to 15 per cent antimony—pumped in. The stereotype plates thus produced are curved to fit the cylinder of the rotary printing press exactly.

(9) The Flatbed Press

The stereotype cylinder cast from a matrix was a printing development caused by the introduction of the rotary or cylinder press. Originally presses were flatbed, which means that printing was done much as proofing is done in a modern newspaper—by inking the actual forme and then pressing paper directly upon the cast type. Some small-circulation weekly newspapers may still be printed this way, but the single sheets of paper must be fed by hand and the maximum attainable speed is around 2,000 copies an hour.

The Cossar press, sometimes called a flatbed rotary (though it is not a rotating press), prints from reels of paper which are then cut and delivered. In America a similar press is the Duplex. With this press it is possible to add one or two colours. The press produces an eight-page paper at speeds of about 3,600 folded copies an hour.

(10) The Rotary Press

The modern high-speed rotary printing press is designed to run almost non-stop once the stereotype plates have been fixed in position on the cylinders. There are two cylinders for the printing of each group of pages. On one are attached the stereotype plates. The other is the impression cylinder, and a continuous reel of paper is fed between them. Adjoining plate and impression cylinders print the reverse pages of a paper almost simultaneously with the obverse. At the end of the machine the papers are cut, folded and delivered automatically.

Such modern presses—the Goss or Hoe-Crabtree—can reach speeds of up to 70,000 copies an hour but normally run at 40,000 copies an hour. They do not have to be stopped to change reels of paper (each of which is about 5 miles long); automatic pasting devices phase in a new reel as an old one ends.

Colour seals—the edition devices usually at the top of a front page beside the newspaper's title—are attached to the cylinders with their own ink fountain, generally in a contrasting colour. Stop-press boxes or 'fudges' are similarly attached.

In printing by high-speed rotary press using hot metal types and half-tone blocks it is noticeable that on many presses half-tones print more legibly on some pages than on others. In planning a newspaper the chief sub-editor will be aware of the fact that a detailed half-tone picture stands a chance of reproducing better in more copies of the paper if scheduled on what are called the 'outer pages'—in an eight-page paper, pages 1, 3, 6 and 8.

Many newspapers are today experimenting with various forms of colour printing, as described below.

(11) The Web-Offset Press

The majority of large-circulation newspapers print by rotary letterpress since it is at present the most efficient way of preparing and printing the largest quantities of newspapers in the shortest space of time. But the established means of production are being substantially challenged by the web-offset process.

In old-fashioned schoolrooms teachers used an offset process (a hectograph) to reproduce copies of maps and diagrams. The illustration would be drawn with a special ink, and then rolled on to a jelly surface. Sheets of paper placed on this surface would then take up the image. The offset process is similar, and it is derived from the lithographic process still used by artists. The original image is drawn on to a porous surface in a greasy substance (such as oil paint). When inked, the ink attaches to the image. It may then be transferred to paper.

In offset printing the plates are produced by photo-lithography. This is a photographic process which works in the same way as grease-and-water lithography except that the variations between inked and non-inked surfaces are produced by making parts of the plate sensitive to light, and other parts not. The printing method is called offset because while in typographical rotary printing the stereotype plates come into direct contact with the paper, in offset printing a third cylinder of rubber is introduced between the plate and the paper. The image is transferred from the inked plate to the rubber roller or blanket, and then picked up from the blanket on to the paper.

In web-offset printing, the paper is fed into the press from a reel, as in letterpress rotary printing. The advantage of this form of printing is that the thin metal plate from which the image is transferred may be produced wholly photographically (which has led to innovations in teletypesetting and computer setting, see below). The resilience of the rubber (or sometimes plastic) blanket gives a more accurate image than is possible with the comparatively crude screens of half-tone blocks, which is why photographs printed by web-offset may sometimes appear not to have been 'screened' at all.

The main disadvantage of web-offset, particularly for large-circulation newspapers, has been the comparative slowness of preparation and production. A photo-offset plate may take up to

40 minutes to produce from a completed page, and the usual maximum printing speed in the 1960s was around 25,000 copies an hour compared with twice that speed with letterpress. But many weekly newspapers have adopted web-offset in Britain, as have some evening newspapers in the provinces. The Irish editions of the *Daily Mirror* introduced web-offset to national daily newspapers, beginning printing by this method in 1966 in Belfast, using facsimile pages transmitted electronically from Manchester.

(12) Gravure

In the gravure process, the image is engraved or etched into the printing plate with acid. The plate is then immersed in ink and then wiped by a 'doctor' blade which removes all trace of surface ink but allows ink to remain in the recessed parts of the plate. When the gravure process is used on a rotary press, the impression cylinder forces the paper against the plate, and the paper takes up the ink to a far greater density or 'weight' of colour than can be achieved by comparable methods.

The gravure process is slow, but because of its accuracy is used to produce fine-quality colour. It is widely used by magazines, including the weekend magazines of the British quality press. The process is costly, and needs considerable skill and time in making ready and retouching the separate colour plates. Handwork with acid is, however, giving way to mechanical methods of producing the same results.

(13) Summary

The printing processes listed above are all mechanical. Most of them still use hot metal at one stage of composition. But a print works that offers a reasonable range of founders' type and slug-cast type faces needs considerable space. Type is cumbersome to store, and weighs heavy. So modern technology has made available new techniques in print, as in other industries.

(14) New Developments

The Teletypesetter

The teletypesetter, or TTS, is used for a process that is also known as autosetting. In character it follows the principle of the Monotype operation. A keyboard is used but the machine instead of setting the type in hot metal produces a punched tape. The punched tape can then be fed into a slug-casting machine.

The message on the punched tape can also be transmitted telegraphically to distant points, where it can control further slug-casters. The TTS has therefore been adopted by newspapers that need to set copy at one point, and print the same copy simultaneously in distant parts of the country. The *Scotsman* was the first newspaper in Britain to use the TTS in this way, in 1934.

The Telex

The TTS is a tool of the printer, but a similar device is used by the editorial departments. This is the Telex. This is a keyboard on which the operator types information, which is then transmitted by cable to another office, where a similar (receiving) machine types out the message in a readable form.

The Telex is similar to the Creed machines used by the major news agencies, on which news stories are typed out at a central point and received simultaneously in every subscribing newspaper office.

Photosetting and Computers

The curved printing plate from which newspapers print may be produced in two ways. It may be produced from a matrix cast from a forme that is made up physically from hot metal, cast in single letters and in lines or slugs. Or it may be produced photographically, by photographing an image that may itself be wholly photographic, or a combination of photography and hot metal setting.

The introduction of complicated electronics into the printing industry has been governed by economics. Whether it is worth while a newspaper investing the large amounts of money needed to change over from existing systems to new ones depends on the amount of capital a management has at its disposal, and the future economic prospects of newspapers. It depends also on the comparative speeds of old and new methods of production.

Photo-typesetting (*Filmsetting*)

Type does not have to be set physically by hand. The Photon-Lumitype is an electronic device that sets a variety of type faces photographically. The machine stores a number of alphabets on glass negative discs. These discs rotate and on signals from a keyboard like that of an electric typewriter, the appropriate letter is photographed on to the film. It is claimed that this machine can set 110,000 characters an hour.

The output of such machines is a sheet of transparent film—or rather, a double-thickness sheet, a blank base and an image sheet on which the image is photographically reproduced. Correcting filmset material is a more complicated matter than correcting lines of metal. Lines with errors have to be 'stripped out'—excised by cutting them out with a scalpel and metal rule.

A correct word or line is then 'stripped in', adhering immediately to the blank base. The corrected sheet is then photographed on to a printing plate ready for the printing press.

Computer Typesetting

A computer is a machine that calculates at a speed much faster than man. But a computer takes decisions only to a predetermined pattern, a programme established by its operator. Computers are now being used to speed up many of the processes of printing. They may be linked with almost any printing process. Thus text may be set in hot metal or filmset with the aid of a computer. And one computer works at such speed that the input from a number of keyboards, and thus many pieces of text being set simultaneously, may be fed through one computer at the same time.

The computer may also be programmed to do many of the processes that the compositor would previously have done manually—such as fixing the column width to a certain number of ems, justifying the lines by inserting appropriate spaces between words, and 'breaking' at an appropriate point words that overrun a line, inserting hyphens where required.

The computer produces punched tape that is unreadable to the operator. But it is possible to build in systems so that the operator can see what the computer is producing. Some have a screen, like a television screen, on which the text being set appears visually before the operator. Or the text may be reproduced as a computer printout. A disadvantage of both a monitor screen and a printout has hitherto been that the text appeared in the capital letters of the 'computer alphabet' and not in the chosen type face. In such cases the text would be interspersed with code symbols indicating type faces, paragraphing, capital letters and the other variants introduced by the compositor to instruct whatever setting machine was being employed. The monitor screen or printout would therefore need skilled interpretation. Now it is possible to build in monitoring devices that give a direct and accurate visual impression, and even produce a conventional proof that can be corrected by reader or author in the conventional manner.

But the computer is a particularly useful aid in setting complicated lists such as telephone directories, timetables, and numerical tables of a similar sort, where the basic setting is likely to be valid for a period of months or years. Such material can be stored on punched computer tape in a much smaller space than would be needed to store an equivalent amount of information in physical metal. Corrections can also be made speedily and comparatively simply, without the hard physical labour of taking out each forme from store, moving it to a stone, and correcting it by hand.

A number of British provincial newspapers—particularly those produced by the Thomson Organisation at Reading and Watford, and also the Shropshire Star group—are now printed using computer typesetting, and this new method of composing newspapers and magazines is being introduced widely in the United States.

Typewriter Setting and Instant Lettering

As the techniques of large-scale newspaper production become more automated and expensive, there have been significant developments in the production of cheap print. Where cost is a vital limiting factor, typewriter setting may be useful. The electric typewriter gives a clear image which can then be combined with display types such as Letraset, a dry-transfer lettering which is manufactured in a wide range of typefaces and merely has to be pressed down, letter by letter, on to the surface.

There is an electric composing machine produced by IBM and based on their 'golf-ball' typewriter which is particularly useful for such desk setting. Little larger than an electric typewriter, it takes a variety of typefaces from 6 pt to 12 pt, each distributed round the surface of the 'golf-ball' typehead which can quickly be clipped into place. This machine also has a justifying device, by which a line can be typed conventionally, and then—after setting the justifying device—re-typed so that the line automatically justifies across the required em-width.

Pages produced in this way take longer to prepare than by a hot metal method, but are a great deal cheaper and reproduce adequately by photo-litho.

There are now tape-controlled automatic typewriters available that can be programmed to produce certain predetermined requirements—indenting, justifying and paragraphing as necessary. The magazine *Private Eye* is produced by this method, which is gaining in popularity for small news sheets and magazines. Some publishers have used it for books such as first novels, which would be unlikely to have a considerable sale and thus cannot cover the rising cost of conventional typesetting.

Teleview

Some newspapers—notably the *Asahi Shimbun* in Japan and *Pravda* in Russia—have adopted the wire system whereby whole pages of a master edition produced at a central point are transmitted by wire (through a British-made Muirhead machine, in Japan) to satellite printing works in subsidiary towns—rather as the *Daily Mirror* transmits facsimile pages to Belfast.

Asahi Shimbun has also introduced a system of home distribution known as Teleview. This system, first introduced at Expo '70 (the World's Fair) transmits whole newspapers direct into the home. There a receiver about the size of a television set prints out an electronically produced copy of the latest edition of the newspaper,

Evening News

and Star
monday 19
october 1966.
26057
price 4d

Late

Prince Charles going to school in the 'bush'

It is known as Eton of Australia

We are all delighted says Menzies

Army of police in new hunt for moor graves

Peter Hall is married at Stratford

Lost envoy mystery deepens

Driver killed

Bauson's trip

Lady Churchill comfortable

Dead on line

Strand Club fire

Magret's most baffling case — see page 8

small ads

Paper round

Abstract art

London market domination

Design: Keith Price, ARCA

A design for a newspaper front page produced at the Royal College of Art in 1966. In the original, the newspaper title is in a second colour (red).

Great newspaper pictures are seldom produced without great patience, sometimes in conditions of real danger. This famous photograph of the blitz over London showing St Paul's Cathedral in smoke and flame was taken on the night of 31 December 1940 from a Fleet Street roof by H. A. Mason of the *Daily Mail*.

He described later how it was taken. 'I focussed at intervals as the great dome loomed up through the smoke. . . . Glares of many fires and sweeping clouds of smoke kept hiding the shape. Then a wind sprang up. Suddenly the shining cross, dome and towers stood out like a symbol in the inferno. The scene was unbelievable. In that moment or two I released my shutter.'

Robert Capa was a Hungarian who at the age of 22 took his camera to the Spanish Civil War. There, on a day in 1936 near Cordoba, he pressed his shutter at the moment when a Loyalist volunteer soldier was struck and killed by a bullet. This picture, probably the most famous of all war photographs, went round the world.

Capa followed war. He went on to photograph the London blitz, the American armies (he became a naturalised American) in North Africa, Italy and Normandy, the 1948 Arab-Israeli war, and finally the Indo-China war. He was killed in 1954 when he trod on a landmine near Thai Binh—the first American correspondent to be killed in what was to become the Vietnam war. With some friends, he founded the great Magnum photo agency in Paris.

Robert Capa picture from Magnum.

Photos: Council of Industrial Design

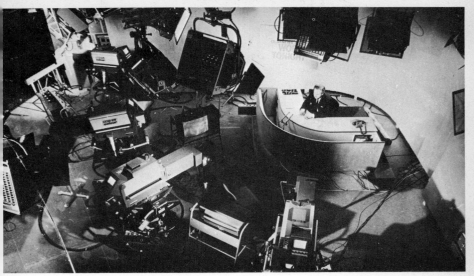

Left: The Marconi colour television camera Mk VII. This contains four tubes, three for colour and one for black and white. There are relay lenses to give a choice of lens; the camera can be switched from 525 to 625 lines. The lower picture shows how the components plug in for easy replacement.

Above: A BBC news studio showing the complex lighting and camera equipment.

Photo: BBC

The BBC television newsroom during the preparation of a bulletin. Beneath the monitor screens are (*left to right*) the Editor of the day, newsreader Peter Woods, and the Copytaster.

The ITN control-room during the transmission of 'News at Ten'. From left: vision mixer, director, production assistant, producer.

The ITN studio set extended to allow for the many participants in a special election broadcast involving newscasters, politicians and pollsters.

The BBC studio set for a special news broadcast about an Apollo moon-shot, showing the model rocket (*left*), the BBC's 'world', and the screen for stills (*right*), with commentators James Burke (*left*), Cliff Michelmore and Patrick Moore.

Television newscasters are frequently reporters who may go outside the studio and conduct interviews. Here ITN's Reginald Bosanquet interviews Edward Heath during an election campaign.

BBC Panorama's reporter Julian Pettifer has specialised in reporting the Far East, particularly the Vietnam war. Here he was photographed in China during the filming of a Panorama programme screened in December 1970—the first independent Western correspondent to go into China since the cultural revolution.

Photo: BBC

Photo: ITN

An ITN camera and reporting team accompanied the climbers up Annapurna. Here Jon Lane (*left*) and John Soldini, ITN cameraman and sound recordist respectively, are checking equipment after they had been hit by an avalanche.

The news magazine programme has recently transformed the presentation of radio news. Here William Hardcastle (*left*), linkman of BBC Radio 4's 'World At One', discusses the programme with producer Andrew Boyle.

Photo: BBC

Photo: The Times

Is this the future of newspapers? The Teleview system (see page 148), now in use in Japan, provides a home receiver (*left*) from which a complete newspaper page unrolls when a button is pressed. The picture shows a demonstration of the system at Expo 70 in Tokyo.

when a button is pressed. At present the machine takes about four minutes to produce one page of tabloid size—one button will issue news, another prints out sports news, a third stock market prices. The blank paper is stored in a reel 100 metres long, and one reel is estimated to last the average family ten days. The manufacturers believe that the machine would cost between £25 and £40 when produced in commercial quantity. Experiments into similar home-printing systems are being conducted in America.

Newspaper Colour Printing

The introduction of colour printing into newspapers was dictated by the financial advantages of attracting colour advertising. A further challenge has been added by the development of colour television. Many newspapers have experimented with colour, but its use is governed by two main factors—the considerable capital cost of colour, and the length of time required to produce colour plates.

A colour transparency must be split up into its primary colours— yellow, magenta (or 'process red') and cyan (or 'process blue'), and three separate blocks made, one for each colour. For the best quality work, a fourth 'black printer' plate is added. Each must then be corrected to obtain the best colour balance. Electronic scanners now enable this to be done much faster, but the problems of register —the exact positioning of one colour over another during the printing process—remain a considerable problem (though in gravure, the process used to obtain the most accurate and satisfactory colour, the register is controlled electronically).

The problem also arises that the reaction of the human eye to colour is to some extent subjective, and there may be great differences between what one man and another may consider a 'true' colour reproduction. There is also the problem that paper may vary considerably in colour, and thus affect the quality of reproduction.

Though many European and American newspapers have used one or two colours in addition to black for many years (for decorations, reversed-out headlines blocks and the like), few British newspapers have used this sort of line-and-tint except for the front-page seal (or edition marker). Full colour was for many years used by large-circulation national newspapers only for advertising.

Advertisements were pre-printed in gravure full colour on reels, usually in continuous designs like wallpaper so that the reverse of the reels could be run through the normal newspaper press in black-and-white (web-offset was later used in the same way). These advertisements are identifiable by the obvious way they 'bleed' off top and bottom of the page, being so designed that each copy of the paper has one complete message and at least two cut-offs.

F

The *Liverpool Daily Post* was the pioneer in Britain of ROP (run-of-press) colour, and developed its own methods of fast block-making for both advertising and editorial colour. Web-offset newspapers, particularly local weeklies with comparatively short runs, have since adopted full colour. But newspapers with large circulations still find that colour slows production unacceptably, and limit the use of colour to a certain number of copies of each run. The London *Evening Standard* has achieved high-quality editorial and advertising colour on this part-edition basis. The London *Evening News* has on many occasions used colour pages that have run through all editions from the second edition.

However, the time required for the preparation of accurate colour blocks still limits the use of colour in daily newspapers to purposes other than hot news—such as sporting slips, fashion pages, and entertainment news, all of which can be prepared some time in advance. The most effective use of colour is in the gravure giveaway magazines, produced by the quality press and pioneered in Britain by the *Sunday Times*. But these are necessarily prepared some weeks in advance of publication and are strictly magazines rather than newspapers. It may be that such magazines depend on the rich advertising to rich readers: the *Daily Mirror* failed to break into this field.

Summary

Printing still provides the most reliable method of recording events in a form that makes them available for easy reference. Computers and electronics have speeded up the techniques of print, but newspaper economics must determine whether the high cost of some of these developments is worth the investment. New techniques such as typewriter composition allied to photo-litho have provided a new and cheaper method of printing, and it may be that as newspapers are polarising into the qualities and the populars, so print will polarise into the very fast and very expensive computer-photoset systems and the slower and cheaper typewriter-composed systems. The cost and complexity of colour will then reserve it to the top end of the market.

But there will still be a place for hot metal, if only in the finest quality and most expensive sector of the trade, where the highest traditions of craftsmanship are maintained.

CHAPTER SEVEN

THE LAW

Most newspapers retain the services of a lawyer. But the fact that he is there, in the office or on call, does not lessen the responsibility of the reporter for what he writes, or of the editor for what is published. Legal actions can be expensive, and involve the journalist, editor and publisher. The journalist who wants to make a name for himself by exposing evils and putting the world to rights must be certain that he has his facts absolutely correct in every detail—and if the case is likely to lead to litigation, must have his report backed with legally witnessed affidavits from those concerned.

If there is any doubt at all about the possibility of legal action following the publication of a story—refer it in typescript to the lawyer. Some newspaper lawyers are more inclined to permit a paper to sail close to the wind than others. But once the lawyer has given his opinion about a story, it is up to the editor to decide what risks the paper will run. It is never the duty of a reporter to take that decision. He should put down all the facts as he knows them: what happens after that is between the paper's lawyer and the editor.

Because the laws affecting publication vary widely from country to country, the contents of this chapter refer specifically to the law as it applied in England and Wales in 1971.

There are two main aspects of the law relating to publication. One concerns the law about the publication of facts, and the other concerns permissible comment on legal proceedings. The first usually relates to libel or defamation. The second is concerned with contempt of court.

(1) Absolute Privilege

The press (and other forms of communication, such as radio and television) are allowed to reproduce statements made in certain circumstances, even though those statements in other circumstances would be actionable because they are incorrect, libellous or malicious. Such statements are said to have 'absolute privilege'.

This applies in the following cases:

1. In the course of debates or proceedings in Parliament. Anything that is said in the House of Commons or the House of Lords

151

may be reproduced as it is said, whether or not it is defamatory. But this freedom applies only to statements made as a part of Parliamentary proceedings: if a Member of Parliament makes a libellous statement outside the House, legal action could be taken against any paper that printed it.

2. In the course of State communications. The officers of State (for example, Government Ministers, senior officers of the Services, and senior Civil Servants) may write what they wish in reports, and these reports are protected by privilege.

3. In the course of judicial proceedings and proceedings before tribunals exercising functions similar to those of a court of justice. If a judge, counsel or witness in a judicial action says or writes anything during the course of that action that is libellous or slanderous, no action can be taken even though the words were said or written out of malice, ill-will or anger.

How far this applies to tribunals is uncertain. No one has cared to risk testing the privilege accorded to statements made during the proceedings of some recent tribunals in Britain. Only a rich newspaper would take the risk.

4. In reports published by order of either House of Parliament. By section 1 of the Parliamentary Papers Act, 1840, all reports, papers, votes and proceedings published by the authority of Parliament are given absolute privilege. *Hansard*, the official report of Parliament, enjoys this absolute privilege, but newspaper reports of extracts from *Hansard* may only enjoy qualified privilege (see below).

5. In fair, accurate and contemporaneous reports in a newspaper or by broadcasting of public proceedings before a court exercising judicial authority within the United Kingdom. The authority for this vital protection is the Law of Libel Amendment Act, 1952, sections 8 and 9 (2). This states:

> A fair and accurate report in any newspaper or by means of wireless telegraphy (as part of any programme or service provided by means of a broadcasting station within the United Kingdom) of proceedings publicly heard before any court exercising judicial authority within the United Kingdom, shall if published contemporaneously with such proceedings, be privileged: provided that nothing in this section shall authorise the publication of blasphemous or indecent matter.

The vital words for journalists in this Act are clearly these: 'fair', 'accurate', and 'contemporaneously'. A report must be fair. If two conflicting accounts of an event are given in court, then both should be given in the report, and not simply the version of one side. It should go without saying that the report must be accurate, but the

Act does emphasise that the facts as published must be correct in every detail. If, for example, a wrong address is given through a transmission error, then this is certainly not protected by privilege. 'Contemporaneously' is taken to mean that a report is privileged if it is published as soon as may reasonably be practicable after the court case has taken place. Thus a daily paper is privileged if it publishes a report in the following day's issue: a weekly paper, if it publishes in the next week's issue.

There can, of course, be no legal objection to the publication of details of a case some time after it has taken place, if the people involved in the case have died—since the dead cannot be libelled. Therefore there are no legal problems about the publication of, for example, accounts of great murder trials of the past.

Law reporters learn to use the sometimes tortuous phraseology of the law with precision. For to vary the precise phrases used might well take the report outside the protection of privilege. Thus if a man has 'elected to go for trial' it would be inaccurate to write that he was 'sent for trial', since that phrase could mean that a lower court had decided that there was a case to answer. In fact the accused might have voluntarily decided—without the evidence being heard—that he wished to be tried by a higher court.

(2) Qualified Privilege

Section 7 of the Defamation Act, 1952, gives newspapers qualified privilege for fair and accurate reports in certain cases. Some statements have this qualified privilege 'without explanation or contradiction'. Other statements are privileged 'subject to explanation or contradiction'. The difference, basically, is that some statements enjoy privilege and an editor does not need to qualify them later, if they are questioned or objected to. Other statements must be qualified later in print, if someone concerned explains that they are wrong.

The following statements are privileged 'without explanation or contradiction':

1. A fair and accurate report of any proceedings in public of the legislature of any part of Her Majesty's dominions outside Great Britain.
2. A fair and accurate report of any proceedings in public of an international organisation of which the United Kingdom or Her Majesty's Government in the United Kingdom is a member, or of any international conference to which that Government sends a representative.
3. A fair and accurate report of any proceedings in public of an international court.

4. A fair and accurate report of any proceedings before a court exercising jurisdiction throughout any part of Her Majesty's dominions outside the United Kingdom, or of any proceedings before a court-martial held outside the United Kingdom under the Naval Discipline Act, The Army Act or the Air Force Act.

5. A fair and accurate report of any proceedings in public of a body or person appointed to hold a public inquiry by the government or legislature of any part of Her Majesty's dominions outside the United Kingdom.

6. A fair and accurate copy of or extract from any register kept in pursuance of any Act of Parliament which is open to inspection by the public, or any other document which is required by the law of any part of the United Kingdom to be open to inspection by the public.

7. A notice or advertisement published by or on the authority of any court within the United Kingdom or any judge or officer of such a court.

The above statements are privileged 'without explanation or contradiction'. The Defamation Act lists certain further statements that enjoy a lesser degree of qualified privilege. A newspaper may publish the findings or decisions of any of the following organisations, or their committees or governing bodies, provided that the report is fair and accurate and published without malice or other improper motive. But if the story is disputed, the newspaper must—if asked—publish 'a reasonable letter or statement by way of contradiction'. The following statements, then, are privileged 'subject to explanation or contradiction':

8. (*a*) An association formed in the United Kingdom for the purpose of promoting or encouraging the exercise of or interest in any art, science, religion or learning, and empowered by its constitution to exercise control over or adjudicate upon matters of interest or concern to the association, or the actions or conduct of any persons subject to such control or adjudication;

(*b*) An association formed in the United Kingdom for the purpose of promoting or safeguarding the interests of any trade, business, industry or profession, or of the persons carrying on or engaged in any trade, business, industry or profession, and empowered by its constitution to exercise control over or adjudicate upon matters connected with the trade, business, industry or profession, or the actions or conduct of those persons;

(*c*) An association formed in the United Kingdom for the purpose of promoting or safeguarding the interests of any game, sport or pastime to the playing or exercise of which members of the public are invited or admitted, and empowered by its constitution

to exercise control over or adjudicate upon persons connected with
or taking part in the game, sport or pastime; being a finding or
decision relating to a person who is a member of or is subject by
virtue of any contract to the control of the association.

9. A fair and accurate report of the proceedings at any public
meeting held in the United Kingdom, that is to say, a meeting
bona fide and lawfully held for a lawful purpose and for the fur-
therance or discussion of any matter of public concern, whether
the admission to the meeting is general or restricted.

10. A fair and accurate report of the proceedings at any meeting
or sitting in any part of the United Kingdom of

(*a*) any local authority or committee of a local authority or
local authorities;

(*b*) any justice or justices of the peace acting otherwise than as
a court exercising judicial authority;

(*c*) any commission, tribunal, committee or person appointed
for the purposes of any inquiry by Act of Parliament, by Her
Majesty or by a Minister of the Crown;

(*d*) any person appointed by a local authority to hold a local
inquiry in pursuance of any Act of Parliament;

(*e*) any other tribunal, board, committee or body constituted
by or under, and exercising functions under, an Act of Parliament; not being a meeting or sitting admission to which is
denied to representatives of newspapers and other members of
the public.

11. A fair and accurate report of the proceedings at a general
meeting of any company or association constituted, registered or
certified by or under any Act of Parliament or incorporated by
Royal Charter, not being a private company within the meaning
of the Companies Act, 1948.

12. A copy or fair and accurate report or summary of any notice
or other matter issued for the information of the public by or on
behalf of any government department, officer of state, local
authority or chief officer of police.

Let us consider some examples of the way this qualified privilege
would work in practice.

Let us suppose that the United Nations General Assembly passes
a resolution describing the British as fascist colonialist exploiters.
Is this statement privileged? The UN is an 'international conference
to which HM Government sends a representative' (clause 2), and the
statement may therefore be published since it has qualified privilege
'without explanation or contradiction'.

Another example. A film star gives her age as 39. A reporter obtains a copy of her birth certificate from Somerset House and discovers that she is 45. May he publish the fact? Certainly, since the birth certificate is an 'extract from a register kept in pursuance of any Act of Parliament which is open to inspection by the public' (clause 6). But the reporter would be wise to check that he has got the birth certificate of Esmerelda Snooks, film star, and not Esmerelda Snooks, housewife; otherwise both Esmerelda Snookses might sue, the one to escape from the fearful drudgery of film stardom and the other from the joys of housewifery and Bingo.

Yet another wholly imaginary case. The General Medical Council bans a doctor from practising and issues a statement that he has been mishandling drugs at a certain address. Is this statement privileged? The GMC is 'an association . . . promoting the exercise of . . . learning, and empowered by its constitution to adjudicate . . .' (clause 8*a*). The statement is therefore privileged. *But* if the doctor's landlord complains that he knew nothing about what was going on, and writes to the editor objecting to his house being branded as a place in which drug trafficking was happening, then the editor *must* publish 'a reasonable letter or statement by way of explanation or contradiction'.

A final case. The Football Association disciplinary committee imposes a fine of £100 on John Farnsbarns, the famous centre-forward (or striker) of Newtown Athletic Football Club, for 'unduly rough tackling leading to his opponent breaking a leg'. Is this statement privileged? Yes, and a paper may publish it, since the FA is an authoritative sports association (clause 8*c*). *But* if John Farnsbarns writes in to complain that the FA got it wrong, that what really happened was that the tackle only bruised his opponent's ankle and then he broke his leg falling against a corner flag, then the editor *must* publish 'a reasonable letter by way of explanation or contradiction'.

In all reports where privilege, absolute or qualified, may be claimed, it is of course essential that these reports shall be 'fair and accurate'. One should, of course, be sure that all reports of any event are 'fair and accurate'—the only difference is that the law sets down extremely heavy penalties where reports that might claim privilege are found to be unfair or inaccurate, and understandably so.

There have, unfortunately, been cases where a reporter has simply misheard a judgement and written a report that totally misrepresented the verdict. In other cases, the reporter may be innocent of misrepresentation but the sub-editor preparing a headline has misread the copy and picked up the wrong end of the stick—a classic case of this occurred in 1925 when a paper published an account of a court case under the heading 'Stole Motor Car—Motor Car Theft'—when the charge of theft had in fact been withdrawn. The reporter concerned had failed to appreciate this fact and the accused man won his case against the newspaper.

Since so many instances of qualified privilege concern associations and institutions, reporters must be careful when dealing with private associations and institutions as distinct from the public associations and institutions with which the Defamation Act is principally concerned. Thus the London Stock Exchange sometimes takes disciplinary action against its members, and issues a public statement announcing the fact. This statement is privileged; but background information about the case is not privileged, and if the background of an individual or a firm that is 'hammered' (that is, forbidden to trade on the Exchange) is described, then those statements take their chance in risking a libel action as if they were statements made about any other member of the public.

The same limitation applies to other 'private' associations and institutions.

(3) Defamation

An individual may claim that he has been defamed if his reputation is attacked in the eyes of the community. Defamation may not always be wrong. Journalism has often been concerned with the righting of wrongs and the exposure of abuses; and if a villain is to be brought to justice, this may involve the publication of facts about him that will certainly injure his reputation in the sight of others. Those facts must be particular and detailed: vulgar abuse in a general sense is not defamation.

This is one of the most delicate grounds on which journalists operate. If the asserted 'facts' are wrong in any particular, the victim may take action in the courts against a journalist or newspaper. That is his right as a citizen. If he can prove that the paper has published a statement that exposes him to hatred, ridicule or contempt, or causes him to be shunned or avoided, or has a tendency to injure him in his office, profession or trade—then he will probably win his action. He might also win if he can prove that the statement made is false, and to his discredit, or if the words printed tended to lower him in the estimation of right-thinking members of society generally.

But what if the accusations are true? Then before publishing them, the editor will be wise to obtain as many legally sworn statements as he can from credible witnesses. Then the newspaper is in a position to plead 'fair comment made in good faith and without malice on a matter of public interest', or that 'in so far as the words consist of statements of fact they are true in substance and in fact, and in so far as they consist of expressions of opinion they are fair comment made in good faith and without malice upon the said facts which are a matter of public importance'.

Sometimes the defence might plead justification—that is, that the words complained of are true in substance and in fact. Justification can be a dangerous defence, since it adds salt to the wound, and may persuade a jury to award higher damages than if the newspaper is properly contrite. Properly, or cynically? Since the 1952 Defamation Act, a defendant does not have to prove that *every* fact printed is true—only that the words that materially injure the plaintiff's reputation are true, provided that the principal charges are true.

The Duke of Wellington may have said 'publish and be damned'. But few newspapers can rely on those whose activities they publicise being so little concerned with public opinion.

If a libel case comes to court, it is for the jury to decide whether the words complained of are defamatory or not. In 1959 the *Daily Mirror* published an article (by 'Cassandra', the great Bill Connor) in which Liberace was described as 'the Summit of Sex—the pinnacle of masculine, feminine and neuter. Everything that He, She or It can ever want'. The article referred to 'This deadly, winking, sniggering, snuggling, chromium-plated, scent-impregnated, luminous, quivering, giggling, fruit-flavoured, mincing, ice-covered heap of mother love.' The jury were asked to decide whether the words (with the exception, for some reason, of 'fruit-flavoured') implied homosexuality. The jury decided that they did, and Liberace won his case: though Mr Justice Salmon in his judgement said that while the words were just capable of that meaning, he himself was 'by no means certain that he would have come to the same conclusion of fact'.

(4) The Right to Report

For many years Parliament fought against the press in refusing to allow official reports of Parliamentary proceedings to be published. Today some local authorities believe that it is in the public interest for the press to be excluded from some of their meetings, if not all. The right of the press to be present at meetings of local authorities is laid down in the Public Bodies (Admission to Meetings) Act, 1960, which enables the press and public to be admitted to meetings of local authorities and their committees. But a local authority may exclude the press and public temporarily from its meetings by a special resolution, if the nature of the business to be discussed makes it in the public interest to do so. Nor, if a matter is to be discussed in private, need that matter be listed on the public agenda of a meeting. This is an unfortunate limitation on the freedom of the press, and has been used as such by local authorities anxious for whatever reason to stifle local comment.

An even more dangerous and uncharted sea for journalists in Britain and many Commonwealth countries (and other countries have similar provisions) is the Official Secrets Act, under which all Government employees, including members of the armed services and civil servants, take an oath promising not to divulge 'official secrets'. This is an Act of all-embracing scope, and technically under it a minor civil servant could be prosecuted for telling his wife what type of biscuit was provided with his office cup of tea. The fact that any prosecution must be authorised by the Attorney-General, and that prosecutions under the Act seldom take place, do not make editorial decisions easier. In 1971, after the '*Sunday Telegraph*' case when Mr Brian Roberts, editor of that newspaper, was acquitted of a charge under the Act, a committee was set up under Lord Franks to investigate its workings.

From time to time governments send editors 'D-notices' warning them about matters that concern the defence of the realm, which the Government believes it would be against the interests of the state to publish. Editors usually observe D-notices, but the decision is theirs, at their risk.

(5) Restrictions on Reporting in Lower Courts

The Criminal Justice Act, 1967, restricted the reporting of committal proceedings in magistrates' courts in England and Wales. This restriction applies only to committal proceedings—if a case is dealt with summarily by the magistrates, it may be fully reported. There are certain exceptions to the general rule that committal proceedings in magistrates' courts may not be reported. These are:

1. Where a defendant, or one of a number of defendants, elects for publicity.
2. Where the magistrates discharge *all* the defendants in a case.

Otherwise, reports of committal proceedings must be strictly confined to the following facts:

1. The identity of the court and the names of the magistrates.
2. The names, addresses, ages and occupations of the defendants and witnesses.
3. The offences, or a summary of them, with which the defendants are charged.
4. The names of the lawyers involved.
5. Any decision to commit a defendant to trial, and any decision on the disposal of the case of any defendant not committed.
6. The charges, or a summary of them, on which a defendant is committed for trial and the court to which he is committed.

7. The date and place to which committal proceedings are adjourned.

8. Any bail arrangements on committal or adjournment.

9. Whether legal aid was granted.

This Act presents reporters with a situation of great complexity. Defendants may be sent for trial without consideration of the evidence if it all consists of written statements made under defined conditions, if the defendants are legally represented, and there is no submission of insufficient evidence.

The magistrates' court rules provide that, where not legally represented, defendants must be told before depositions of witnesses are taken that they have the right to have the restrictions on publicity lifted: but they may exercise this right at any stage of the hearing in the lower court.

Where a defendant elects for publicity during the course of a committal hearing, the fact is announced at the time and also at the beginning of the resumed hearing. From the time a defendant elects for publicity the whole of the committal proceedings, including anything that was said in the case *before* he elected for publicity, may be reported. Where one or more defendants among several elects for publicity, he or they must be clearly identified in reports.

In other words, a court reporter must take a full note of every lower court hearing, in case at some stage one of the defendants may elect to have the case reported—in which case his part in the trial must be disentangled retrospectively from the rest.

Sometimes during a committal hearing the magistrates may decide to try one or more of the defendants summarily, while committing other defendants for trial. The Newspaper Society, in consultation with the Home Office, has produced this summary of what may then happen:

Where at any time during the committal proceedings, the court proceeds to try summarily the case of one or more of the defendants under the Magistrates' Court Act 1952 (summary trial of indictable offences), while committing one or more defendants for trial, it shall not be unlawful to publish or broadcast a report of the summary trial, including evidence relating to the summary trial which was given as part of the committal proceedings before the court determined to proceed summarily in the case of one or more of the defendants.

In such a case the evidence given during the committal proceedings, before the court determined to proceed summarily in the case of some of the defendants, does not have to be given again for the purpose of the summary trial; it automatically becomes part of the summary trial and is therefore reportable without restriction to the extent that it is relevant to the cases of the defendants being tried summarily.

It will frequently happen that the same evidence constitutes part of the case against those committed for trial; indeed this will often be inevitable where the defendants were jointly charged with the same offence. However, this is not a bar to the reporting of that evidence since it will sometimes be impossible to prepare a meaningful report of the summary trial without it.

(6) What to Write When

In court reporting, it is vital that newspapers publish nothing that might be said to prejudice a fair trial. The main reason for the passing of the Criminal Justice Act, 1967, was a fear that when a case had been widely publicised in a lower court, the trial in the higher court would inevitably be prejudiced since it would be virtually impossible to find a jury that had not read some of the evidence in the newspapers, and probably formed some view about the guilt or innocence of the defendant.

Many journalists and some lawyers believe, however, that publicity of the case in the lower court was often a good thing since defence witnesses sometimes came forward as a result of reading about the case in the papers.

However, the law is the law, and reporters must be careful that they phrase every report of legal proceedings so as to avoid any possible accusation of prejudicing those proceedings. Leslie Sellers* gives this vivid example of what may be written and when:

STAGE ONE: Charlie Broome finds a head on his doorstep, and doesn't have much difficulty in identifying it as belonging to Gloria Pole, with whom he spent the previous weekend in Southend. At this point, the newspapers can tell the lot, subject of course to the laws of libel.

On Day 2 clues are being followed up and the dreaded finger of suspicion is pointing at Fred Grudge, who is not only Gloria's regular boy-friend and an insanely jealous chap, but a butcher to boot.

Still no contempt risk arises, because there is no question of proceedings. If Fred chooses to talk his head off at a time when proceedings are not imminent ('I know things look black for me') that's all right, provided the reporter has got a witness in case he denies everything later.

STAGE TWO: Just when this splendid tale is about to go into the newspaper the police pull Fred in and charge him with murdering Gloria. Out it all comes. No longer can Fred or Charlie or anyone else who might be witnesses be quoted.

* In *The Simple Sub's Book* (Pergamon Press, 1968).

No longer can there be talk of the girl being murdered except as part of the charge; instead she must have been found dead. No longer must the paper say that it happened just before the pubs shut, because the time might be vital to the defence. No longer can Fred's picture be used, because a question of identity may arise.

The police statement naming Fred and giving the charge can be quoted because that's privileged, and some lawyers argue that strictly speaking that is all that should appear. But in practical terms it's possible to get in a few other facts which are unlikely to be disputed or prejudice a trial. Like this:

A man was accused last night of murdering 16-year-old artists' model Gloria Pole, whose head was found on a doorstep in Wapping last week.

Fred Grudge, 43, was taken in a police van from his terraced house in The Creek. Later his wife arrived and stayed for half an hour.

Gloria, who left Pickover comprehensive school six months ago, had been modelling since she was three. Her mother, Mrs Jessica Pole, runs a herbal store in Ealing.

This kind of thing is about as far as it can be stretched. It avoids anything which might create either hostility or sympathy towards Fred, such as saying that he was a quiet, homeloving man or that she was a quiet, homeloving girl. It even leaves out his occupation, which would normally be used: the word 'butcher' is a bit pointed in the context.

STAGE THREE: Here we come to the stage of deadpan reporting. Committal proceedings have to be dealt with according to the new rules outlined above. The case in the higher court can be reported 'fairly and accurately', and that's all.

STAGE FOUR: When it's all over, and Fred has been found guilty and sentenced, it's back to Square One. Then all the old Fiend-of-Wapping stuff can be trotted out *ad infinitum* and indeed *ad nauseam* if your paper likes that kind of thing.

To this may be added a warning—be careful to stick to the formal phrases conventionally used before a charge is made. When someone goes to a police station voluntarily—and indeed, when they go with a little gentle persuasion—they are 'helping the police with their inquiries', which is nice of them. To suggest that the police are looking into their alibis for the night a crime was committed would certainly be actionable. It might also, for all we know, be incorrect—which would be as serious.

(7) Obscenity and Blasphemy

Even when 'fair and accurate' reports of court cases, duly privileged, get back to the office, the editor has another hurdle to leap over. The criminal fraternity is not renowned for the purity and inoffensiveness of its language. Some fruity words are frequently heard in court, and some of the details of (in particular) murder cases might bring a blush to the cheek of a well-brought-up schoolgirl. As Mr Mervyn Griffith-Jones asked of the book *Lady Chatterley's Lover*: 'Is it a book that you would even wish your wife or your servants to read?'

What is considered obscene or blasphemous may change from period to period. Much is now published openly that only a few years ago would not have been published. It is for an editor to decide what is, and what is not, fit to publish. His readers may thereafter disagree with him, and the courts may possibly uphold the readers' point of view: but it is the editor's decision in the first place. A reporter should give the facts fairly and accurately, and leave censorship to his editor.

(8) Comment

A newspaper is free to comment on any subject—within the limitations of the laws of libel and the special provisions relating to the prejudice of legal proceedings. But even in the latter case, custom seems to be changing. When he was Lord Chancellor, Lord Gardiner said to the House of Lords (May 1966):

> The law is not in any doubt. It is a free country. Anybody is entitled to express his honest opinion about a sentence and about the way in which the judge has conducted the case, though it is desirable that it should not overstep the bounds of courtesy and should not be a virulent personal attack on a judge. But subject to that, the administration of justice is not, as Lord Atkin once said, a cloistered virtue, and anybody is entitled to express an honest opinion about it.

This is a more liberal view of the law on newspaper comment than has sometimes been taken. It suggests that if comment is fair and reasonable, the press is free to say what it thinks of a sentence, even when a sentence may later go to appeal. It will always be dangerous to comment on a case that has yet to go before a jury. But these days the judges appear to take the view that they are unlikely to be influenced by press comment on a case, once the case has been taken beyond a jury (who, being laymen, might possibly be influenced by such comment). It would however be rash even now to suggest that a judge must be out of his mind to impose a certain sentence.

(9) Election Reporting

Newspapers enjoy considerable freedom in reporting elections, but there are special responsibilities to be borne in mind.

(*a*) *Libel.* While a candidate has as much protection as anyone else and may take action on libels that concern his private life, his public life is a matter of public interest and a newspaper may plead 'fair comment' if that comment is based on fact.

Fair and accurate accounts of public meetings are privileged, subject to three conditions.

1. Publication must be for the 'public benefit', and what is published must be 'of public concern'. If someone stands up in the hall and makes slanderous and abusive remarks about the speaker, such interruptions are *not* privileged, and the reporter takes risks if he reports them.
2. If a candidate considers that a report is unfair he has a right to request that an explanation or a denial shall be printed, even if the report was fair and accurate.
3. If a newspaper report is reprinted and published separately, this reprint is *not* privileged as the newspaper report is.

(*b*) *Untrue Statements about Candidates.* It is a criminal offence to publish any untrue statement (whether libellous or not) about a candidate at a Parliamentary or municipal election for the purpose of affecting the return of any candidate if

1. The statement concerns his personal character or conduct as distinct from his public conduct, and
2. It is a statement of fact (not just opinion), and
3. The newspaper did not have 'reasonable grounds' to believe it to be true.

An injunction can be obtained to prevent the repetition of the statement, even if there were 'reasonable grounds' to believe it to be true. The penalty for such a criminal offence is a maximum fine of £100 and loss of voting rights for five years.

Remember that the untrue statement may be a criminal offence even though it is not libellous. Thus in a Protestant district it would be an offence to say that a candidate was a Catholic if he were not, even if he had not claimed to be of any particular faith.

It is not an offence to make a statement, even if untrue, about a candidate's political or public character or conduct, as distinct from his personal character or conduct. Thus to say that as a councillor he had never attended a meeting would not be an offence.

But this would be an offence if the candidate had in fact attended many meetings, and had claimed this in public: for then the statement would implicitly accuse him of dishonesty or hypocrisy, which would concern his personal character or conduct (and be libellous also).

Though untrue statements about a character of a candidate

opposed by your newspaper are obviously most likely to provoke trouble, untrue statements in favour of a candidate your newspaper supports (e.g. that he lives in the constituency when he does not) may also be an offence.

An untrue statement may be an offence even if it is a fair and accurate report of another candidate's speech, or in a letter, or merely quoted from another newspaper. It is therefore important to be careful when reporting what one candidate says of another.

If the matter comes to court and the court must decide whether a paper had 'reasonable grounds' for believing a statement to be true, a journalist should be able to say where the statement came from. If it comes from someone who is known to be responsible, and who is likely to be in a position to know the truth of what he is saying, this could be a defence. But overhearing something said in a pub by strangers certainly could not.

(*c*) *Incurring Expenses.* A newspaper may not take part in an election in a way that might incur any expense to promote or procure the election of any candidate without the written consent of the election agent. So a newspaper may not organise public meetings or displays, publish bills or circulars, or photographs of the candidate except in the news or editorial columns. Nor may a newspaper publish an advertisement of political significance during elections (even if the name of the candidate is not mentioned) unless the advertisement is concerned with the general policy of a party and covers all constituencies. Thus a newspaper could publish an advertisement about nationalisation if that were an election issue, but could not publish an advertisement giving a local candidate's views on nationalisation if not paid for by his election agent. If it did, the company and directors would be liable to imprisonment for one year, a fine of up to £200, and loss of voting rights for seven years.

(*d*) *Imprints.* A printer who produces election literature, of whatever kind, must print on the face of it the name and address of the printer and publisher. The penalty for not doing so is a £100 fine.

This also applies to hand-written bills giving election news and it is therefore advisable to have blank bills on which such news is to be written pre-printed with the publisher's name and address.

CHAPTER EIGHT

TRAINING FOR JOURNALISM

One reason why journalism used to appeal so much to young people as a career was that it did not seem to need long and boring periods of study. After all, what more does a reporter need than a nose for news, a notebook and pencil, and ambition? Many famous journalists of today did start in exactly that way. They talked themselves on to some small-town newspaper, and then learnt how to do the job as they went along. Many senior journalists look back on those days with nostalgia. They sympathise with youngsters who want to get away from their books and make a reputation in the outside world.

But today it is not so simple. Would-be journalists need a higher standard of school qualifications before they can get a job in the first place. And then they must agree to follow a course of training laid down by the National Council for the Training of Journalists, and they must pass their examinations before they can be sure of holding their jobs.

The NCTJ operates in Britain, but there are similar bodies being established in most countries. In those countries, such as the United States, where a high proportion of youngsters go on from school to college, there are university courses in journalism and the best jobs go to graduates. Though there is only one embryo course in journalism in a British university (at Cardiff), more graduates are entering the profession and as training schemes become more formalised, the chances in journalism of a boy or girl who dislikes school and cannot study or pass exams are very slight.

(1) The Training Council

Training for journalism in Britain is organised by the National Council for the Training of Journalists (Harp House, 179 High Street, Epping, Essex—telephone Epping 2395). The NCTJ was set up as a result of the recommendations of the Royal Commission on the Press (1949). This stated:

The problem of recruiting the right people into journalism whether from school or from university and of ensuring that they achieve and maintain the necessary level of education and technical efficiency, is one of the most important facing the Press, because on the quality of the individual journalist depends not only the status of the whole profession of journalism, but the possibility of bridging the gap between what Society needs from the Press and what the Press is at present giving it.

The Council (it took its present title in 1955, though its work began in 1952) has representatives from the Newspaper Society (proprietors and managers of provincial papers in England and Wales and London suburban papers), the Newspaper Publishers' Association (national newspapers), the Guild of British Newspaper Editors, the Institute of Journalists, the National Union of Journalists, and from newspaper and journalists' organisations in Scotland, Northern Ireland and the Republic of Ireland. There are four educational representatives on the Council, one nominated by the Department of Education and Science.

The aims and purposes of the Council include the establishment of standards of qualification for entry into journalism, and the formulation and administration of schemes for the training and education of journalists, including press photographers.

In 1956 an International Centre for Advanced Training in Journalism was set up in Strasbourg under the auspices of UNESCO, and the Director of the British NCTJ is one of the five-member international executive committee of that Centre.

The training schemes run by the Council became compulsory for new entrants to journalism from 1961, when about 500 trainees were registering each year. To regulate the training courses around the country, the Council has 15 Regional Committees based on various towns. These committees supervise the operation of the training schemes in their areas, liaise with the local education authorities in arranging courses, and advise local editors on methods of vocational training, and provide the experienced journalists to conduct proficiency tests.

The revenue to run the National Council for the Training of Journalists comes from the member societies and organisations, with contributions from individual national newspapers and broadcasting and television organisations. Contributions have also been made by big companies with a special interest in the improvement of standards of journalism, e.g. in popular science writing.

(2) Training Schemes

There are basically two ways of entering the training schemes organised by the NCTJ: either by getting a job on a newspaper and then applying to enter the training scheme which combines practical journalism with part-time study, or by taking the one-year full-time course organised by the NCTJ.

(3) Getting a Job

How does the ambitious school-leaver get into journalism? This is the most difficult part. The NCTJ is not an employment agency. Each new entrant must find his first job for himself (or herself—one in four new entrants to journalism in Britain is now a girl).

Most new entrants will join a newspaper. The British Broadcasting Corporation and the television companies usually recruit experienced journalists rather than trainees, although it is occasionally possible to find a job as a studio assistant and hope to climb the promotional ladder that way.

So the young hopeful must apply to the editor of a provincial newspaper, and hope to get an interview. Sometimes newspapers advertise for bright juniors in the jobs vacant columns, but there is more often no shortage of applicants who write in. The basic educational qualification for a school-leaver is three Ordinary Level passes in the General Certificate of Education (including English Language) or the equivalent. Three top-grade passes in the Certificate of Secondary Education are accepted as an equivalent. The NCTJ's own recommendation to editors, however, is five 'O' levels, and there are often many applicants with 'A' levels which are obviously no disadvantage. Journalism appeals as a career to many arts graduates emerging from universities, so the school-leaver with minimum educational qualifications may find himself battling for a job against people with far better academic qualifications.

That said, it must be added that academic qualifications are not everything. Personality counts for a lot. Journalists must meet many people, however briefly, throughout their working careers. They must be able to persuade strangers to talk easily to them, often about worrying or intimate aspects of life, and often in times of crisis or stress. So an editor interviewing a potential reporter looks for confidence and ease of manner: not arrogance or extreme self-assertiveness, for the reporter who does all the talking will seldom get the story from the person he is interviewing. Secondly, an editor looks to see whether the potential reporter is interested in newspapers and in the sort of work he will have to do.

An applicant who turns up for an interview for a job on a provincial paper and admits that he has never read that paper, and that his ambition is to get out of the provinces and into Fleet Street or television as quickly as possible, is unlikely to get a job.

An editor is conscious that his reporters are the ambassadors of the paper around the town. So he expects his reporters to have a presentable appearance. Some editors (for they are ordinary men) may be prejudiced against shoulder-length hair in men, dyed tee-shirts or fringed jackets. They may not mind these expressions of individuality personally, but they may think that a reporter looking like that is not going to get much of a story at a factory gate or the town hall. Fashions are changing and brightly floral ties may now be acceptable. But the general reporter has to be sensitive to the environment around him: it is not for him to make dramatic and assertive gestures. Very long hair or brilliantly colourful clothes tend to be conspicuous in provincial towns, which are not as liberated as the King's Road or Carnaby Street. If a young applicant cannot understand that, then he is lacking in sensitivity to atmosphere—one of the prime requirements of a good journalist. His function will be to report what is actually happening, not to lead the glorious revolution of the proletariat. If he wants to do that, he must do it outside office hours.

A reporter must have a reasonable knowledge of current affairs. An eighteen-year-old of moderate intelligence, for example, would be expected to know the names of the President and Vice-President of the United States, the name of the first man to walk on the moon, the name of the local member of parliament and his or her political allegiance. The aspiring reporter should also have some idea of the character of important local industries, and have a general knowledge of his area's social problems.

Last but far from least, the school-leaver will be expected to be able to write a straightforward piece of English prose, with properly shaped sentences, accurate grammar and accepted spelling. No one expects the new entrant to be able to do shorthand or type (these things are taught in the training scheme), though an ability to do either or both would be taken as evidence of keenness and an awareness of the requirements of the job.

If the editor likes the way the interview has gone, and if there is a job available, he will offer the applicant a job for six months on probation, so that he can be tested out. This six-month period is important. The new entrant will probably be given many of the tedious routine chores on the paper, and it will be up to him how he handles them. If he carries them out with accuracy, efficiency and good nature, he may be offered an apprenticeship. If he rebels at being treated like an office-boy instead of God's gift to the written word, then he won't be.

(4) Apprenticeship

If after six months the editor likes the new entrant's work, and the new entrant feels at home in journalism and wants to continue, then he and his employers sign articles of apprenticeship. These form a legal contract under which the employer undertakes to

provide thorough training and observe agreed conditions of payment
and employment for a period of three years (two years for graduates);
and the trainee, for his part, promises to take his training seriously.
The trainee is then formally registered with the National Council
for the Training of Journalists. (This scheme refers to junior trainees,
under the age of twenty-four and with less than one year's experience
of newspaper or news agency journalism.)

(5) The Pattern of Training

Newspaper offices are not academic institutions. They exist to
produce newspapers, and the training of juniors is an incidental.
Therefore a good deal of responsibility rests with the trainee to
make the most of the opportunities offered to him, and to use his own
initiative to read and study outside working hours. There are two
ways in which the academic side of training is done: by day-release
courses, and by block release.

Day Release. Where suitable courses are being run in the neigh-
bourhood, trainees attend day-release courses on one day a week over
a period of two years. They follow the Council's courses in English
(over two years), local government (one year), newspaper law (one
year) and they study shorthand (over two years). Some local authorities give grants to cover the cost of these courses, or the newspaper
may pay for them—leaving the student to pay for his own books.
The trainee takes the Council examinations in June, and failures re-
take them in the autumn. Current affairs and practical journalism
are included in the courses.

Block Release. If there are no day-release courses nearby, or if the
editor of the paper prefers to lose his trainee's services for two periods
of eight weeks rather than one day a week, the trainee will attend
block-release courses, usually held about twelve months apart.
These cover the same subjects as day-release courses, but more
intensively: these long courses allow the students time to produce
their own newspaper. Examinations are held at the end of each block-
release period. These courses are residential: local authority grants
or the employer usually pay the cost of fees and half the accommodation cost, leaving the trainee to find half the cost of accommodation
and the cost of books.

Other Methods. There may be cases where neither of these schemes
is practicable for one reason or another. In such cases, if the National
Council is notified and can make arrangements for appropriate
examinations trainees may take correspondence courses (the National
Council runs its own correspondence course in newspaper law, and
has an approved list of other correspondence courses) or join
classes at local colleges of further education in the particular subjects
required. But these methods are not encouraged unless it is quite

impossible for the student to take a day-release or block-release course.

Subjects. The main subjects studied are shorthand and typing, English, local government, newspaper law and current affairs.

English is studied so that journalists have an effective command of their own language, with clarity of thought and expression. The course includes references to the Council's textbook *Daily English*, and students are encouraged to read a number of twentieth-century authors. They must also produce an original piece of writing of at least 2,500 words on a subject of their own choice, based on detailed research.

Local government is studied, and only marginally the way central government impinges on it, since most young reporters are practically concerned with the structure and operations of local government. This course is based on a booklet produced by the National Association of Local Government Officers as part of its correspondence course.

Newspaper law is studied not only so that journalists may avoid getting themselves and their papers into trouble, but also so that they know what protection and liberty the law permits them in their work.

(6) Development of Training

During the probationary period before he signs his indentures the new entrant will have started to learn shorthand, to learn how his newspaper office functions, and to cover a few local events supervised by a senior member of the staff. One member of the staff is responsible for training, but if he is a full-time newspaper executive he is unlikely to be able to watch every detail of every trainee's progress.

First Year. In his first year of indentures the trainee will be expanding his experience of reporting, assessing news values and learning how to interview. He may attend courts, inquests and local government meetings, and though his shorthand may not be good enough for him to be given full responsibility to report these for the paper, he may write 'shadow' reports and then, with the training officer, compare them with the actual reports that appeared in the paper. He will be discovering how the production processes work, and outside the office will be reading widely in the literature of journalism.

Second Year. In his second year the trainee should be reaching the speed of 100 words per minute at shorthand, and be reporting independently such occasions as juvenile courts and minor cases at magistrates' courts, and the meetings of local authority committees. He should be carefully briefed for these assignments, but encouraged to accept full responsibility for them. There may be opportunities to do some specialisation (e.g. in sport, or the arts). The results of his first examinations will be available and give a yardstick of achievement. They also warn the trainee which subjects he must improve his grasp of.

Third Year. In his third year the trainee will try to improve his shorthand to reach a higher speed. He will be given more experience of court reporting—Assize, Quarter Sessions, County Courts and divorce courts, and ideally be given a wider experience of all aspects of local government. He will also be given a chance to sub-edit copy (prepare other reporters' copy for the paper) and may have a chance to write feature articles, leaders, and criticism. At the end of the third year the trainee sits the Council's Proficiency Test.

Proficiency Test. The test is held twice yearly, usually in April and October, in a number of centres throughout Britain. On the panel of assessors are local editors, senior journalists, and sometimes managers and proprietors. They have before them a confidential report from the trainee's editor about his progress, and he must take with him three specimens of work (one from a recent copy of his paper).

The trainee is given a printed briefing instructing him that in fifteen minutes he is to conduct an interview to obtain a factual story. He carries out this interview in the presence of two assessors, who are experienced journalists. The candidate then has an hour to write or type his report of the interview, as if for his own newspaper. This is read by the two assessors.

He is then given a handout or piece of promotional material asked to rewrite it for his own newspaper, and say how he would use local or regional sources in following it up.

Then (usually in the afternoon) the candidate is tested in the reporting of the spoken word, and takes papers in current affairs and newspaper practice, including newspaper law and local government.

If he passes, the trainee receives the Proficiency Certificate of the National Council for the Training of Journalists and is qualified to work as a journalist out of indentures (the usual pass rate is around 60 per cent of candidates).

(7) Freelance Journalists

Journalists employed by freelance news agencies may be admitted to the training scheme and registered as candidates for the training scheme under certain conditions, the most important of which is that the agency for which they work must be approved for this purpose by the National Council. Youngsters who consider joining a freelance news agency in the hope of progressing to a newspaper should therefore check with the National Council, before they join, that the agency concerned is suitable.

National Diploma. There is a higher qualification available to older journalists—the National Diploma in Journalism. This is awarded on the evidence of a written examination, of practical work over a period, and of a thesis of 10,000 words on some aspect of journalism or the newspaper industry.

Full-time Courses. The training schemes listed above, based on day-release and block-release courses conducted simultaneously with practical experience in a newspaper office, are how the majority of new entrants to British journalism have learnt their trade. Within the past few years the National Council has introduced full-time preparatory courses, lasting one year.

In 1970–1 there were seven such courses, held at colleges in Darlington, Harlow, Portsmouth, Preston, Sheffield, Cardiff and Edinburgh. Entrants for these full-time courses must hold at least two Advanced level certificates and be under twenty years of age when the course starts. Selection for these courses is made early in the New Year by panels of editors and senior journalists who interview candidates at certain regional centres. The candidates also take aptitude tests to assess their suitability for journalism. Grants are usually available from local authorities for suitable candidates, who are expected to live in lodgings near the college where the course is held.

The course consists of practical journalism, law, government, current affairs, shorthand and typing. At the end of the first term there is an examination, after which students who are not up to standard leave. Those who complete the course are helped by the National Council to find jobs as trainee reporters on local news-papers, where they serve the customary three years' apprenticeship.

(8) Photographers

There is now a comparable full-time course for trainee newspaper photographers at the Department of Photography, West Bromwich College of Commerce and Technology, Staffordshire.

Block-release courses for photographers employed as trainees on newspapers are already held at this centre.

Candidates for the full-time course must hold at least four Ordinary level certificates (including English language) and be under nineteen years of age when the course starts. Selection is by interview at Wednesbury, organised by the National Council.

Trainee newspaper photographers are encouraged to take the intermediate examination of the Institute of Incorporated Photographers (38 Bedford Square, London WC1) or of the City and Guilds of London Institute (76 Portland Place, London W1).

(9) Group Training Schemes

Two British newspaper groups run their own training schemes for journalists: these are the International Publishing Corporation (publishers of the *Daily Mirror*, *Sunday Mirror*, the *People*, the *Glasgow Daily Record* and many magazines) and the Thomson Organisation (publishers of *The Times*, the *Sunday Times*, and sixteen provincial newspapers).

The Mirror Group and IPC Schemes

The Mirror Group accepts as trainees (*a*) graduates up to twenty-four, preferably with arts degrees, e.g. English, History, Economics, Languages, or Sociology and allied subjects, or (*b*) school-leavers under twenty with a minimum of five Ordinary level passes and one Advanced level pass, preferably English, in the General Certificate of Education examination. More 'A' levels are an advantage.

The training course is conducted on the lines of that laid down by the National Council for the Training of Journalists, with some differences. To launch this scheme, IPC bought six newspapers in South Devon—a regional Sunday newspaper serving Devon and Cornwall, and five local weeklies. All six were grouped into one company, West of England Newspapers Ltd, a subsidiary of the Mirror Group Ltd.

IPC trainees take indentures with the company, lasting two years for graduates and three for non-graduates. In each case, they serve six months' probation, after which they can leave if they or the newspaper feel that they are unlikely to be happy in the job. About a third of the trainees are girls.

Trainees receive tuition in four compulsory subjects—shorthand, local government, newspaper law and the use of English, and sit the NCTJ's examinations in each subject. The standards are those of the NCTJ, except that in shorthand trainees are required to reach a speed of 120 words a minute, instead of the NCTJ's stipulated pass speed of 100 words.

The trainees are found accommodation in Plymouth when they arrive, and afterwards may find lodgings or share a house with other trainees—the only requirement being that they must live in the area of the paper on which they are working. As the six papers vary in style—two are broadsheet (large size) while the other four are tabloid —trainees get a variety of newspaper experience (they usually work on three different papers during their training).

By living in the area covered by the paper, the trainee learns what his readers think about the paper, and has a wide opportunity to do a variety of jobs—even to specialise, for example in sports reporting. But initially, for the first three and a half months, the trainee is mainly in the classroom, learning the elementary principles of newspaper work. Then he goes to one of the papers, and immediately can begin reporting (though on his first few assignments he is accompanied by a senior member of the staff). During this first period of the course, everything a trainee writes for the paper is commented on privately by a training officer and he is given guidance on whether his work is developing satisfactorily.

Towards the end of the course, trainees are attached to one of the newspapers for a period of up to two months. This enables them to see how things are done on a national newspaper. Finally, they take the NCTJ Proficiency Test. If they pass, they are qualified journalists, and may be offered a job on 'a Mirror Group' newspaper or magazine.

In this scheme there is no commitment to find the successful trainee a job at the end, but conversely there is no commitment by the trainee to continue working for the Mirror Group.

During their training, trainees are paid either a special house scale which recognises the additional expense of living away from home, or the current salary scales agreed between the Newspaper Society and the journalists' organisations, whichever is higher. Rates are the same for men and women. IPC Magazines Ltd also runs a training scheme for technical experts wishing to join its trade and technical publications.

The Thomson Organisation

About 800 graduates each year apply for jobs on Thomson newspapers. Of these, some 350 are interviewed, having been selected on the basis of their written applications. The number accepted each year depends on the number of available jobs on Thomson regional (provincial) newspapers—each editor tells the Thomson Organisation each year how many places he can offer. There are never more than thirty—so fewer than one in ten of those interviewed obtain jobs.

The qualifications for graduates are a degree, preferably in History, Politics or Economics, though Classics, English or Law are acceptable. One foreign language is useful. The ability to write plain English is essential. Graduates must normally be under twenty-four when joining their paper. The Thomson Organisation does not particularly favour people who have worked on a university newspaper, but looks for men or women who can be trained as competent general journalists, with the emphasis on news and news-feature work.

On specialisation, Thomsons are interested in graduates who want to go into financial journalism; in that field they are able to specialise sooner. Ambitious would-be foreign correspondents are warned that they must normally spend about ten years in general reporting, some in the provinces and some in London, before they would be considered for a foreign posting. In addition, complete fluency in one foreign language is essential: *The Times* demands two.

Graduates join the Thomson Organisation in August and spend four months at one of the two training centres at Cardiff or Newcastle, working at pre-entry study of shorthand, typing, law and the other subjects required in the NCTJ syllabus. Most graduates take the NCTJ newspaper law paper during this period, and before they join their regional newspaper as an apprentice in January.

The indenture period lasts for two years, and in that time the graduate trainees work for the NCTJ Proficiency Certificate, often taking it successfully in twelve or fourteen months. Provided they pass that test, they are fully qualified members of their local newspaper's staff. In due course they may want to move to another paper, or to London (*The Times* now requires its new recruits to have worked for a minimum of three years in the provinces). But as job opportunities become fewer in Fleet Street, many graduates who have trained in the provinces are seeing the advantages of staying there.

The Thomson Organisation also introduces its graduate entrant to the business side of newspapers—advertising, production, sales and distribution. (The Organisation also recruits graduates into the other fields of its operations—marketing, sales management, magazine and book publishing, financial and accounting services, holiday tour administration and personnel management.)

A similar scheme for school-leavers with the basic qualification of at least two 'A' levels, one of which must be English, is being planned for Thomson regional papers. Candidates would be recruited by their own home-town newspapers (having the particular advantage of local knowledge) and would study for a five-month pre-entry course on the pattern of the graduate courses at Cardiff or Newcastle before taking up their indentures on the papers.

It is clear that such schemes, whether organised by the NCTJ or by independent companies, will become the pattern for entry into all the media. All require a good basic education, usually to 'A' level. Therefore the young man or woman who leaves school before taking 'A' levels in the hope of achieving success in journalism will soon find it hard to get a foothold on the lowest rung of the ladder.

(10) International Training Scheme

In 1962 Mr Roy Thomson (now Lord Thomson of Fleet) set aside £5 million to form the Thomson Foundation. This is for the 'advancement of knowledge and spiritual enlightenment of all peoples, enabling them to achieve closer understanding and to play an informed and responsible role in the affairs of their nation and the world'.

The Thomson Foundation—which is independent of Lord Thomson's commercial interests in newspapers and television within the Thomson Organisation—provides courses in journalism and television production and engineering for journalists mainly in the developing countries who want to improve their knowledge and understanding of modern newspaper and television techniques.

The Press. At the Foundation's Editorial Study Centre in Cardiff, three courses are held each year, each lasting twelve weeks and with twelve students. There is a long waiting list for these courses. The Foundation pays for tuition, board and lodging and travel within Britain. The student or his sponsor (for each student must be sponsored and recommended by his employer, usually his newspaper) must pay the fare to and from Britain (though occasionally candidates are helped from Government Technical Assistance Funds).

Candidates for these courses must have had at least three years' practical experience in full-time journalism, and be fluent in English. The courses cover most aspects of newspaper journalism in both editorial and management functions, and each course produces its own newspaper, called *Scope*. Usually the summer course each year has a specialised interest—sports writing and editing, industrial and commercial journalism, or agricultural journalism.

Some courses have been geared to the performance of specific functions on newspapers—one has been run for potential editors, another for chief sub-editors. The Editorial Study Centre is run on severely practical lines, since from experience it was found that journalists from the developing countries were concerned primarily with the practical aspects of the profession. The Centre is directed by a former newspaper editor.

The Centre also organises short courses sponsored by the Commonwealth Press Union.

Television. At the Foundation's Television College at Newton Mearns, Glasgow, there are two regular courses each year, lasting sixteen weeks, each with twenty students who must be working in television in their own countries. Each course contains both a production and an engineering stream. There are also specialised courses, e.g. for news editors, women's and children's programmes, etc.

The cost arrangements are similar to those for the newspaper courses. But the basic need that the Television College answers tends to be different. Often, when new television services are being started, the staff is assembled at the same time as the equipment. The staff may have experience in newspapers, radio or film, but few have any experience in the novel medium of television.

The Television College has therefore set out to provide this basic training in all aspects of television production and engineering, based on the College's own fully equipped studio.

Applications. Details of these courses are available in the developing countries from British Council offices, or from Information Offices of British High Commissions or Embassies.

In the first five years, students came to Britain for these courses from Aden, Afghanistan, Australia, Bahamas, Barbados, Bermuda, Bolivia, Brazil, British Honduras, Ceylon, Chile, Cyprus, Ethiopia, Fiji, Ghana, Gibraltar, Greece, Guyana, Hong Kong, India, Indonesia, Iran, Iraq, Israel, Jamaica, Japan, Jordan, Kenya, Korea, Kuwait, Laos, Lebanon, Liberia, Libya, Malawi, Malaysia, Malta, Mauritius, Mexico, Nepal, New Zealand, Nicaragua, Nigeria, Norway, Pakistan, Peru, Philippines, Rhodesia, Rumania, Sarawak, Sierra Leone, Singapore, Somali Republic, South Africa, South Vietnam, Sudan, Syria, Taiwan, Tanzania, Thailand, Trinidad, Turkey, Uganda, United Arab Republic, Uruguay, Venezuela and Zambia.

Overseas Courses. In addition, the staff of the Thomson Foundation have travelled overseas to provide specialised courses on-the-spot where requested.

Newspaper journalism courses have been held in Afghanistan, Cyprus, India, Malawi, Philippines, Thailand and Uganda. Television courses have been held in Ethiopia, Lebanon, Pakistan and Uganda. Film courses have been held in Cyprus, Nigeria and Zambia.

The interchange of information between the more experienced communicators of Britain and the rapidly developing information services of the emerging world has proved a most valuable experiment.

(11) The Local Newspaper as Training Ground

Most training for journalism is done through the local newspaper. But this is only incidental to the functioning of such a newspaper. It is a living thing, an organisation with its own tensions and its own pace. The trainee, whether he enters it direct from school or from university, will find it very different from anything he has experienced before.

The pattern of a daily paper and a weekly is in contrast. On a daily paper the moment-by-moment pressures are acute. There is an ever-present awareness of speed, and of the need to get the paper out at all costs. On a weekly paper this pressure may be less, yet it can be felt building up as press-day approaches.

Journalists become accustomed to the rhythm of the paper on which they work. They attune their own lives to it, and they subordinate their private lives to it. One of the most important things that the young trainee has to learn is how he fits into the scheme of things.

Though ideally training schemes would be run for the complete benefit of those taking part, the intensity of newspaper work hardly makes this possible. On a daily paper the newcomer may be disturbed by the triviality of much that is done: but if it is news, and interests the readers, then it justifies its place in the paper. The ordinary newspaperman's cynicism is often a shield against this flood of triviality. He must somehow preserve a sense of proportion and an awareness of ordinary life as it is lived by ordinary people.

The world of a newspaper is geared to reflecting that ordinary world, with all its faults and failings, its joys and achievements. But everything is processed, put through the machine. It must be: the technical requirements of producing a newspaper demand it.

There is never enough time, newspapermen often feel, to do anything properly on a newspaper. Never enough time to get quite all the facts into a story, never enough time to write it quite perfectly, never enough time to sub-edit so that it fits the page precisely without having to be cut.

And there is never enough time or energy to explain all this to trainees. There is never enough time to point out that an apparent shell of toughness does not mean a complete absence of all human feelings.

The local paper is the voice of a town or a region, and that voice must be clear and articulate. The mental shorthand of a newspaper office, where men who have been working together for years do not say everything they mean or think because they *have* worked together for years and know what they mean or think without putting it into words (and they have enough traffic with words anyway)— the trainee reporter has to learn all this by intuition, and learn how he can usefully contribute to the paper.

For it is by playing a valuable part in the production of even the smallest local paper that the potential journalist can become the responsible newspaperman.

(12) Student Journalism and the Employment Prospects of Graduates

Many students enjoy working for university newspapers during their university career. Some of these papers, such as *Varsity* at Cambridge, reach a high standard of professionalism in presentation and production, and sometimes in writing. But there is no direct link between student journalism and Fleet Street. It used to be the custom for student journalists to spend some time during their vacations working as 'holiday reliefs' on national newspapers, but this system has now ended and student journalists must take their chance with other entrants to the profession. Union agreements on recruitment make it impossible for even the brightest university whizz-kid to hope to start at the top on national newspapers. He must go through the provincial newspaper hoop like everyone else.

Some may regret that this has shut off a fertile source of youthful enthusiasm and new ideas from Fleet Street, since now graduates can scarcely hope to reach a national newspaper before they are twenty-five or twenty-six. But that is the position.

It may still be possible for the young critic—of music, say, or the arts—to get a foothold into criticism through student journalism where the information network of the arts may from time to time signal to the London magazines and television media the arrival of a new incisive, witty and prodigiously polished voice. But that is a matter of luck, and might happen to one in a thousand—that one in a thousand who is prepared to starve in a garret or work as a dustman while reviewing concerts in the evening for a little magazine, waiting for the gap to happen on the arts pages of one of the literate Sunday papers.

The graduate in Britain who wants to enter journalism can best do so through the training schemes of the National Council for the Training of Journalists, the IPC or Thomson Organisation training schemes (see above), or by applying to one or other of the following organisations and papers who recruit graduates:

The Director, Centre for Journalism Studies, University College, 34 Cathedral Road, Cardiff CF1 9YG, Wales.

Group Training Officer, The Kent Messenger, Maidstone, Kent.

Personnel Adviser, East Midland Allied Press Limited, Oundle Road, Woodston, Peterborough, Northants (up to April each year).

The Secretary, Reuters Limited, 85 Fleet Street, London EC4.

Group Personnel and Training Officer, Yorkshire Post Newspapers Limited, Albion Street, Leeds 1, Yorkshire.

The Editor, Bristol Evening Post, Silver Street, Bristol.

The Editor-in-Chief, Eastern Counties Newspapers, Norwich NOR 87.

The Editor, Halifax Courier and Guardian, Courier Buildings, Halifax, Yorkshire.

Group Personnel and Training Manager, Express and Star, Queen Street, Wolverhampton, Staffordshire.

Group Editorial Director, Morgan-Grampian Ltd, 28 Essex Street, Strand, London WC2.

The Editor-in-Chief, Tillotsons Newspapers Ltd, Mealhouse Lane, Bolton, Lancashire.

The Editor, Morning Telegraph and/or The Star, Telegraph and Star Building, York Street, Sheffield 1.

The Editor-in-Chief, Liverpool Daily Post and Echo Ltd, 46 Victoria Street, Liverpool, Lancashire.

(13) Practical Requirements

Shorthand

Shorthand systems enable the reporter to take down verbatim accounts of speech at whatever speed it is spoken, by the use of symbols to represent sounds or words (so the systems are variously described as 'phonographic' or 'orthographic'). Good shorthand is an asset to any journalist.

The shorthand systems in common use are:

Pitman's   The oldest and most widely used system in Britain, devised by Sir Isaac Pitman in 1837. Tuition books may be ordered from booksellers, and further particulars obtained from Sir Isaac Pitman and Sons Ltd, Pitman House, Parker Street, Kingsway, London WC2.

Pitman Script   A new and abbreviated system devised by Miss Emily D. Smith of Pitman's and launched in 1971. It combines symbols representing sounds with letters from the orthographic system.

Gregg   Devised by Dr John R. Gregg in 1888, Gregg shorthand is based on the movements of the hand in ordinary handwriting: it is widely used in the United States. Gregg is marketed in Britain by the McGraw-Hill Publishing Company Ltd, Shoppenhangers Road, Maidenhead, Berkshire.

Notehand   A basic system based on Gregg shorthand intended for those who do not need speeds of more than about 80 words per minute.

Speedwriting   This was developed in the United States in the early 1920s by Emma Dearborn and Dr Alex Sheff. It uses the letters of the conventional alphabet, and so may be learned fast. The British headquarters are Speedwriting International, Avon House, 360/366 Oxford Street, London W1.

Teeline   An orthographic system devised in 1968 by James Hill, a Nottingham shorthand tutor. Recommended by the National Council for the Training of Journalists, Teeline is published by Heinemann Educational Books Ltd, and may be ordered through booksellers.

Typing

Clear and accurate typing is a necessity for journalists. The pace of newspaperwork means that there is seldom time to retype or correct a page. When a news story is being written at speed, it may be sent to the printer page by page and the reporter cannot revise.

There are a number of stages in newspaper production at which errors can creep into copy—the news desk, the sub-editor, the compositor, the reader, the stonehand. So it is important that the original copy should be 'clean'.

Never type over mistakes to correct them—the mark of the amateur. You may know which of the two overtyped letters you intend to be set, but the compositor has every right to choose the wrong one. Much better delete the incorrect word and retype it 'clean'. Always make particularly certain that names appear accurately on your copy: they may not be familiar to the compositor, and no newspaper error is more irritating to the subject of the story than finding that his name has been misprinted.

Leave plenty of room on your copy for the sub-editor's marks (see 'How to prepare and lay out copy', below). Always end a sentence on one page rather than continuing it on to the next, which involves the copy-desk in time-wasting work with scissors and paste before setting. Always put your name, the date, and the time of completion of the story on your copy. But above all, type 'clean'.

The Tape Recorder

An increasing number of journalists now use the tape recorder, especially since the production of light, battery-powered casette-loaded machines. They have the advantage that every word that is said is recorded, can be played back, and can be stored as evidence in case the interviewee announces after your story has been printed that he never said any such thing.

On the other hand, the tape recorder is an inhibiting factor in some interviews, for its presence is a constant reminder that the subject is being reported and must be careful what he says.

Casette recordings are seldom acceptable for radio broadcasting (unless they are of some particularly newsworthy or startling occurrence, and can be transcribed). The machine generally used by BBC sound radio reporters is the Uhuer, recording at $7\frac{1}{2}$ r.p.s.

Keeping to the Deadline

Newspapers run on edition times. Those edition times are vital. If they are missed, because a page is late being made up, then production is late, newspaper trains leave without that edition, and readers in distant parts of the country may never get a copy of the paper at all. If this happens once, it is serious. If it happens several times, it can be disastrous for the commercial success of a newspaper.

So if journalists are asked to produce a report by a certain time, known as the 'deadline', they must produce a report by that time. If it is not as complete as it would later be, if it is not phrased with that precision that the journalist would wish, provided the facts have been checked and are accurate as they stand then the report must go forward. Otherwise it is not worth writing at all.

For the purpose of journalism is to produce newspapers. If journalists miss their deadlines not once but many times, then they will not hold their jobs for long. The deadline is not a flexible moving feast, but a predatory ogre that cannot under any circumstances be denied. Keep to the deadline, or don't be a journalist.

(14) How to Prepare and Lay Out Copy

Copy will be either typed in the office, or telephoned in to a copy-taker. If it is typed in the office, it should be prepared so that it needs practically no sub-editing and could almost be photographed and put in the paper as it stands. At the top of each sheet put a 'catchline'. This is a key word, since it identifies all sheets of the copy during production, and is printed with each stick of metal so that the printers can collate the whole story. Choose, therefore, a slightly uncommon word, rather than a word that may well figure in half a dozen stories in that edition of the paper, such as 'Crime'.

From the above paragraph, for example, I would not choose 'office', 'copy', 'edition' or 'paper'. About the only suitable words in that paragraph are 'key' or 'stick'. The word need not have a close identification with the story, though there should be some mental link.

Put the catchline and the folio (page) number at the head of each sheet. Type also your name, and the date.

Leave a good two inches above the opening of the story, and at least one inch of margin at the left. Sub-editors like to use thick pencils and thick felt-pens (it gives them a sense of power) and these take up a lot of space.

Always end a page at the end of a paragraph: never continue a sentence on to another page. At the end of each folio type the words 'more' or the letters 'm.f.' ('more follows') and at the end of the last page, 'end'. These details are not decoration: they may save vital minutes when your story is being translated into print, and may prevent some brilliant sentence of yours from being lost forever in the printers' limbo.

Follow 'house style' scrupulously. Every paper has its whims and fancies when spelling certain names. Don't ask why your paper always spells the country Iraq 'Irak'. If it does, it does. Yours not to reason why. It was probably because Lord Northcliffe laid it down that it would be spelt that way in 1900: and unless and until the Editor changes the house style, you must spell it that way. If you don't, the eagle-eyed sub-editors will change your spelling to the one the paper uses. It saves time, and the subs' tempers, if you use the house style in copy.

Some papers have a house style book, in which these peculiarities

Wainwright　　22 Apr 71　　　　　　　Publish 1

(Thurs)　　　　　A new book on journalism, to be published tomorrow,

deals with many of the problems that concern newspapers,

television and radio today.

Entitled "Journalism Made Simple", the author has

tried to define the job of communications in the context

of the technical changes of recent years, to point to the

various developments that are on the way and to suggest

how journalists, printers and those working in radio and

television might cope with them.

mf

This is how a page of copy should be laid out in typescript. The second paragraph deliberately contains a grammatical howler that no reporter should perpetrate: it is included so that the sub may demonstrate how he would correct it. See page 131

and customs are spelt out. If the paper has one, study it and follow it. Other papers rely on the subs to hand down the house style generation to generation like folk legend, and on the 'readers' (the men who sit reading galleys to check that the printers have followed author's copy) to correct errors of style as well as errors of fact, spelling and sometimes grammar. But it is not the readers' job: it is the reporter's job to present his copy in a form that needs the least possible processing.

(15) Dictation to Copy-takers

Copy-takers take copy. They sit in front of typewriters with earphones clamped to their heads. They translate into words on paper the speech of reporters.

They take down urgent accounts of train crashes from news reporters, solemn accounts of government changes from lobby correspondents, frothy accounts of hemline changes from fashion writers. They take down complicated legal reports, the sophisticated criticism of fire-night plays, the racy reports of sporting events.

They are expected to know the jargon of these very different worlds. They are expected to be able to spell correctly all the names that are in the news.

But the sensible reporter does not assume that the copy-taker whose typewriter is rattling at the other end of the telephone line knows everything. The reporter is wise to treat the copy-taker with civility and with care, since his typewriter is the first of many hurdles that the reporter's incomparable words must surmount in the race to get into the paper.

A correspondent who rings up a newspaper at the busiest time of the day or night and spends twenty minutes dictating an overlong and tortuous story of no great importance will find that the copy-taker (who has usually achieved, over the years, a sound news sense) becomes impatient, and with good reason. So the reporter who dictates 'to copy' is well advised to keep his story short, sharp, and effective.

Few reporters can stand in a draughty telephone box and dictate fluently without notes. At least get the opening paragraph down on paper, and list the main facts of material importance in the story. It pays to prepare these before picking up the telephone: the copy-taker will not thank a reporter who wants to revise a story on the phone.

Give your name (and, if a freelance, address) and telephone number. If you are speaking from a telephone box, give the number.

State the department on the paper the story is intended for. ('For Sport', 'for News', 'for Diary'.) Give a catchline word.

It is not necessary to give detailed punctuation to copy-takers unless there is some significance in it—unless, for instance, the punctuation completely alters the sense.

For example:

The Prime Minister spoke first. Against a background of noise the Leader of the Opposition followed him.

Unless you dictate the full-point between those sentences the passage could reasonably be printed thus:

The Prime Minister spoke first against a background of noise. The Leader of the Opposition followed him.

It might not, because the copy-taker would judge from your voice which version you meant. But why should he have to do the work?

Spell out all names that are not completely obvious. Thus 'James Heath (as in Prime Minister), but 'Sir Basil Smallpeice (spelt "Small-papa-echo-India-Charlie-echo")'.

There are several acceptable dictation alphabets (and most older reporters use the older British system beginning 'Able, Baker, Charlie, Dog . . .').

The most modern dictation alphabet, used by international air lines and police, is:

Alpha	Juliet	Sierra
Bravo	Kilo	Tango
Charlie	Lima	Uniform
Delta	Mike	Victor
Echo	November	Whisky
Foxtrot	Oscar	X-ray
Golf	Papa	Yankee
Hotel	Quebec	Zulu
India	Romeo	

(16) Writing for the Market

Most newspapers, magazines, radio programmes or television programmes have a style. It may be brief and popular, or florid and intellectual. Whatever the style, analyse it and then write to it. That does not mean 'writing down'. It is an illusion to suppose that popular tabloid journalism is easier because its stories are briefer than in the quality papers. If is often a great deal easier to write a story in a thousand words than to tell the essential facts of that story in fifty words, not one of which may be wasted.

Freelances often make the elementary mistake of sending material to newspapers and magazines that a moment's thought should tell them would be entirely unsuitable. The London *Evening News* runs a short story nearly every day, and nearly every day it is 1,150 words long, give or take a sentence. But day after day contributors send in short stories varying from 250 words to 2,500.

Writing to style does not mean hack writing. Nor, occasionally, does it necessarily mean writing the story you are told to write. A reporter is expected to have a sense of news values and to be able to use his own initiative. You may be given a detailed briefing for a certain assignment, and when you get there you may discover a far better story. There is a story of an Irish reporter sent to cover a country funeral. The day came and went, and no sight of a story from him. Eventually they tracked him down in the nearest pub. Where, they asked, was his report? 'Oh, there wasn't a funeral after all,' he said. 'The priest had an accident on the way there and didn't turn up, so there wasn't a funeral to report.' If there is a better story, get on the phone and warn the office, and then write it.

CHAPTER NINE

PICTURE JOURNALISM

(1) News Photography

The news photographer has one of the most difficult jobs in journalism. The reporter may observe an incident or a situation over a period of time, even if it is only seconds: he then mulls over what he has seen, and writes his report. The photographer must anticipate the key moment, have his camera poised to catch it, and then press the button at precisely the right second. You cannot turn back time to recapture a missed moment; and the occasions on which the press photographer can pose his subject are rare.

Of course not all moments are captured, and there is an element of luck in the best news photography. Too often the great photographs are associated with war and with death—for example, the classic picture taken by the young Robert Capa during the Spanish civil war, at the precise second when a bullet found its mark and a soldier fell back dying, to be held in mid-air for ever by the pressure of Capa's finger on the button.

The news photographer will be trained in the techniques of his craft. He must know how the camera works, how the exposure meter works, how filters will exaggerate definition and produce cloud effects. Definition is particularly important in news photography since the process of reproducing pictures in half-tone by screening, and then printing on crude newsprint, blurs the black and white. There is no room for subtle shading and lighting in news photography. Light effects must be strong, features well outlined.

The photographer must do his homework as thoroughly as the reporter. He must have some idea what his picture is going to be; but as the reporter is always on the lookout for new angles and developments of a story, so the photographer will have one eye on the unusual picture. He will be briefed as fully as possible on the required subject, and perhaps told that the most useful picture shape would be 'portrait' (vertical) or 'landscape' (horizontal)—this may be dictated by certain predetermined elements (for example, advertisements) on the page.

It is up to the photographer to do what research he can. Like the reporter, he may sometimes check with cuttings or reference books before going out on an assignment. If he is to photograph someone who is not too familiar to him, he may check with the picture library beforehand and look at previous pictures of the subject so that he will not miss him.

The news photographer does not simply point his camera at a scene and hope for the best. He composes a picture, as an artist does. He will look for strong vertical and horizontal lines, for a balanced picture. To this end he will try to get to the assignment as early as possible and examine the setting. He then picks a vantage-point. There is not often time to pose the subject (particularly in photographing hard news) so if the picture is of someone emerging from a doorway—say the doorway of No. 10 Downing Street—the photographer will focus his camera in advance on some point on the step. If he allows himself some depth of field, the subject will be in focus from the doorway to the edge of the step.

All too often the setting changes. A policeman moves the photographers back, a split second before the door opens and the subject emerges. Or even worse, the policeman stands immediately in front of the camera. Then the photographer must move, and fast.

He learns to manipulate the controls of his camera with little more than a glance. He must be able to play the camera as a pianist plays a keyboard, without looking at his hands. Most press photographers now use a single-lens reflex camera (such as the Nikon) which takes telephoto, wide-angle and standard lenses, considerably simplifies the controls and with fast film avoids the time-wasting tedium of the old plate cameras with magnesium flash.

In these days there is often competition with television cameramen, who may have lights that can radically affect the press pictures. If the TV people switch on their lights as a subject emerges from No. 10, the press photographers must adjust their cameras to the changed lighting. They may, of course, be using flash (the electronic flash attachments linked to the camera).

The best press pictures are seldom 'set up' but are the result of a photographer snatching the precise moment of action. A good series of photographs, for a photographic feature, should lead up to a climax and will illustrate how the man behind the camera has anticipated a developing theme, and built up its development. But this is where the element of luck comes in, and this is why many newspapers print 'readers' pictures' from time to time—the reader happens to have been at the right place at the right time to capture a pictorial incident.

A vital skill for news photographers is caption writing. Most newspapers have a standard caption-label that is attached to each print. The photographer has to be sure that he has clearly identified each principal figure in his pictures with his full name.

He must also give a brief and factual description of the action and the setting, if possible adding any other relevant details. It is the editorial caption writer's job to put this information into suitable form for the paper, but to do his job properly he must be given the basic facts.

Many photographers belong to the Institute of British Photographers (38 Bedford Square, London WC1), the official body which maintains a Register of Incorporated Photographers—photographers working in all fields who have satisfied the exacting standard of membership.

(2) Magazine Photography

Photography for magazines is a specialisation that provides work for a limited number of photographers. Some, like the late Larry Burrows or Don McCullin, become famous for news feature work, sequences of pictures that tell a story. Other specialise in—for example—the photography of food to accompany the recipes that are a feature of the women's magazines.

Much of this photography is in colour, and usually done in the studio. While it does not involve the harsh pressure of news photography, it demands high technical skill and an awareness of many tricks of the trade. Often this type of magazine photography is combined with photography for advertising.

(3) Line Illustration

There is not a great deal of opportunity for line illustration in newspapers, though some has in recent years been combined with original graphics to form page-headings, titling for special features, and column-heads for specialist columns. But the chances of breaking into this field are severely limited.

Newspapers do occasionally use line illustrators (as distinct from cartoonists) on assignments were the camera is forbidden or inappropriate. For instance, drawings may be released of a wedding dress to be worn by royalty, and a line illustrator may be commissioned to produce a drawing showing how the royal personage will look in the dress.

Another instance is the court case. Cameras are not allowed in court, and so it is not possible to illustrate the proceedings photographically (there are also strict rules about the use of cameras in the precinct of a court, though the precise definition of 'precinct' is a matter of contention between the press and the law). Line illustrators may be asked to attend a session of the court and produce an impression of the proceedings.

Some newspapers use occasional line illustrations as column-breaks. These are usually thumbnail sketches, often humorous, and give a twist to some point in a reader's letter or a feature article. Line illustrations may also be used in strip-cartoon form, for example to teach golf, or do-it-yourself home improvements—where the simple line of the draughtsman can often give a clearer impression than the photograph in half-tone.

There is much more scope for the line illustrators in magazines, particularly the women's magazines. Articles on home-making and interior decoration are often illustrated with drawings, sometimes in colour, since it is more practicable to have the writer's concepts drawn than to create a life-size room setting and have it photographed. The line illustrator is usually asked to provide a romantic drawing to set off the opening double-page spread of a piece of romantic fiction, and perhaps to provide linking illustrations for subsequent instalments.

(4) Cartoons

The newspaper cartoon is a curious phenomenon. It is one man's view of the world. At its best the cartoon makes the reader stop short and think about some aspect of the news. The cartoonist is an artist. But some cartoonists are better at ideas than at drawing, and others draw superbly but have fewer brilliant ideas.

Cartoonists arrive at their jobs in a variety of ways. Some are commercial artists by training, who sell drawings to magazines and so gradually build up a reputation. Some of the most famous cartoonists have no art-school training at all. The job is one of those in journalism for which it is almost impossible to 'train', in that there are very few opportunities and it is largely a matter of chance if the right man is in the right place when an opportunity arises.

In the nineteenth century, and in the early years of this century, the political cartoon was a meticulously drawn commentary on some serious point in the news (for example, Sir Bernard Partridge's weekly political page in *Punch*). Today the cartoon—particularly in the popular newspapers—is more often a light-hearted personal comment on the news.

The main challenge of daily newspaper cartooning lies in the problem of producing a drawing a day, five or six days a week. It is too much to expect that each one will be of an equal standard.

In the past few years a new brutalism has come into cartooning, with the eighteenth-century vigour of Gerald Scarfe and Ralph Steadman. Though each cartoonist fixes his own recognisable style—a Low, a Vicky or a Giles is always instantly identifiable—there is always room for new development.

The 'pocket cartoon', a single-column comment often relying as much on a witty caption as on the humour of the drawing, is also an asset to a newspaper since it provides a smile on a front page often given over to the world's disasters and troubles. Osbert Lancaster maintains an enviably high standard in the *Daily Express*: the late Timothy Birdsall developed his own personal style.

Most newspapers run strip cartoons, often syndicated by international feature agencies. These command a considerable following.

On the following pages are some cartoons from the past fifty years illustrating the variety of approach and line that has proved successful.

POCKET CARTOON
by OSBERT LANCASTER

"Sure, Father, an' I thought it was just an aspirin"

© Osbert Lancaster

— LITTLE CARTOON —
By TIMOTHY

"What are you going to be if you grow up?"

© Mrs Jocelyn Starling

The 'pocket cartoon', in a single column, demands a technique of its own —demonstrated in these two examples by Osbert Lancaster of the *Daily Express* and the late Timothy Birdsall of the *Sunday Times*

PEACE AND FUTURE CANNON FODDER

The Tiger: "Curious! I seem to hear a child weeping!"

© Syndication International (*Daily Herald*)

This remarkable cartoon by Will Dyson appeared in the *Daily Herald* at the time of the Versailles Peace Treaty of 1919. It shows Lloyd George (back), Clemenceau (front) and President Wilson (right), and the infant 'Class of 1940' who—as Dyson so presciently realised—were to pay for this agreement

THE KINDEST CUT OF ALL.

Welsh Wizard. "I NOW PROCEED TO CUT THIS MAP INTO TWO PARTS AND PLACE THEM IN THE HAT. AFTER A SUITABLE INTERVAL THEY WILL BE FOUND TO HAVE COME TOGETHER OF THEIR OWN ACCORD—(*ASIDE*)—AT LEAST LET'S HOPE SO; I'VE NEVER DONE THIS TRICK BEFORE."

Reproduced by permission of *Punch*

For many years Sir Bernard Partridge drew an incisive political cartoon for *Punch*—such as this vigorous illustration of Lloyd George partitioning Ireland

"Here you are! Don't lose it again!"

Philip Zec drew this for the *Daily Mirror* to mark the end of the war in
Europe, in 1945. It demonstrates that with a strong line and poignant
meaning a cartoon does not have to be funny to be effective

Sir David Low made his name with 'Colonel Blimp' and the 'TUC carthorse'—but this more political cartoon, at the time of the 1936 Disarmament Conference, demonstrates the vigour of his line and the sharpness of his imagination

"ALL RIGHT! FOR THE LAST TIME. WHO'S THE BRAINS BEHIND THIS?"

Jak of the London *Evening Standard* is one of the most consistently funny cartoonists. Here he exploited the imprisonment (for CND demonstrations) of the philosopher Bertrand Russell

"HE SAYS HE WANTS TO JOIN — ON HIS OWN TERMS . . ."

Vicky made a particular study of Prime Minister Harold Macmillan (whom he christened 'Supermac'). He often portrayed him, as here, in the guise of the Edwardian Englishman

'I suppose we *did* send them to the right schools?'

© Associated Newspapers Group Ltd (*Daily Mail*)

Trog (Wally Fawkes) has an exaggerated yet simple line that carries great force

"Ladies and Gentlemen, Miss Chris—"

London Express

Giles of the *Sunday Express*, with his regular cast of Grandma and the dreadful infants, often steps out to comment on social events—such as the embarrassment caused in public life by the political scandal involving Miss Christine Keeler

"Mister Swigert, am I glad to see you! My name is Walter H. Flugenheimer and I represent the United States Internal Revenue Service..."

© Associated Newspapers Group Ltd (London *Evening News*)

Bernard Cookson drew this cartoon for the London *Evening News*. Swigert, an astronaut on the ill-fated Apollo 13 mission, had been rumoured to be in trouble with the tax authorities. This cartoon was published on the evening Apollo 13 splashed down safely—and was almost immediately overtaken by events, when Swigert's colleagues told him the taxman wanted to see him

198

THE WIZARD OF ID

by Brant parker and Johnny hart

Two of the most famous strip cartoons—'Peanuts' by Charles Schulz, and the 'Wizard of Id' by Brant Parker and Johnny Hart.

CHAPTER TEN

RADIO AND TELEVISION

(1) The Development of Radio and Television

The Italian Marconi demonstrated a 'wireless' system in 1895, transmitting messages through the air by electronic impulses. The practice of journalism was about to be revolutionised. Its potential was well demonstrated when in 1910 the murderer Dr Crippen was arrested after the captain of the ship, SS *Montrose*, in which he was trying to escape to America sent a wireless message to London from mid-Atlantic identifying him.

The newspapers were slow to recognise the way in which radio, and later television, would transform journalism by changing the pattern of communications around the world. Radio was initially sponsored by the manufacturers of wireless and electrical equipment. In 1922 the British Government granted a two-year exclusive licence to the British Broadcasting Company, a commercial organisation formed by merging the broadcasting interests of six manufacturers. By 1926—when the original company's licence has been renewed twice—there were two million radio receivers in Britain, and the Government established the British Broadcasting Corporation by Royal Charter as a system of public service broadcasting.

Under John Reith (later Lord Reith) the BBC created a worldwide reputation for independence and authority, despite its nominal subservience to governments. Since it was financed by licence fees, it was free of commercial pressures and the need to gather in advertising, which has increasingly burdened the British press and debased the commercial radio networks of other countries.

It was not until the second world war that radio news became a significant challenge to newspapers. But then the work of the BBC's war reporters brought a sound-picture of the truth of war into people's homes. Churchill's broadcasts were a rallying-point for Britons, as de Gaulle's were for Frenchmen: and in America, Franklin Delano Roosevelt began his 'fireside chats' to the people of the United States, while Ed Murrow, broadcasting from London, revealed to them the facts and emotions of wartime London.

One of the remarkable achievements of the BBC was in widening public appreciation of classical music; and in 1946 the Third Programme was founded. The development of an international 'pop' culture in the 1960s led to a proliferation of 'pirate' radio stations offshore, and in 1967 the Government took action to close these down. Shortly afterwards, in its schedule of Broadcasting in the Seventies, the BBC revised its channel divisions to provide one channel of 'pop' (Radio 1), one of light music (Radio 2), one of music and the arts (Radio 3), and one of news, documentaries and plays (Radio 4). In place of the old regional specialisations, the BBC set up eight local radio stations, concentrating on local news and affairs—the BBC proposed to increase these to forty.

In 1971 the Government announced the creation of an Independent Broadcasting Authority, to control sixty independently financed (commercial) radio stations through Britain. These changes paralleled the development of newspapers, where local newspapers were becoming increasingly significant for regional news while the major news stories became the province of the BBC's national news on radio and television.

On radio there was a revolution in journalism when to the straightforward narrative news bulletin was added on-the-spot telephoned or recorded reportage with a mixture of commentary, as in such programmes as 'The World At One', 'PM', and the 'Ten O'Clock' programme. These were perhaps a feedback from the techniques of television news, where the impact of on-the-spot film reporting is dramatic.

The principle of television was first demonstrated in Britain by John Logie Baird at the Royal Institution in 1926. Baird devised a system of mechanical scanning: that is, the picture was divided into lines for transmission by mechanical means. Meanwhile the Marconi–EMI system, using electronic scanning, was evolved in America and developed in Britain. When on 2 November 1936 the BBC began regular television transmissions in Britain, putting out two hours of programmes each day, six days a week, the Baird and Marconi–EMI systems were used in alternate weeks. After three months the Marconi–EMI system was adopted as standard. Regular television programmes began to be transmitted in the United States on 30 April 1939.

During the second world war television transmission was suspended in Britain, and resumed in 1946, again by the BBC. In 1954 the Television Act established an Independent Television Authority to provide alternative television programmes supplied regionally by programme contractors who finance their programmes by advertising (but not, as in the United States and other countries, by allowing advertisers to 'sponsor' specific programmes). The first independent television programmes were transmitted in September 1955, and in the following year the number of households in Britain with TV sets rose above 80 per cent.

Hard news bulletins on Independent Television, as distinct from news documentaries, are provided by Independent Television News Limited. This is an autonomous company financed by the independent television contractors who are its shareholders. ITN operates as a newspaper's editorial department, with its own editorial staff and reporters. On Mondays to Fridays ITN produces a ten-minute news bulletin at 5.50 pm and a half-hour programme, 'News at Ten', which has consistently appeared high on the ratings of viewer interest. ITN also produces special programmes for major news events, which are then networked, i.e. put out on all the independent television regional stations. Such programmes have been produced for parliamentary and local elections, Budgets, party conferences, US presidential elections and moon landings.

Following the Pilkington Committee on broadcasting (1960) the BBC was given a second television channel, BBC 2, which began transmissions in April 1964, on 625 lines. In 1967 BBC 2 began regular colour transmissions, and shortly afterwards colour was introduced by BBC 1 and ITV.

Both the BBC and ITA are responsible to Parliament, reporting through the Minister of Posts and Telecommunications. The British Broadcasting Corporation is run by twelve governors, appointed by the Queen on the advice of the Government. There is a General Advisory Council, regional councils and specialist councils (e.g. for religious broadcasting, schools broadcasting, etc.). The permanent staff of the BBC is headed by the Director-General.

The Independent Television Authority is run by a chairman and twelve members, appointed by the Minister of Posts and Telecommunications. The ITA builds, owns and operates transmitting stations, and licenses programme contractors, retaining overall control over programme standards and advertising through its permanent staff led by its Director-General.

The programme contracting companies, each of which produces regional news programmes in addition to networking the news bulletins of ITN, are:

Anglia Television Ltd
ATV Network Ltd
Border Television Ltd
Channel Television Ltd
Grampian Television Ltd
Granada Television Ltd
Harlech Television Ltd
London Weekend Television Ltd
Scottish Television Ltd
Southern Television Ltd

Thames Television Ltd
Tyne-Tees Television Ltd
Ulster Television Ltd
Westward Television Ltd
Yorkshire Television Ltd.

While no newspaper group may wholly own a programme contracting company, several companies are partly owned by newspaper groups.

(2) How They Work

The microphone picks up varying impulses which are then transmitted electrically. Picked up by a sensitive aerial, these impulses are then fed into an amplifier and loudspeaker, producing an approximation of the original sounds.

The television camera is a more complicated development of the same principle, picking up picture images as the microphone picks up sounds. In the camera there is a lens which focuses the scene on to a light-sensitive surface (as in the ordinary camera the lens focuses the scene on to a light-sensitive film). Behind the light-sensitive surface is an electron gun. This fires a continuous beam of electrical particles (electrons) at the light-sensitive surface, producing an electrical current that varies in proportion to the brightness or darkness of the line that is being scanned.

This current is the video or picture signal. The complete screen is scanned 25 or 30 times a second: this is too fast for the human eye to catch and so each swift image appears to be complete as it is transmitted. In fact the beam scans the odd lines (1, 3, 5 etc.) of the picture first, and then the even lines (2, 4, 6 etc.). In America TV pictures have 525 lines. The BBC began with 405 lines but is moving over to the European definition, 625 lines.

In the home television set there is a cathode-ray tube with an inner coating of fluorescent powder. This glows when hit by electrons. The video or picture signal activates an electron gun which sweeps over the cathode-ray tube, producing images of varying brightness that (if the set is correctly adjusted) are the same as those picked up by the studio camera.

Colour television uses the same principle, but instead of the single electron gun in camera and receiver, there are three.* One scans the red images, a second the green, and a third the blue. The tube of the home receiver is covered with a multitude of tiny dots that pick up each colour, red, green and blue. Colour variations are produced

* Sony, the Japanese company, has now introduced a single-gun colour system that effectively improves on the performance of the three-gun colour system.

by the intensity of each dot and by the overlapping of one colour on another (as in colour printing).

Television journalism may use three types of camera: the studio camera, the OB (outside broadcast) camera, or the film camera. The studio set (as used—for example—in discussion programmes) has the basic advantage that it can be pre-planned. The people appearing before the camera can be placed with reasonable accuracy before the programme, and lit to the best advantage. The director can be sure that backgrounds do not clash and that his cameras are so placed that he can cut from one speaker to another appropriately.

The conventional OB camera used to be as large as a studio camera, and was frequently mounted on a tower-platform or car roof. This had the disadvantage of only limited mobility, and of virtually no control over lighting, particularly in the British climate. The development of the hand-held camera and the directional microphone (which can pick up speech at considerable distances) has provided television journalists with much greater flexibility. The camera can, of course, lie—particularly if equipped with a variety of lenses. The telephoto lens makes a subject seem much closer to the camera than it is, with a consequent distortion of the foreground and middle distance by foreshortening. The wide-angle lens, useful for photographing a large group, has the reverse distorting effect: it makes distances from the camera seem greater than they are. Most modern studio cameras use zoom lenses which avoid the need to rotate lenses during a programme.

The film camera (usually 16 mm) is widely used in television journalism, especially for foreign reporting where it is impracticable to televise direct or to record on video-tape. Video-recording works on the same principle as the conventional sound tape recorder, except that it records vision as well as sound. In order to play-back incidents in sporting fixtures—the scoring of a goal in football, the action of a horse in show-jumping—the BBC has developed a video-recorder that is almost instantaneous, and can be played back virtually immediately after the action itself, and stopped still if required.

Now that video-tape can accurately reproduce even 8-mm 'home movies' it seems probable that the cassette revolution that has conquered sound tape recording will do the same for television. Instead of sending back cumbersome film and sound tapes, the television journalist will send back his whole story in cassette form. Though the introduction of video-cassettes at home will have greater immediate impact on televised variety shows and plays, its application to the technique of preparing hard news is being considered.

The news report will always have to be edited to suit the editorial requirements of a bulletin; but the convenience of cassettes for quick loading and unloading may bring them into use by reporters.

(3) The Presentation of News

The main skill of radio and television journalism is to achieve accuracy in the briefest possible space. Says Milton Shulman, TV critic of the London *Evening Standard:* 'A ten-minute news bulletin on the BBC does not contain the number of words in a single page of a tabloid. A half-hour on TV, such as ITN's "News at Ten", contains fewer words than the front page alone of *The Times.*' Three minutes on the air is a long time, while 500 words in a newspaper (about the same number of words) is a short article.

The reporter for radio or television must therefore be a highly skilled précis-writer. He must be able to distill the essential facts of a situation into his brief report, together with whatever background or local colour he can find room for. He is circumscribed always by time. The same thing applies, even more intensively, within the radio or television newsroom. Reports from many parts of the world will be coming in simultaneously, and the editor must decide which is the most important and interesting, and which merits how much time. A report from a foreign correspondent that runs to five minutes of film or tape may need to be cut to two minutes of running time.

Therefore the report must be written in short, sharp sentences. Involved prose that develops an argument phrase by phrase, hanging conditional clauses on the main clause like decorations on a Christmas tree, are a handicap to the editor. Especially if the reporter raises his voice at the end of a subordinate clause, thus making it impracticable to cut the report at that point. The reporter has to find the right balance between the brisk short-sentence news delivery, and the use of voice variations to make the report easy on the ear.

Radio journalists usually tape their own interviews on battery-operated recorders they carry and control themselves. A popular type is the Uhuer, recording at $7\frac{1}{2}$ revolutions per second. Not all radio reporters, of course, will record interviews. They may use a 'radio car', which gives them a direct link with the studio so that they can broadcast their report 'live'; or they may telephone a report on a conventional Post Office line. Tape has the advantage of actuality, but the disadvantage that it needs to be edited—and that takes valuable time.

The television journalist often travels, particularly on foreign assignments, with a camera and sound crew. He is responsible for selecting the subjects to be reported, selecting the backgrounds, writing the report and delivering it 'to camera'. The camera and sound crew are responsible for capturing the report as the journalist intends it, and obtaining the best possible technical quality. Occasionally the television journalist will recruit a local camera and sound crew in the country of his assignment.

Television news, even more than radio news, is a presentation. That is, it is not enough merely to report the news. As a newspaper displays different news items in different-sized type, with different-sized headlines and varying quantities of picture illustration, so the television news bulletin must have pace and variety. The producer is making a programme that must grip the viewer as powerfully as a play or a variety show. Perhaps the news producer has an advantage in that the viewers, for the most part, are basically curious to know what has happened in the world and so the proportion of information to entertainment can be greater. Nevertheless the news must be made palatable. This does not mean suppression or deliberate distortion: it means that complex subjects must be analysed to their elemental parts, and obscure subjects clarified.

Apart from the straight reports from his correspondents and from news agencies, the television news producer has other visual aids he can use. He may use still photographs—for example, of people mentioned in the bulletin. He may use graphics and cartoon film—for example, to illustrate changes in tax rates during a budget. He may bring in specialists—the political correspondent, or the medical correspondent—to comment 'to camera' on news items that affect their specialisation and need explanation.

As on a newspaper, all the material that comes into the newsroom is read by the copytaster. He passes anything that may be of interest to the chief sub-editor, whose team of writers and specialists prepare this news for the bulletin. Later the producer and the newscasters (who 'front' the news bulletin before the cameras) meet to determine the order of items and the balance of the programme. Meanwhile film is being edited, tape edited, still photographs prepared, and the studio itself lit and checked for sound.

Around three-quarters of an hour before transmission, there is a rehearsal, to check timing. But even after this, new items may be added and others discarded to make room. During the transmission the director sits in the main control room before a bank of monitor sets. Beside him (or her) is the vision mixer, whose job is to switch from one camera to another, and to cue in video-tape or film as directed. There is a separate sound control room, and often (for complicated productions) another for lighting. The pressure in both studio and control room is intense, and the newscaster must be prepared to ad-lib if anything goes wrong.

At this stage the production aspect of television takes precedence over the news aspect, rather as at the climax of a newspaper's production.

Television is the medium now most capable of exploiting the news action 'scoop', provided only that a camera can be got to the points of action in time. The moon-walks, when the American astronauts became their own reporters, are one example. Vietnam has continuously been another. Yet another was the blowing-up of airliners hijacked to Jordan by Arab guerillas in September 1970. An Arab cameraman shot film of the explosions. ITN producer David Phillips joined with the American network CBS to charter a Caravelle jet from the Royal Jordanian Airways at a cost of £6,000 to fly the film to London.

(4) Microphone and Camera Techniques

Remember to check the recording controls—and the level of the battery, if this is visible—before embarking on an interview, and never be frightened to do a test recording and play-back before starting some important interview. Record a brief introduction or conclusion giving the subject, place, date and time of the interview so that it is on tape together with the interview. Labels can easily be lost.

Remember that the microphone placed in even a slight breeze is likely to obscure the human voice with what sounds like a howling gale. While background effects may add atmosphere to a tape report, make sure the balance between background and foreground speech is correct. Remember when using a directional hand microphone to direct it towards whoever is speaking.

When interviewing before the camera, remember that the camera has a limited field of vision and never point to something or someone out of shot without identifying it verbally in case the camera fails to catch it. Go over with the cameraman in advance what you plan to say, and any gestures you are likely to make. Warn him if you intend to wave dramatically, to illustrate a measure with your hands, or otherwise need him to change from close-up to a general shot. Try not to invent new 'business' in the middle of an interview: it may all be wasted. Learn the camera's capabilities and stay within them.

On overseas assignments reporters try to find appropriate backgrounds (otherwise they might as well be reporting from base). These must be chosen with care. There are still countries where small boys find the camera of such obsessive interest that they must rush in front of it and wave. Choose a background that is interesting yet not distracting. A long line of vehicles passing behind the speaker at speed might well be distracting.

Wheeled vehicles are often distracting because they create a stroboscopic effect: at certain speeds, the wheels seem to be turning backwards (the actual speeds are 60 revs per second on American

TV, 50 revs per second in Britain). Harsh light contrasts are also best avoided. If the foreground speaker is in shade and the camera is set to focus on him, he will be clearly outlined while the background will be little more than a white haze.

Some news reports start with the camera on a landscape while the reporter talks over it, and the camera slowly pans round to him. It is generally better the other way round: start with the camera on the reporter—to identify the voice—and then if necessary pan away from him to the landscape. If possible avoid a wholly static background—it might just as well be a still photograph, and wastes the cost of sending a reporter to film.

CHAPTER ELEVEN

FREELANCING

(1) Examining the Market

Few freelance journalists manage to carve a livelihood for themselves starting from scratch. Most move to freelancing after a period on the staff of some newspaper or magazine, from which vantage-point they can discover the particular specialisations on which they subsequently work. The freelance is highly susceptible to the condition of the market. In times of recession it is the outside contributor who is most quickly dispensed with.

The freelance cannot afford the time and effort required to send copy to newspapers and magazines on the chance that it may be accepted. He cannot afford to write for the spike (on which unused material is 'spiked' in a newsroom), and must make every contribution acceptable. This presupposes a detailed knowledge of what each newspaper and magazine requires, what length of article is acceptable, and in what style. There is no point in sending a popular newspaper a 2,000-word academic thesis on minor metaphysical poets.

There are one or two freelances who distribute blurred carbon copies of their stories. This is an immediate indication to the recipient that the top copy has gone elsewhere. Never send copy that is dog-eared with travelling from office to office, and stained with the marks of a dozen rusty paper-clips that once held rejection slips.

(2) Building up Contacts

The keys to successful freelancing are a competent filing system and address book, constantly kept up to date. The freelance depends on staff journalists buying his work: he must discover where the power of decision lies on a newspaper or magazine, and keep his name and his interests in the eye of the executive who holds that power.

There is a fine line to be drawn between oppressive persistence—the freelance who repeatedly rings up just before edition time with unimportant stories will soon find himself brushed off—and a too reticent approach that fails to capitalise on success.

209

How much time the freelance can afford to dedicate to the simple business of maintaining contacts depends on the field in which he operates. He has to apportion out his own time—so much for researching information, so much for writing, so much for maintaining contact with the market.

(3) Putting Forward Ideas

Freelances are more common in magazine journalism than in newspapers. In magazines the man (or woman) who can be relied on to produce a workmanlike article, readable and accurate and well researched, and delivered on or before the deadline, stands a good chance of success.

Some combine this type of journalism with the authorship of books, but it requires singular determination to slot into one working life two forms of creation with radically different preparation times.

(4) Exclusivity

If a story is offered to a newspaper or magazine exclusively, then it must be exclusive and is bought on that understanding. For a longer piece of work, an author may specifically sell first British serial rights, and then sell second British serial rights elsewhere. But 'exclusive' means what it says, and if the word is used, it must be honoured. The successful freelance who builds up a substantial business will probably, in any case, leave the negotiation of rights to an agent.

CHAPTER TWELVE

ON THE FRINGE

(1) Public Relations

The concept of public relations as a distinct branch of communications is comparatively recent, though the practice is of course ancient. Any organisation wants to present itself to the public in the best possible light. Government departments and transport undertakings —particularly the Post Office and London Transport—were among the first to tackle this form of self-presentation.

The Post Office in the 1930s made several excellent films as a public relations exercise, the most famous (and still a classic) being *Night Mail*, directed by Harry Watt and Basil Wright with a script by W. H. Auden and music by Benjamin Britten. London Transport led the way with its excellent graphics and directional signs designed by Edward Johnston for Frank Pick, and a series of posters of uniquely high standard.

Today public relations embraces all these visual and practical aspects of a company's public 'image', and also controls the relations between the company and the press and television. Where a company takes its public relations seriously and where the department has direct access to the highest decision-making strata of the company at Board level, public relations may be useful. Where the public relations department is a comparatively minor outpost, a front-line pillbox to warn the company of imminent attack by predatory inquirers, public relations is useless and indeed dangerous, since it confirms the view of many journalists that public relations officers ('PROs') are mere whitewashing agents paid to disguise what is really happening.

The public relations officer must work out the best way of introducing his company or organisation usefully to the media. This may be by means of handouts—circulars sent through the post—or printed publicity material; by special events such as press conferences or receptions; or on a more personal level by introducing the company's executives to journalists, sometimes over lunch. Not all the most successful PROs work over substantial expense-account lunches, though; and many journalists are sceptical of this form of softening-up, however readily they may accept a good lunch.

It is for each PRO to determine what is the best and most cost-effective method of communicating his company's interests. This presupposes that the initiative comes from the PRO.

The other function of public relations departments is to answer queries from the press and television. This is almost more important than the previously mentioned approaches. If a public relations department earns a reputation for finding the answers to press queries swiftly, effectively and accurately, and presenting them in a form that is usable by the media, then what that department says is likely to be believed, trusted and used. If, on the other hand (as too often happens), a public relations department treats press and television inquiries as tedious interruptions in the day's work, to be dealt with casually and at whatever pace may suit the PRO, then the department will earn a reputation for awkwardness and must not be surprised if journalists are constantly trying to get into touch with the company bosses direct.

(2) How to Prepare a Handout

Remember that a handout is intended to be read, often by very busy people to whom it will be one more piece of paper (or sheaf of pieces of paper) among hundreds in the morning mail. While every PRO must believe that the information he is putting out is of vital importance, it may not seem that way to the recipient.

Just as a journalist writing a news story must contrive an opening sentence that attracts and holds the attention of the reader, so must the handout writer catch the attention of journalists who are pre-disposed not to be interested in what they read.

If the subject of the handout is long and complicated, it is a good idea to summarise the subject at the top of the first page, or on a covering sheet, to explain why the subject deserves to be treated at length.

Much the same applies to speeches by chairmen, managing directors and chief executives. Some PROs circulate ten-page speeches by their lords and masters to the press, and are then disappointed and surprised that not a line appears in print. Better to extract one or two short, sharp and (if possible) controversial sentences as a lead-in.

The same principles of layout apply to handouts as to copy for the press. Use one side of the paper only, of course. Leave wide margins. Never run a sentence from one sheet on to another. And always check spellings, names, dates and figures. Newspapers have in general only one filing system, the waste-paper basket, and corrections to handouts sent by the following post seldom catch up the original mistake.

Keep it simple. If technical terms must be used, work in an

explanation of what they mean. If the handout is to be issued in advance (e.g. the advance text of a speech) make sure the embargo time and date is clearly marked on each sheet.

Finally, check the circulation list. It is wasteful to send handouts to people who obviously have no interest in them (e.g. to send handouts about food and cooking to magazines with no cookery column). Many PROs have an annual weed-out of the handout circulation lists; but be careful not to offend those who can be useful to you. Sometimes over-enthusiastic departments send arrogant demands that if the recipients want the handouts, they should ask for them. Some who would be quite glad to receive the handouts are not prepared to go through this routine, and a useful channel of communication might become blocked through false efficiency if the recipient takes offence.

Remember that it is the PRO who needs the publicity for his message, not the other way round.

(3) Contacting the Press

The customary reference books—*Willings' Press Guide*, and the *Newspaper Press Directory*—list newspaper 'specialists'. But these change from time to time and it is as well to check periodically by telephone that the names on the circulation list are still doing the same job. Many thousands of handouts are sent annually to journalists who retired and even died many years ago.

Read the papers. Too few public relations departments evidently do. They demonstrate that they have no awareness of what is suitable for one newspaper or another, and what might interest this or that television programme. The blanket coverage seldom works, while the exclusive story given to the appropriate newspaper might stand a chance of being published with considerable prominence.

Decide whether a story should be given across-the-board to all the papers, or exclusively to one, or to one group (the mornings, the evenings, the Sundays). Learn the press times of the columns and pages you wish to interest. Never telephone with a casual story within half an hour of press time—or if you do, never expect to be listened to with much care or enthusiasm unless what you have to say is truly newsworthy in the context of the newspaper.

Try to meet as many journalists as possible personally. This does not necessarily mean taking them all out to extravagant meals. At a press reception, keep an eye on the signature-book and introduce yourself to the journalists you need to meet.

Never try the hard sell, the hail-fellow-well-met approach. Few journalists appreciate being addressed familiarly as 'Charlie' on the telephone by people they have never met. After that, they will take particular care to avoid you.

(4) How to Organise a Press Campaign

Let us suppose your company wants to launch a new product. You produce handouts about it, and perhaps a 'press kit' complete with photographs. You decide to hold a press reception to launch the product. Compile a list of the people you want to be there, and see that they are invited a fortnight or so in advance. Some PROs telephone round on the day before to 'check' whether those they have invited are coming. Make sure that this is done delicately: few journalists plan their day in detail far ahead, and some columnists will not know until the day itself whether they have a more pressing engagement. Don't push them too hard.

Most hotels are geared to preparing standard receptions. You will soon learn which are good at it, and which are not. If there are to be speeches, make sure that those who are to speak are fully briefed on what they are going to say. If the chairman or managing director is to speak, he will probably have asked the public relations department to prepare his speech. Try to persuade his secretary to make time for him to study it before delivery: nothing is so off-putting as a chairman being thrown by the little joke he has not seen before he read it out. See that those speaking are clearly identified and introduced, and that the press have copies of the speech. If the chairman is likely to interpolate remarks of his own, make sure the speech is marked 'check against delivery'.

See that as many journalists as possible are personally introduced to the firm's executives, and make sure that the introductions are carried out clearly so that each knows who the other is.

If there are specialist writers present, see that points of particular interest to them are drawn to their attention. You may well be mainly concerned here with the technical and trade press: see that they get full information, since they will probably use it verbatim. Afterwards, check with the signature-book and send copies of the press kit to those journalists who did not attend.

Alternatively, you may decide to introduce the product to one or two specialist journalists who will have a special interest in it. Each case has to be measured on its merits. Sometimes the general campaign will be more effective, sometimes the exclusive story (or story given slightly in advance) will obtain more meaningful coverage.

(5) How to Handle TV Interviews

Most senior executives in industry recognise that their jobs require them to stand up and speak in public. Some do it well, some do not. Most are coming to recognise that they may have to appear on television, and that this requires a technique totally different to that of public speaking.

There are now several organisations (among them the Institute of Directors) which run courses for senior executives to train them for television. There are one or two simple rules.

First, never hesitate. The television camera is voracious and abhors a vacuum. At all costs keep talking.

Secondly, be concise. Never embark on a long and tortuous explanation—it will certainly be cut off in mid-flood, and if the main point is coming at the end, it will never be heard.

Thirdly, keep still. Use your hands as little as possible; and try not to lean forwards. It is best to assume as comfortable a fixed position as possible, and stick to it. Techniques of boardroom debate—leaning backwards, pausing dramatically for effect, thumping the table—are all disastrous on the screen.

Finally, remember that the most aggressive interviewer is always disarmed by sweet reason, quietly, courteously and concisely expressed. Television interviewers are aware that conflict makes good TV and are keen to get an argument going: the opponent who calmly refuses to be ruffled generally wins.

GLOSSARY OF PRINTING TERMS

Ad	Abbreviation for advertisement.
Add	A later addition to copy.
Alignment	The ranging of type along its base line. Also the horizontal and vertical ranging of columns.
Ampersand	The typographical sign for 'and' (&).
AP	Associated Press news agency.
Arm	The horizontal stroke of capital letters (E, F).
Art Department	The picture department of a newspaper.
Artwork	Photograph, drawing, illustration, etc., prepared for photographic reproduction.
Ascender	The stroke of a lower-case letter extending above the x-height (b, d, h, k, l).
Asterisk	A star-shaped character (*) used in text to link with a footnote, or occasionally to represent missing letters in 'obscene' words.
Back-bench	The senior editorial executives of a newspaper.
Banner	A main headline right across the top of a page.
Beard	The portion of type body below the type face.
Bearer	(*a*) Type-high metal included in a forme for moulding, to protect type and blocks.
	(*b*) The load-carrying part (i.e. the steel bars on the sides of the type-bed) of a printing machine on which the cylinder rotates.
Beat	(*a*) When a story is obtained before rival newspapers.
	(*b*) A particular subject or area covered by a reporter.
Black	Carbon copy of a sheet of typescript.
Black Letter	Type face derived from mediaeval script (Old English Text, Goudy Text).
Blanket	In offset printing, a sheet of natural or synthetic rubber clamped round a cylinder which transfers the image from a plate to paper.
Bled-off or Bleed	An illustration placed to the edge of a printing area, so that when the paper is trimmed the picture is at the edge without margin.

Block	An original letterpress plate, when mounted. Usually an illustration engraved or etched on a metal plate: line blocks for drawings, half-tones for photographs.
Blocking Out	Eliminating undesirable backgrounds and portions of a negative by opaquing the image.
Blower	The telephone.
Blow-up	An enlargement.
Body	(*a*) The metal base forming the mount for the face of the type, also known as the shank. (*b*) The viscosity or consistency of a printing ink.
Bold Face or Bold	Heavy-face type, in contrast to light-face type, and used for emphasis in headings, sub-headings, etc.
Bowl	The space on printed letters entirely or almost entirely enclosed by the curved strokes of a letter (b, c, d).
Box	(*a*) An item ruled off on all four sides with a rule or border. (*b*) See *Fudge*.
Break	The moment when a news story begins.
Break for Colour	To separate the parts to be printed in different colours.
Brevier	Old name for 8 pt type.
Brief	A short news item.
Broadsheet	A page the full size of a rotary press plate, usually applied to a newspaper's size (often with a page about 23 ins by 16 ins) as distinct from *Tabloid*.
By-line	A reporter's name printed above his story (by . . .).
Cap-line	The imaginary line level with the top of capital letters.
Caption	The descriptive wording beneath or beside an illustration.
Carbro	A full-colour photograph, often used as an original for colour reproduction.
Casting	(*a*) In electrotyping, backing the copper shell with molten metal alloy to the desired thickness. (*b*) Injection of type metal alloy into a mould or matrix to produce type or stereos.
Cast Off	To estimate the space a typescript will take when set up in a certain type size.

Catchline	A word or phrase written or typed at the top of a sheet of copy for later identification, and reproduced on the takes on galley.
Chase	A metal frame in which type and blocks are assembled and then locked before printing.
Classified	Small ads, consisting only of type and classified by subject, e.g. House sales.
Coarse-screen	Half-tone screen containing 85 or less lines to the inch.
Colour Separation	Process, usually photographic, by which colours are filtered to produce a set of 3 or 4 negatives from which printing plates may be made for colour printing.
Column Rule	The light rule frequently used to separate columns of type.
Comp	Abbreviation for compositor, the man who 'composes' or translates typescript into metal type.
Composing Stick	A small tray in which single type characters are assembled and justified by hand.
Copy	Editorial material prepared for setting.
Copy Paper	Paper on which editorial matter is typed or written, frequently interleaved with carbon paper to provide blacks.
Creed	The telegraphic printer by which newspaper offices receive messages from news agencies.
Crit	Abbreviation of criticism.
Crop	To cut down a photograph or a plate in size.
Crosshead	A heading, often a single line, placed in the text of a story and centred in the column width.
Curtain	A headline ruled off on three sides (also called a hood).
Cut	(*a*) A deletion of matter in typescript or print. (*b*) Old term for a printing plate (from 'woodcut').
Cut-off	(*a*) A full rule across one or more columns. (*b*) The depth of sheet of a rotary-printed page.
Cut Out	Letterpress half-tone plate in which only the subject proper appears, the background having been removed by hand cutting and routing.
Cuttings	Extracts from newspapers filed in a newspaper library under subjects or personalities (in USA, known as *Clippings*).
Date-line	The place from which a story and its date is sent, usually appearing above foreign news.

Deadline	The time at which a piece of copy is required.
Deck	(*a*) A part of a headline, usually its subsidiary section.
	(*b*) The levels of a rotary printing press.
Deep-Etch	(*a*) In offset, a plate for long runs where the inked areas are slightly recessed.
	(*b*) In letterpress, where certain areas of dot images are removed (usually from highlight areas).
Descender	The part of the type extending below the x-height (g, p, y).
Didot	The Continental system of measuring type sizes: the Didot point is 0·148 ins or 0·38 mm (see *Point*)
Display Ads	Large advertisements, usually containing drawings or photographs, often provided by agencies (cf. *CLASSIFIED*).
Distribute	(*a*) With hand-set type, the return of individual letters to case or store ready for further use.
	(*b*) With machine-set matter, breaking up pages for melting.
Dot	The individual element of a half-tone plate.
Double	The same item appearing twice in the same issue of a newspaper.
Drop Letter	A larger initial letter, often extending down two or three lines of type.
Dummy	(*a*) An unprinted blank version of a paper often in miniature, used for page planning.
	(*b*) An experimental printing, not for public view.
Ear	The advertising spaces at the top left and right of a newspaper front page, on either side of the title.
Electronic Engraving	Flat or curved letterpress printing plate, metallic or plastic, made by cutting or burning into the surface with a stylus activated by the amplified output of a photoelectric cell.
Electrotype	A duplicate letterpress plate produced from a wax graphite or plastic mould of the original by an electrolytic process.
Em	(*a*) A space of the same point width as the depth of the body, so named because the letter M in early founts was usually cast on a square body.
	(*b*) A standard unit of measurement equal to 12 points (the pica em), known as a 'mutton'.

Embargo	The fixed time (sometimes to be found on public relations handouts) before which a story should not be published.
En	A measure of space equal to half an em, known as a 'nut'.
End	The conclusion of a story, required to be put at the end of the final sheet of copy.
Engraving	A printing plate produced by an etching or cutting process.
Face	The part of the type or plate that makes an impression on paper.
Feature	An article of background information or personal opinion, usually by a named writer, appearing on the 'feature pages'.
Feature Writer	A journalist who principally writes feature articles as distinct from news reporting.
File	To telephone or cable a news story.
Filler	A *Brief* when in type.
Filling-in	In letterpress printing, when ink fills the area between half-tone dots or the open areas in type.
Fine Screen	A half-tone screen containing 100 or more lines to the inch.
Flash	A short message of no more than a few words by telephone or teleprinter giving the first information on an important news story.
Flong	In stereotyping, a moist mixture of papier-mâché, which, when impressed against the forme, and dried, becomes the matrix from which a stereo plate is cast.
Flush Left (or Right)	In composition, type matter set to line up at the left (or right) of the column.
Flush Paragraph	A paragraph without indentation.
Folio	A sheet of copy, usually associated with numbering (first, second, third folio of a story).
Forme	Typematter, including blocks, locked up in a *Chase* ready for printing.
Forme Rollers	The inking rollers which deposit ink on printing surfaces.
Fount	A complete set of type consisting of all letters of the alphabet and other symbols in their normal proportions.
Frame	The compositor's workbench, with racks of type cases containing upper and lower case letters.

Freelance	A journalist not on the staff of one newspaper, but usually contributing to several.
Fudge	The Stop Press areas on the front and/or back pages of a newspaper, into which late news may be inserted during the print run of a newspaper.
Furniture	Metal used to fill in the blank spaces in a forme.
Galley	A metal tray on which type is assembled.
Galley Proof	A proof taken of the metal in a galley, before it has been made up into a page.
Gossip Column	A personality column usually written under one real or fictitious name (now obsolescent).
Half-double	A rule or dash half the width of a column indicating the end of a story in print—so called because for many years a double rule, thick and thin, was used, where today a single rule is customary.
Half-stick	A portrait block half a column width, also known as a thumbnail.
Half-tone	A photograph reproduced on newsprint by simulating the variations in tone value by varying sizes of printed dot to give the illusion of tone variation. The term also applies to the letterpress printing plate used (see *Screen*).
Handout	A story sent round to newspapers by a public relations company for the benefit of its client.
Hanging Indent	A setting device by which the first line of a story is set full out across the column width, and the remaining lines of the paragraph are indented by one em. This is signified by the instruction 'nought-and-one', or '0 + 1'.
Hold	An instruction marked on copy (usually as 'set and hold') to ensure that a story is prepared for publication but not put into the newspaper—e.g. a pre-prepared obituary of some public figure.
Hood	A headline ruled off on three sides
Hot Metal	Composition from molten type metal, as distinct from photographic composition.
House Organ	A company magazine or newspaper.
House Style	Domestic rules governing type faces, layout styles, peculiarities of spelling and punctuation, etc., sometimes set out in a House Style book.
Indent	The indication of a paragraph opening by beginning the first line one or two ems further

	into the column than the remainder of the paragraph.
Ink Fountain	The reservoir or duct for ink on a printing press.
Intaglio	A printing surface where the type or illustrations have been cut or etched out below the surface, as in steel-plate engraving or gravure printing.
Intertype	A machine that casts solid lines of type in a slug, like a Linotype.
Intro	The introduction to a story.
Italic	A variant of many type faces with the lettering sloping to the right.
Italtype	A line casting machine similar to Linotype, developed in Italy.
Job	A reporter's particular assignment.
Justify	In composition, to add appropriate spaces between words to make a line of regular column width.
Keep Down	Use lower-case letters
Keep Up	Use capital letters.
Kern	The part of a type face which projects over the edge of the body.
Key	To identify copy as it appears in a dummy by means of symbols—numerals or catchlines.
Keyplate	In colour printing, the particular printing plate used as a guide for the register of other colours.
Kill	Discard a story at any stage, e.g. because a better account is available to replace it, or it has been disproved.
Knock Down	A reporter's action in disproving a story, perhaps a story in a rival paper.
Layout	The newspaper page designed in pencil by the sub-editor and sent to the compositor for guidance.
Lead	The main story in a newspaper, or the first paragraph in a news story giving the main facts.
Leader	A newspaper editorial, its official view of events.
Leads	Thin strips of metal placed between lines of type to space them, e.g. to make the story fill out a given space.
Leg-man	A contact who helps a reporter, or a reporter who goes out of the office instead of relying on the telephone.

Letterpress	The printing process that uses a raised surface for the printing image.
Lift	To extract a section of type from one edition to use it in a subsequent edition, perhaps in an otherwise rewritten story.
Ligature	Two or more letters joined together in recognised form (ff, fi, fl, ffi).
Lineage	Old method by which contributors to newspapers were paid on the rate of the number of lines published.
Line Block	A metal printing plate used for letterpress printing, produced photographically from a black-and-white original (e.g. drawing) by etching away non-image areas.
Linotype	Composing machine which is operated by a keyboard and sets lines of type by casting them in hot metal.
Literal	An error in setting, e.g. a mispelling, transliteration, etc.
Lithography	A printing process using a planographic printing surface. Originally litho printing was from stone, but printing plates are now usually made from a variety of metals including zinc and aluminium.
Lockup	To secure type and blocks within a chase.
Logotype	Two or more letters cast in a single type body, e.g. a company name or trade mark.
Long Ink	An ink that has a good flow in the fountain.
Long Primer	LP or Long Primer, the old name for 10 pt.
Lower Case	(*a*) The small letters in a fount of type, as distinct from the capitals.
	(*b*) Originally, the case in which these letters are stored together with punctuation marks, etc.
Ludlow	A composing machine which casts lines of type from matrices assembled by hand: used for headlines and display type.
Magazine	The case holding the matrices on Linotype or Intertype machines.
Makeready	Correcting an imperfect impression from type formes by pasting paper on low or weak areas of a pull, then placing in packing to register with the forme: also correcting register, improving tonal values of half-tones, etc.

Make-up	(*a*) The sheet on which a sub-editor indicates to a stonehand where the various items will go on a page. (*b*) The process of assembling a page.
Mangle	The stereotyper's press (usually hydraulic) for producing a matrix from a forme.
Masthead	Generally, the newspaper's title at the top of p. 1. Strictly, its title above the editorial on the leader page.
Mean Line	The imaginary line along the top of lower-case letters that have no ascenders (a, c, e).
Measure	The length of a line to which type is set, expressed as a multiple of 12 pt (pica) ems.
m. f.	Abbreviation for 'more follows'—to be typed at the foot of every folio of copy up to the last.
Minion	Old term for 7 pt.
Monotype	Composing machine that casts single pieces of type.
Mould	See *Matrix*.
Must	An editorial item which must appear, often by order of the management, e.g. a legal correction.
Mutton	Printer's slang for an em space.
Negative	An image in reverse from the original print.
Newsprint	A cheap mechanical paper, generally used for newspapers, containing approximately 80 per cent of mechanical wood pulp.
n.f.	No fly—printer's slang for the cancelling of an instruction.
Nonpareil	Old name for 6 pt.
Nut	Printer's slang for an en space (half an em).
Obit	Abbreviation for obituary, a pre-prepared account of a famous person's life set and held in anticipation of his death.
Offset	The printing process by which ink is transferred from the printing plate to a blanket or rubber-covered cylinder, and from the blanket to the paper, as distinct from *Letterpress*.
Overmatter	Type that has been set but for which there is no space in the page or forme.
Overprinting	Printing on an area that has already been printed.
Overset	More text than is required for the space available.
PA	Press Association news agency
Page Proof	Proof of a single madeup page of type.

Pagination	Numbering of pages.
Panel	A short item indented each side, sometimes in bold or italic type with a rule or border top and bottom.
Para	Abbreviation for paragraph.
Pasteup	Preparation of copy by putting the elements on to a preparation sheet before photographing.
Photostat	A process for producing copies of printed matter etc. by photography (see *Xerography*).
Pica	Old name for 12 pt (rhymes with *striker*).
Piece	A news story or feature article.
Pigment	The solids used to give body to printing inks.
Pix	Abbreviation for pictures.
Planographic	Printing from a level surface (see *Lithography*).
Plate	The curved metal plate used for printing on a rotary press.
Point	(*a*) The unit of type measurement—0·0138 ins, 12 points to the pica, approximately 72 points (pts) to the inch.
	(*b*) A full-stop (full-point).
Positive	An image corresponding to the original print: the reverse of a negative.
Primary Colours	Three lights, red, green and blue, of specified wavelengths are the light primaries. The pigment primaries are, as near as is practical, complementary to these—generally called yellow, magenta (or process red) and cyan (or process blue).
PRO	Public Relations Officer.
Process Plates	Printing from a series of two or more plates in half-tone to produce other colours and shades; usually (in four-colour process) magenta, yellow, cyan and black.
Progressive Proofs	In colour printing, the engraver or platemaker prepares a set of proofs showing each colour separately and then in combination.
Proof	A print taken from type or other printing plate for checking and correcting purposes.
Proofing Chromo	A superior quality chromo paper.
Puff	A free advertisement (often about an individual) in editorial matter.
Pull	A proof taken from galley or forme.
Quad	(*a*) Abbreviation for Quadrat—a blank piece of metal less than type height for spacing between letters.

(*b*) Blank spacing material used to fill out lines. (*c*) A sheet four times the area and size of the given sheet, thus: Quad Crown is four times Crown (20 ins × 15 ins), i.e. 40 ins × 30 ins.

Quarto   One-fourth of the given sheet, thus Crown Quarto is one-fourth Crown, i.e. 10 ins × 7½ ins.

Quire   The unit of newspaper distribution, usually 26 copies. In other paper uses a quire may be 24 or 25 copies, or one-twentieth of a ream (which may variously be 480, 500, 504 or 516 sheets).

Quoin   In letterpress, small wedges or expanding devices used to lock type and blocks in a chase to produce a forme.

Quote   Indication of quotation marks beginning in telephoned copy (ends by '*Unquote*').

Raised Initial   A capital letter two or more sizes larger than the text, its base line ranged with the base line of the text.

Random   The rack on which sections of type being set are assembled and collated before being proofed in galley and distributed to the stone.

Reader   A proof corrector who marks corrections on galley and page proofs.

Reel-fed   A printing press into which paper is fed from a reel rather than flat sheets.

Register   When pages, columns and lines of type are truly aligned, or when two or more colours meet exactly, they are 'in register', otherwise they are 'out of register'.

Rejig   The rewriting of existing editorial text (in the light of new information).

Replate   During an edition run of a paper, the positioning of a new stereo plate to give late news; also the editorial process that leads to this.

Reproduction Proof   In letterpress, the proofing of a type forme for photographic purposes.

Retainer   A regular fee paid to a freelance correspondent to retain his services, often exclusively.

Retouching   Alteration by hand of a photograph, negative or positive.

Reuter   The Reuter news agency, principal agency for foreign news in Britain.

Reverse Indent   see *Hanging Indent*.

Reverse Plate	A printing plate in which the parts that are usually black or shaded are the opposite, or reversed, so as to appear white or grey.
Revise	A proof of set matter after corrections.
Roman	Upright type with serifs, as distinct from italic.
r.o.p.	Run-of-the-press (or Run of production), where in newspaper work colour is printed simultaneously with the edition, instead of being pre-printed.
Rotary Press	Printing press in which both the impression and printing surfaces are on revolving cylinders, and the paper is fed from a reel. Rotary presses may be letterpress, lithography or gravure.
Rough	A preliminary layout, sketch or design.
Round-up	A comprehensive inquiry on one subject, often involving several reporters.
Routing	Cutting away the non-printing surfaces of a letterpress stereo plate.
Rule	A strip of metal that prints as a single line, see *Column Rule*.
Run	The period of printing an edition.
Run-on	Where matter is not broken up into paragraphs, but run on from one full line to the next.
Sans Serif	A typeface without serifs (see *Serif*).
Scanner	An electronic device used for making colour separation negatives and positives. Used also for monochrome.
Screen	Photographs to be reproduced by lithography or letterpress are photographed through a fine mesh which breaks up the illustration into dots of varying sizes. Usual newspaper screens are 55 to 65 dots to the square inch of a half-tone block.
Seal	Decorative feature usually beside the title on the front page, indicating the edition, often in a second colour.
Serif	The short cross-lines at the ends of the strokes of letters in certain type faces.
Set and Hold	See *Hold*.
Set-off	When the ink of a printed sheet rubs off or marks the next sheet being delivered.
Shank	See *Body*.
Shoulder	The top plane of the body of a type from which the type face is raised.

Show-through	The appearance of print on paper as seen through another sheet of the same paper.
Side	A sheet of teleprinter copy.
Sidehead	A subheading set left or right of the column.
Side-stick	Furnishing of a chase at the side of a page.
Slant	The flavour given to a newspaper story by editorial policy or prejudice.
Slip	A special edition for a particular area or event (football slip, dog show slip), or the change of one or more pages.
Slug	A line of type or blank line set on Linotype or Intertype.
Small	See *Filler*.
Small Caps	An alphabet of small capital letters, usually the height of the fount's normal x-height.
Smalls	Small advertisements, see *Classified*.
Snap	A brief news message slightly less important than a *Flash*.
Solid	Lines of type set without leads.
Sorts	Individual pieces of type.
Space	The metal units for spacing out a line of type, namely hair, thin, mid, thick.
Spaceband	The metal wedge that spaces lines on a Linotype.
Spike	A metal filing spike for unwanted copy: thus a story that is written but unpublished is 'spiked'.
Splash	The main news story on the front page of a newspaper.
Standing Type	Type which has been set and stored for future use.
Stereo	A flat plate made by stereotyping from type or blocks, usually applied to advertisements supplied as plates.
Stereotype	In letterpress, a printing plate cast in one piece from a matrix containing the mould of the matter to be printed.
Stick	See *Composing Stick*.
Stone	The smooth metal surface in the print works on which pages are made up—so called because it was originally marble.
Stonehand	A compositor making up a page.
Story	An editorial item.
Strap	A minor headline placed over a main headline.
Streamer	A multi-column headline at the top of a page, not necessarily across it—see *Banner*.
Strike-through	Penetration of printing ink through a sheet so that it shows on the reverse side.

Stringer	Usually a local correspondent or overseas correspondent, who may assist a staffman.
Stripping	In offset preparation and photo-engraving, the arranging and affixing of negatives or positives.
Style	The special rules of a particular office in relation to spelling, punctuation, layout, etc.
Sub	Abbreviation for sub-editor, or the act of preparing copy by subbing.
Supercaster	A Monotype machine that casts large sizes of type for headlines etc.
Supplement	A special section of a newspaper on a single subject, usually planned with the advertising department as a means of gaining additional revenue.
Surface Plate	In lithography, plates in which the printing image is on the surface of the grained metal, as distinct from *Deep-etch*.
Switch	The newspaper telephone system or switchboard.
Tabloid	A page half the size of a broadsheet—usually applied to popular newspapers of this page size (approx. 16 ins × 12 ins).
Tag	A short line in small type following a main headline, or an agency acknowledgement at the end of a story.
Take	A short piece of copy being dictated by a reporter, or a section of copy as distributed to one compositor among several for speed of setting.
Tape	News agency copy, in teleprinter sheets.
Text	Solid matter as distinct from headlines, display types etc.
Thick Space	A space of one-third of an em in hand composition.
Thin Space	A space of one-fifth of an em in hand composition.
Tints	Dots, lines and textures which simulate tone effects in what would otherwise be line blocks (e.g. cartoons).
Tip-off	Information passed on to a newspaper by the public.
Titling	Capital letters cast full face on the type body, from a fount with no lowercase letters.
Transparency	A full-colour photographic positive with the image on a transparent base.

Transpose	To exchange the position of one letter, word, group of words, or illustration with another.
Tube	A pneumatic device for carrying copy from one part of a newspaper office to another.
Turn	Continuing a story in another column or page.
Type Face	The printing surface of type.
Type Height	0·918 inches from the face to the foot of a piece of type.
Type Metal Alloy	Alloys of tin (3–12 per cent), antimony (11–24 per cent) and lead, but may contain small proportions of copper or other substances.
Typography	The craft of letterpress printing—composition, imposition and press-work. The term now refers to the planning of printed work, the choice of type face and size, and the layout of type and illustrations.
Underscore	To set a rule under a word of group of words or headline for emphasis.
UPI	United Press International news agency.
Upper Case	(*a*) Capital letters. (*b*) The type case in which capital letters, small capitals, figures, reference marks and accents are kept. When in use with *Lower Case*, it is mounted above it, whence the name.
Vehicle	The liquid component of printing ink,.
Vet	To examine a story for possible legal implications or dangers.
Web	(*a*) In papermaking, the continuous reel of paper being made. (*b*) In printing, the length of paper being fed through the press from a reel rather than in sheets.
Web-Offset	The printing process whereby the image is conveyed to a rubber-covered cylinder and thence on to a continuous reel of paper (see *Offset*).
White	Areas on a newspaper page not covered by type or illustration.
Wire Machine	An electronic machine for transmitting photographs by the telegraphic wire.
Wrap-around Plate	In rotary letterpress, a thin one-piece relief plate wrapped around the press cylinder.
Wrong Fount	w.f., a letter from a type fount other than the one specified.

Xerography	(*a*) Dry writing invented by C. F. Carlson in 1938. The sensitive material consists of a plate carrying an electrical charge which is destroyed on exposure. Charged areas, representing the shadows, become the printing image, in powdered pigment.
	(*b*) A process used to make small lithographic plates, by transfer of image formed by a light-sensitive electro-static charge on a special base.
x-height	The height of a lower-case x in any size of type, and thus of all letters without ascenders or descenders.
Zinco	A line block etched on zinc.

GLOSSARY OF RADIO AND TELEVISION TERMS

Audio Control	Control of studio sound so as to match sound with picture.
Barndoor	Adjustable flaps fitted to studio lights to limit light-spill.
Boom	A suspended microphone boom.
Camera Script	Script for television programmes listing camera movements, telecine and video-tape etc., as well as the spoken word.
Console	The switching desk in the control room at which the vision mixer works.
Control Room	The gallery from which a director controls a television programme, equipped with monitors and electronic switchgear.
Crane Up/Down	To move a camera (mounted on a dolly) up or down.
Creeper	A low dolly with camera lens about two feet high.
Cue	Signal for a programme or performer to begin.
Cue Cards	Outline script giving cameramen their technical cues.
Cut	Change from one picture to another.
Cutaways	(1) 'Audience reaction' shots. (2) Questions separately filmed by an interviewer after a recorded interview, and then 'cut in' to the interview before transmission.
Cyclorama	The curved light-blue or grey background cloth in a television studio.
Directional Microphone	Microphone that must be aimed at the subject, picking up sounds from one direction only.
Director	Executive who directs a television transmission.
Display Screen	A 'blackboard' screen behind a newsreader on a television set, on which films or still pictures appear by back-projection.
Dolly	Platform on wheels, sometimes motorised, on which a camera is mounted that can be raised or lowered for high- or low-angle shots.

232

Electron Gun	A gun that fires electrons at the cathode-ray tube screen, the basis of the television signal.
Eurovision	An organisation of European television networks, founded in 1954, for the exchange and transmission of each other's programmes and the production of shared programmes.
Flicker	Flickering picture effect usually caused by parallel lines, e.g. in fabrics and clothing coinciding with the picture scanning.
Flips	Titles on a series of sheets that flip over.
Floor	The studio, as compared with the control room.
Floor Manager	Studio manager.
Gallery	Control room.
Graphics	Words and figures used on television screens, often specially drawn, as titles, illustrations of statistics, etc.
Inlay	Machine by which captions are flashed on top of pictures, and which also produces split-screen effects, inlays on picture within another, etc.
Key, To	To set studio lights before a transmission.
Keylight	Predominant direction of studio light.
Kill, To	To turn off a studio light, or to remove an unwanted shadow by moving light or camera.
Lines	The divisions of a television picture, which may be horizontal or vertical, which the electron-gun scans to transmit a television image; usually 525 (USA) or 625 (UK and Europe) lines per picture.
Live	A studio performance transmitted as it takes place, compared with telecine or video.
Monitor	Television screen in control room or studio so that producer, performers and technicians can see what is being transmitted.
OB	Outside broadcast, i.e. live transmission from outside a studio.
PAL	Phase Alteration line—the Colour TV Standard used in Western Europe, except for France and Spain.
Pan, To	Move a camera from side to side, e.g. to follow or close up on a performer or subject.

Ped	or Pedestal: a metal tripod on wheels on which a television camera is mounted and moved around by hand.
Presentation Studio	Studio that links all transmissions from one station, provides between-programme information, and cues in successive programmes.
Primary Colours	The basic colours for colour transmission—red, green and blue (with black and white).
Producer	Executive who plans a television transmission and may, or may not, direct it.
Ratings	The measurements of the number of viewers who watched a particular programme, obtained either by market research or by meters attached to a sample number of television sets to record when they were switched on.
Roll Film	Cue instruction to start telecine.
Roller	Caption machine for 'rolling' programme titles.
Scanner	Mobile control van for outside broadcasts.
SECAM	The colour TV system used in France and Russia.
Set	The setting—desks, chairs, props—for a television programme.
Shot	Picture taken by a television camera, e.g. long-shot, mid-shot, close-shot.
Signal	Series of electronic impulses that form a television picture transmission, i.e. video.
Stroboscopic Effect	When wheels appear to turn backwards; it happens when a wheel is turning at precisely the scanning speed of the picture, i.e. 60 revolutions per second (USA) or 50 revolutions per second (Europe).
Studio Manager	The producer's representative on the studio floor, directing performers and technicians on the spot.
Talk-back	The producer's sound-system by which he communicates from control room to studio.
Telecine	Equipment that feeds prepared film into television programmes (cued in between three and eight seconds ahead of cue); using 35-mm, 16-mm and recently also 8-mm film.
Teleprompter	Machine mounted beside camera lens, or printing electronically on the camera lens itself, by means of which a performer can read a script unrolling before his eyes as he apparently talks straight to camera.

Tilt, To	To move a camera shot up or down.
Titles	Introductory captions, or closing captions, for a television programme.
Tracking	Movement of a dolly-mounted camera.
Transmission Monitor	Main control-room screen, showing the picture being transmitted.
Tube	Cathode-ray tube, the basis of television camera and receiver.
Video	(1) Video signal, the transmitted signal. (2) Video-tape recorder, a recorder that puts both sound and vision on tape.
Vidicon	The simplest television camera.
Vision Mixer	Control-room technician who at the director's instruction switches from one studio camera to another, introduces film or video-tape etc into a programme.
Zoom Lens	The general television camera lens with variable focal length, quickly adjustable from long-shots to close-up.

SUGGESTED FURTHER READING

General

Dodge, J. D. and Viner, G. (eds.). *The Practice of Journalism*. Heinemann, 1963.

Evans, H. *Editing and Design* (5 vols). Heinemann (for National Council for the Training of Journalists), 1972–75.

Evans, H. *The Active Newsroom*. International Press Institute, 1965.

Harris, G. and Spark, D. *Practical Newspaper Reporting*. Heinemann, 1966.

Sub-editing

Garst, R. E. and Bernstein, T. M. *Headlines and Deadlines*. Columbia University Press, 1963.

Sellers, L. *Doing it in Style*. Pergamon Press, 1968.

Sellers, L. *The Simple Sub's Book*. Pergamon Press, 1968.

Design and typography

Hutt, A. *Newspaper Design*. (2nd edition) Oxford University Press, 1967.

Simon, O. *Introduction to Typography*. Faber, 1963, and Penguin Books.

Printing

Brewer, R. *An Approach to Print*. Blandford Press, 1971.

Printing Reproduction Pocket Pal. IPC for Advertising Agency Production Association.

Use of English

Ashe, G. *The Art of Writing Made Simple*. W. H. Allen, 1972.

Gowers, Sir E. *The Complete Plain Words*. HMSO, 1954, and Penguin Books.

Partridge, E. *Usage and Abusage: A Guide to Good English*. Hamish Hamilton, 1965, and Penguin Books.

Law for Journalists

Lloyd, H. *The Legal Limits of Journalism*. Pergamon Press, 1968.

McNae, L. C. J. *Essential Law for Journalists*. Staples Press, 1963.

National Association of Local Government Officers' notes on local Government. Available from National Council for Training of Journalists.

Smith, R. Callender. *Press Law*. Sweet & Maxwell, 1978.

Press Photography

Baynes, K. *Scoop, Scandal and Strife*. Lund Humphries, 1971.

Press Background

Boston, R. ed. *The Press We Deserve*. Routledge & Kegan Paul, 1970.

The British Press. Central Office of Information reference pamphlet 97, HMSO, 1970.

Cleverley, G. *The Fleet Street Disaster*. Constable, 1976.

Cohen, S. and Young, J. *The Manufacture of News*. Constable, 1973.

Merrill, J. C. *The Elite Press*. Pitman, New York, 1969.

Murphy, D. *The Silent Watchdog*. Constable, 1976.

The National Newspaper Industry: a Survey. Economist Intelligence Unit, 1966.

Science and the Media. British Association for the Advancement of Science, 1976.

Seymour-Ure, C. *The Political Impact of Mass Media*. Constable, 1974.

Tunstall, J. *Journalists at Work: Specialist Correspondents*. Constable, 1971.

Tunstall, J. *The Westminster Lobby Correspondents*. Routledge & Kegan Paul, 1970.

Whale, J. *Journalists and Government*. Macmillan, 1972.

Williams, F. *Dangerous Estate, the Anatomy of Newspapers*. Longman, 1957.

Television

Elliott, P. *The Making of a TV Series*. Constable, 1975.

Halloran, J. D., Elliott, P. and Murdock, G. *Demonstrations and Communications: a Case Study*. Penguin Books, 1971.

Halloran, J. D. *The Effects of Mass Communication*. Leicester University Press, 1968.

MacNeil, R. *The People Machine: the Influence of Television on American Politics*. Eyre & Spottiswoode, 1970.

Millerson, G. *The Technique of Television Production*. Focal Press, 1969.

Sound and Television Broadcasting in Britain. Central Office of Information reference pamphlet 61, HMSO, 1969.

Newspaper Histories and Biographies

Ayerst, D. *Guardian: Biography of a Newspaper*. Collins, 1971.

Braddon, R. *Roy Thomson of Fleet*. Collins, 1965, and Fontana.

Clarke, T. *My Northcliffe Diary*. Gollancz, 1931.

Cook, Sir E. *Delane of 'The Times'*. Constable, 1915.

Driberg, T. *Beaverbrook*. Weidenfeld & Nicolson, 1956.

Gollin, A. M. *'The Observer' and J. L. Garvin*. Oxford University Press, 1960.

Hammond, J. L. *C. P. Scott*. Bell, 1934.

McLachlan, D. *In the Chair: Barrington-Ward of 'The Times'*. Weidenfeld & Nicolson, 1971.

Morison, S. *The History of 'The Times'*. Oxford University Press, 4 vols., 1935–52.

Pound, R. and Harmsworth, G. *Northcliffe*. Cassell, 1959.
Taylor, A. J. P. *Beaverbrook*. Hamish Hamilton, 1972.

Some collected Journalism and Memoirs
Boardman, H. *The Glory of Parliament*. Allen & Unwin, 1960.
Cassandra at his Finest and Funniest. Daily Mirror/Paul Hamlyn, 1967.
Cockburn, C. *I, Claud*. Penguin Books, 1967.
Coleman, T. *The Only True History*. Hutchinson, 1969.
Cudlipp, H. *Publish and Be Damned*. Dakers, 1953.
Whitehorn, K. *Social Survival*, Methuen, 1968.

A few Novels about Journalism
Dale, C. *Trial of Strength*. Cape, 1955, and Viking Press.
Forster, P. *The Spike*. Hutchinson, 1969, and Penguin Books.
Frayn, M. *Towards the End of Morning*. Collins, 1967, and Penguin Books.
Harling, R. *The Paper Palace*. Chatto & Windus, 1951.
Harling, R. *The Enormous Shadow*. Chatto & Windus, 1955.
Harling, R. *The Hollow Sunday*. Chatto & Windus, 1967.
Hodson, J. L. *Morning Star*. Gollancz, 1951.
Lindop, A. E. *The Tall Headlines*. Heinemann, 1950, and Pan Books.
Montague, C. E. *A Hind Let Loose*. Methuen, 1910.

Index

The page references in bold type are of particular importance.